BEYOND GOING POSTAL

SHIFTING FROM WORKPLACE TRAGEDIES AND TOXIC WORK ENVIRONMENTS TO A SAFE AND HEALTHY ORGANIZATION

AN INSIDER'S VIEW

OF POSTAL WORKPLACE VIOLENCE,

ITS PREVENTION,

AND THE CULTURE

WITHIN THE

U.S. POSTAL SERVICE

STEPHEN MUSACCO, PH.D.

ISBN: 1-4392-2075-1
ISBN-13: 9781439220757

Visit www.booksurge.com to order additional copies.

PREFACE

This book is written from an insider's perspective. It is based significantly on my thirty-four years experience with the United States Postal Service. I felt compelled to write the book for two important reasons: First, the postal culture, beginning in 1997, progressively worsened. Second, the last postal district I worked at became a toxic workplace for many of its employees during the last year of my employment as an internal consultant.

In good conscience, I could not turn a blind eye to postal management's blatant display of arrogance at the highest level of the organization. I couldn't ignore the *lack of accountability* for unethical organizational practices and behaviors and not bring it to the attention of the American public, the press, and, most importantly, to Congress. In chapter ten, I argue that it is a moral obligation for public and private organizations to create healthy organizations. It is no less a moral obligation for public policy makers to create the tone and the legislative requirements to ensure that healthy organizations become the norm in this country.

In writing this book, it became my mission to *comprehensively investigate* these concerns and lack of accountability in the context of workplace violence in the Postal Service and its postal culture. As a result of this examination, I provide an answer to the question: **Why has there been so much violence in the Postal Service and what can be done to prevent it?**

Accordingly, as a chief part of my motivation for writing this book, it became necessary to demonstrate how, as a result of this *comprehensive investigation*, the Postal Service could shift from an unsafe and unhealthy organization to a safe and healthy one. It would have served no useful purpose just to explore what was not working and not offer viable solutions.

In Part 1 of the book I explore the prevalence of workplace violence in the United States and the Postal Service. In this examination, I discuss twenty-seven incidences of postal tragedies, from 1983 to 2006.

In Part 2, I review the notion of "going postal", especially in the context of the Califano Report. This review is critical because the Califano Report has been a central part of the Postal Service's public relations efforts to frame the notion of going postal as a myth.

The Califano Report's importance is revealed by how the national media reacted to it, especially national magazines and newspapers. If you Google "going postal as a myth," for example, there are still archived articles from the national media emphasizing the major conclusions and findings of the Califano Report.

In Part 3, from an insider's perspective, I examine the Postal Service's workplace violence prevention efforts. The building blocks of the postal culture are detailed in Part 4. I discuss in detail the impact of this postal culture, from an insider's perspective, on postal employees and their families.

Finally, in Part 5 of the book, I provide requirements and recommendations to top postal management and congressional leaders that, if implemented, will serve to make the Postal Service a safer and healthier organization for its employees.

The Postal Service is at a crossroad in its history. The private mailing industry has aligned itself with the Postal Service Board of Governors (BOG) and the Bush administration to contract core postal operations. Since 2006, these events have heated up and employees have been caught in the middle.

Besides contracting of city letter positions in cities across the country in 2007, the Postal Service also submitted a plan to Congress in 2008 to consolidate their network of processing centers and to contract out mail processing and transportation services. In 2008, the Postal Regulatory Commission (PRC) contracted with a private vendor to conduct a comprehensive study on the Postal Service's "Universal Service Obligation."

If the universal service requirement can be relaxed by congressional legislation, or the USPS is allowed to contract postal core services, this means huge profits for many of these contractors involved in the mailing industry. It would mean the "Wal-Martinizing" of future employees who will transport, process, and deliver public and private mailings. No major action is likely on these issues until after the new Congress is sworn in on January 21, 2009.

In addition to well-orchestrated efforts to contract delivery, mail processing, and transportation services, there have been efforts to expand contracting for retail services. A prime example of these efforts is the Postal Service agreement in 2008, to the dismay of postal unions, with retail chain stores named "Goin Postal," an agreement that gives the "Goin Postal" chain, with three hundred stores nationwide, the benefits of being part of the USPS "Approved Shipper" program. It is very telling and interesting that the Postal Service would enter an agreement with a company bearing this name. For the last fifteen years, they have engaged in an arduous publicity campaign to combat the assignment of this stereotype to postal employees.

The uncertainty and anxiety of postal employees is probably higher than anytime in recent history. Like other companies, the Postal Service is struggling under the impact of a national recession. Mail volume has declined while delivery points have increased. Besides the contracting efforts previously mentioned, early-out opportunities, with penalties, have been offered to all employees. In light of a 7.9 billion dollar deficit for the last two years, the Postal Service is reviewing its option of lay-offs for the first time in its history and all positions have been "frozen." Furthermore, the Postal Service requested that the management associations consider agreeing to have their salaries frozen.

When turmoil, anxiety, and anger are at high levels, there is an increased potential for workplace violence. How the Postal Service reacts to the numerous changes that are transpiring, both externally and internally, is critically important. Besides attention to the "bottom line," the organization needs to pay careful attention to the well-being of its employees by creating a "participative culture" with its unions, management organizations, and its employees.

In writing this book, multiple audiences were considered, including: 1) rank and file postal employees and their family members, 2) postal management and union officials, 3) human resources professionals, 4) arbitrators and administrative judges, 5) professionals in the field of workplace violence, organizational development, organizational psychology, business management, and occupational health psychology, and 6) members of Congress and their staff.

It is important to note as background information: The United States mailing industry is a 900 billion dollar enterprise, employing about three million employees. The Postal Service is the third largest employer in the country, behind Wal-Mart and the Department of Defense. It employs approximately seven hundred thousand employees and has a vast network of over four hundred mail processing plants and thirty-seven thousand post offices. The Postal Service had a 5.1 billion dollar debt in fiscal year 2007 and a 2.8 billion dollar deficit in fiscal year 2008.

TABLE OF CONTENTS

Book Sections ....

*Part One (Chapters 1-2)   The Specter of Workplace Violence   1-20

Part Two (Chapters 3-4)   "Going Postal": Myth or Reality?   21-34

Part Three (Chapter 5)   Overview of the U.S. Postal Service's
                                  Workplace Violence Prevention Efforts   35

**Part Four (Chapters 6-9)   Looking at the Big Picture: The "Fallout" of an
                                  Unhealthy Organizational Culture   45-108

Part Five (Chapters 10-11)   Shifting to a Safe and Healthy
                                  Organization   109-137

*Includes Appendices A-B

**Includes Appendices C-E

Book Chapters ....

Chapter One   Introduction: What is Workplace Violence?   1

Chapter Two   Specter of Workplace Violence in the
                      United States and Postal Service   11

Chapter Three   Making the Case: "Going Postal" a Myth?   21

Chapter Four   Let's Examine the Record: "Going Postal"
                      a Reality?   27

Chapter Five   A Closer Look: The Postal Service's Violence
                      Prevention Efforts   35

Chapter Six   Building Blocks of the Postal Culture   45

Chapter Seven   A Paramilitary, Authoritarian Postal Culture?   53

Chapter Eight   Postal Culture from an Insider's Perspective   73

Chapter Nine   Impact of Postal Culture on Postal Employees,
                      Families, and Organization   97

Chapter Ten   Creating and Maintaining a Healthy
                      Organization   109

Chapter Eleven   Oversight and Accountability:
                      Open Letter to U.S. Congress   123

Book Appendices..

Appendix A   Psychological and Physical Aggression
                      in the Workplace: Its Prevalence,
                      Source, and Impact   139

Appendix B   Profile of Workplace Tragedies in the
                      U.S. Postal Service   149

Appendix C   Impact of Strategic Plans and Congressional
                      Oversight on Postal Culture   163

Appendix D   Impact of Internal Stakeholders
                      on Postal Culture   179

Appendix E   Impact of Postal Law Enforcement
                      on Postal Culture   209

DEDICATION

I would like to thank postal employees throughout the country for sharing their sorrows and hopes with me, in my role as an Employee Assistance Program (EAP) representative and as a Workplace Improvement Analyst. This book is dedicated to them. My hope is that information contained herein is used to enrich their workplace environments, well-being, and family life.

This book is also dedicated to Patricia Anne Shea, M.S.W. She was steadfast in her encouragement and belief that I was capable of completing this challenge. Without Patricia's support during the beginning of this effort, it is unlikely that I would have accomplished this task. Finally, this book is dedicated to my beautiful daughter Dominique and a very special person, Neila Jean Bowden.

CHAPTER ONE
Introduction:
What is Workplace Violence?

Despite the attention and focus on this important topic over the last forty years, scholars and practitioners in the field have reached no real consensus in defining workplace violence. In this chapter, I attempt to answer the question: What is workplace violence? Two broad categories of workplace violence are psychological aggression and physical aggression. Based on the review of these two categories of workplace violence, I provide a comprehensive definition of workplace violence.

Understanding and Defining Workplace Violence

To define workplace violence, the first requirement is to arrive at an understanding of the nature of violence itself. The *American Heritage Dictionary* defines violence[1] as a) physical force exerted for the purpose of violating, damaging, or abusing, and (b) abusive or unjust use of power. There are several other definitions provided, but these two definitions provide a deeper understanding of the two key components of violence, physical and psychological.

In focus groups, the term "workplace violence" was tested for one particular study.[2] Focus group participants were reported to quickly reach consensus that workplace violence included both physical and psychological harm. The groups concluded both physical and psychological violence were equally implicated in psychosomatic illnesses. Experts in the field of workplace violence[3] generally agree that violence in the workplace is an act of aggression and these acts of violence can be expressed either in the form of psychological aggression or physical aggression.

For these reasons, I explore the two forms of workplace violence below in the context of how each form manifests itself in the workplace. After this review, I provide a comprehensive definition of workplace violence.

Psychological Aggression in the Workplace

> Cruelty can be both contagious and aimless, and the worker knows that if people can be cruel to each other, some day he himself might become the victim of cruelty. As a result of harassment, then, an atmosphere is created in which trust is minimal and fear is increased…[4]

By far most workplace aggression is verbal and of a non-physical nature. In the past forty years, labels or terms to identify psychological aggression in the workplace have surfaced in both academic and popular literature; the most common terms identified include **harassment, mobbing, bullying**, and **emotional abuse**. Each of these terms is briefly discussed, including a very brief account of origin, definition, and a real life example.

Harassment

In 1976, Carroll M. Brodsky's seminal book titled *The Harassed Worker* was published. Dr. Brodsky was the first author and medical doctor to comprehensively address workplace violence in terms of psychological aggression and its impact. She described in detail how the harassment of employees in the workplace impacts their mental and physical health, including costs to employers. Dr. Brodsky defined harassment as "repeated and persistent attempts by one person to torment, wear down, frustrate, or get a reaction from another."[5] It is important to note, she did not limit harassment to psychological aggression.

In the following, an actual example of harassment in the workplace, reported to me in my capacity as an internal consultant with the Postal Service, is presented.

Real Life Example of Harassment

Wayne is a letter carrier at an office with about eighty employees. For the past several weeks, his supervisor has been focusing more and more on his office performance. Wayne is about six feet six inches, while his supervisor is about five feet nine inches tall. In the last two days, the supervisor began monitoring nearly every move the carrier made in the office for two or more hours. He was forbidden to talk to his peers while working in the office. The employee was verbally criticized and belittled in front of his peers. He was so demoralized and demeaned that he broke down and cried in the workplace and went home sick. When he returned to work the next day, the supervisor began where he left off from the previous day. Again, the employee broke down crying in the workplace. The employee later sought help through the Employee Assistance Program (EAP), and the union called me to report the situation.

Mobbing

In Scandinavian countries, "mobbing" became the term principally used by scholars studying the impact and effects of psychological aggression in the workplace. Their focus on the extent and impact of psychological aggression in the workplace paved the way for national workplace environment legislation in Sweden, Finland, and Norway in the late 1980s and into the 1990s. Heinz Leyman,[6] a chief researcher in Scandinavia on the topic of mobbing during this time period, defined mobbing as: "Psychological terror . . . in working life that involves hostile and unethical communications, which is directed in a systematic way by one or a few individuals mainly towards one individual . . ."[7]

Leyman claimed he deliberately chose the term mobbing over the term bullying because the word bullying used by the English, Australians, and Americans conveyed physical aggression and threat.

An actual example of mobbing in the workplace, reported to me as an internal consultant with the Postal Service, is provided below.

Real Life Example of Mobbing

John is a manager at a large postal facility with over one hundred fifty employees under his command. For the past several months, John had reportedly received demeaning e-mail messages and phone calls about his performance. He had been reportedly yelled at and his decision-making latitude was taken over by his manager. Even John's supervisors claimed that they were yelled at in front of their employees on the workroom floor. John received demeaning e-mail messages and discipline from his supervisor's boss. He was being "mobbed" by two employees who had position power over him. During this timeframe, he was in a car accident while on duty. Later he became very sick and was on sick leave for several weeks with an immune deficiency disorder, manifesting itself in high temperatures and intestinal problems. Arguably, there was a causal link between the mobbing of John and these aforementioned events.

Bullying

In the 1990s, after debating the relevance of Leyman's argument for the use of the term mobbing, most international researchers in Europe and Australia favored the use of the term bullying to convey psychological aggression. The attributes of bullying, as generally accepted by these researchers,[8] include a) repeated actions and practices that are directed against one or more workers, b) are unwanted by the victims, c) may be carried out deliberately or unconsciously, d) cause humiliation, offense, and distress, and e) may interfere with job performance and/or cause unpleasant working conditions. Similar to the terms harassment and mobbing, the notion of bullying emphasizes psychological aggressive acts toward employees in the workplace.

In the following, an actual example of bullying in the workplace, reported to me as an internal consultant with the Postal Service, is presented.

Real Life Example of Bullying

Sandra is a manager at an office with about fifty employees. At a staff meeting, she spoke out against a policy that did not take into account the necessary resources to get the job done. After the meeting concluded, a higher level manager met with her privately and chided her for speaking her opinion. This superior then reportedly suggested to Sandra that she got her job because she was an attractive female. This particular superior reportedly later suggested to Sandra's immediate boss that he had selected her because she was an attractive female. Almost immediately after these events, Sandra had at least four outside teams audit her operations. These events created a great deal of fear and stress for Sandra regarding her job security. She began to suffer migraines, stomach problems, and sleep disturbances.

Emotional Abuse

The term emotional abuse in the workplace is primarily associated with the American researcher Loraeigh Keashly.[9] In the 1990s, Keashly claimed she favored the use of the term emotional abuse because she wanted to clearly distinguish it from physical abuse in the workplace. The word "abuse" itself is striking in its connotative meaning, implying a severity of mistreatment. Keashly[10] wanted to rigorously measure the defining features of emotional abuse, which she delineated as: a) verbal and non-verbal (excluding physical contact), b) repetitive or patterned, c) unwelcome and unsolicited by the target, d) violations of a standard of appropriate conduct toward others, e) harmful or cause psychological or physical injury to the target, f) intended harm or controllable by the actor, and (g) exploiting position power of the actor over target. In the context of these dimensions, Keashly and Harvey defined emotional abuse as "repeated hostile verbal and non-verbal behaviors (excluding physical contact) directed at one or more individuals over a period of time, such that the target's sense of self as a competent worker and person is negatively affected."[11]

An actual example of emotional abuse in the workplace that was reported to me as an internal Employee Assistance Program (EAP) representative with the Postal Service is provided in the following.

Real Life Example of Emotional Abuse

Fred is a mail handler at a mail processing plant. He was outspoken about policy and management style concerns. Because of this outspoken behavior, the plant's managers and supervisors targeted him and disciplined him based on minor offenses and treated him differently compared to his peers. One manager in the plant told me in private that Fred was being singled out because management needed to show the other workers that management was in control, not the employees. He was continually monitored, criticized, and ridiculed in front of his peers. As a result of this treatment, Fred had a complete mental breakdown and was hospitalized with major depression.

Discussion

Harassment, mobbing, bullying, and emotional abuse can be viewed as severe social stressors because of their potential to engender harmful effects for those who experience it. The four terms share more commonality than differences and some researchers use the terms interchangeably. The important thing to keep in mind about each of these four terms is each are thought to form a pattern of behavior in which one or more individuals had the intention or effect of causing psychological harm toward another person or persons. In definitions provided by scholars and researchers in the field of workplace violence regarding these four terms, the notion of sexual harassment is considered a separate phenomenon.

In this examination, I intentionally did not review some important and relevant terms found in the workplace violence literature. For example, the terms "incivility" and "counterproductive behaviors" have been the focus of a significant number of scholarly articles. These two terms were not, however, reviewed in the foregoing because they do not convey the severity of psychological aggression and its persistence in terms of *frequency of occurrence*, *variety of abusive behaviors co-occurring*, and *harmful effects* – like harassment, mobbing, bullying, and emotional abuse convey. From the perspective of this book, incivility and counterproductive behaviors are less important to what is emphasized in the context of workplace tragedies and toxic workplace environments.

This is not to say that incivility and counterproductive behaviors are not important to the understanding or defining of workplace violence. They are important because sometimes they are precursors of more severe forms of aggression in the workplace. Some lower threshold behaviors that may fall under the notions of incivility and counterproductive behaviors include teasing, offensive joking, pranks, swearing, and insults. Each of these lower threshold aggressive behaviors could lead to a violent incident in the workplace, especially when it is not an isolated occurrence.

Two journal articles in the field of workplace violence illustrate the importance of viewing workplace aggression on a continuum, from low threshold to high threshold. For example, one article is titled *"Workplace bullying: Escalated incivility,"*[12] suggesting that workplace aggression can be viewed on a continuum. Similarly, in another article the author stated in the introduction section that *"[w]orkplace bullying is a particularly insidious form of counterproductive behavior,"*[13] suggesting that workplace aggression can be viewed on a continuum.

Three major factors related to harassment, mobbing, bullying, and emotional abuse are a) the severity of aggression on a continuum, b) its persistence or frequency, and c) the variety of abusive behavior co-occurring. The first factor was previously discussed. The implication of the second factor is that psychologically aggressive behaviors are directed toward an employee(s) frequently, with a duration of several months or longer.

The third factor, the variety of abusive behavior co-occurring for each of the four terms may involve: a) personal insults, b) invading personal territory, c) threats, intimidation, verbal and nonverbal, d) sarcastic jokes and teasing used as a delivery system, e) blistering e-mails, f) status slaps intended to humiliate victims, g) public shaming or status degradation rituals, h) rude interruptions, i) two-faced attacks, j) dirty looks, k) treating people as if they were invisible, and l) invading individual's personal territory. These types of aggressive acts over time, for many employees, lead to psychological and physical harm and secondary harm to their families and the organization itself. These harmful effects are discussed extensively in chapter nine.

The notion of psychological aggression in the workplace is complex, requiring the examination of many factors to determine level of severity and potential for harm. The notion of physical aggression is more straightforward, and most people view this form of aggression as a clear act of workplace violence.

Physical Aggression in the Workplace

Although some international researchers include physical aggression in their definition of the terms of harassment, bullying, and mobbing, virtually all in-depth research studies using these terms as measures of workplace violence have focused solely on psychological aggression. For that reason, in the previous discussion, these three terms were intentionally placed under the category of psychological aggression along with emotional abuse, which Loraeigh Keashly clearly distinguished from physical aggression.

The notion of physical aggression is easier to address and define compared to the notion of psychological aggression. Physical aggression in the workplace can range from inappropriate touching to murder. It includes shoving, kicking, pushing, and the use objects to cause physical harm to another. It also includes deliberate sabotage or destruction of workplace property.

Comprehensive Definition of Workplace Violence

In developing a comprehensive definition of workplace violence, both the psychological and physical components of workplace aggression are incorporated. Accordingly, a broad and workable definition of workplace violence is offered: *Workplace violence is defined as an incident where one or more individuals has been psychologically abused or threatened, or physically assaulted (including suicide), or there has been an incident of deliberate sabotage or destruction of workplace property.* Although this definition includes three areas of focus, this book does not consider incidences of deliberate sabotage or destruction of workplace property. Consistent with the purpose of this book, its focus is limited to incidences of psychological abuse and physical assault in the workplace.

Concluding Remarks

As indicated earlier, "lower levels" of workplace violence cannot afford to be ignored. If they are ignored, they can lead to a violent incident. The FBI, in one of their publications, noted:

> Mass murders, on the job, by disgruntled employees are media-intensive events. However, these mass murders, while serious, are relatively infrequent events. It is the threats, harassment, bullying, domestic violence, stalking, emotional abuse, intimidation, and

other forms of behavior and physical violence that, if left unchecked,
may result in more serious violent behavior. These are the behaviors
that supervisors and managers have to deal with every day.[14]

The implicit warning in this statement is that, if left unchecked, psychological aggression can eventually lead to physical violence, including workplace suicides and homicides. In chapter three and chapter eight the instances in which psychological aggression was noted as a contributing factor to these types of postal tragedies are highlighted.

In this introductory chapter, we looked at two components of aggression in the workplace, psychological and physical aggression. The purpose of the examination was to provide the reader with an appreciation for the complexity of workplace violence and a framework to understand it. I provided a comprehensive definition of workplace violence.

In chapter two, I consider the prevalence and impact of workplace violence in the United States for both psychological and physical aggression. Besides briefly discussed in chapter two, the prevalence and impact of workplace violence in the Postal Service are explored in the context of physical aggression in chapters three and four. In chapter four, I also consider the impact and prevalence of psychological aggression in the Postal Service in the context of the Califano Report[15], and from an insider's perspective, in chapters eight and nine.

CHAPTER TWO

Specter of Workplace Violence in the United States and the Postal Service

In the last twenty years, there have been numerous books and articles written on the subject of workplace violence in the United States in both the popular and academic press. The Internet has been another useful source of information on workplace violence, especially for obtaining statistics on physical acts of physical aggression from government agencies. I use all three sources of this information as the basis for the review of workplace violence in the United States for this chapter and Appendix A. As a result of this review, it is clear that both psychological and physical aggression in the workplace are epidemic in the United States.

The main focuses of this chapter include the examination of the prevalence and impact of workplace violence in the context of psychological aggression and physical aggression. The chapter is divided in four sections: in section one, the focus is on psychological aggression in the workplace. I present findings on the prevalence and impact of psychological aggression from four national studies, which are: 1) The Northwestern Study,[16] 2) United States Hostile Workplace Study,[17] 3) The American Workplace Survey,[18] and 4) U.S. Workplace Bullying Survey.[19] In Appendix A, I present more in-depth information on each of these four landmark studies.

In section two, the focus is on physical aggression in the workplace. I present findings of two national studies regarding *nonfatal physical violence*, which are: 1) The Northwestern Study and 2) National Survey of Workplace Health and Safety.[20] I provide relevant findings pertaining to *workplace homicide*. In Appendix A, I present more in-depth information for both nonfatal physical violence and workplace homicide. In the third section, I analyze factors involved in workplace violence separately in the context of workplace bullying and workplace homicide. In the last section, I present a brief summary of workplace tragedies in the USPS. A brief narrative for each of these workplace tragedies is discussed in Appendix B.

Psychological Aggression in the Workplace: Its Prevalence and Impact

Since 1993, there have been four major national surveys on the scope and impact of psychological aggression in U.S. workplaces. Accordingly, workplace violence studies from the perspective of psychological aggression (harassment, bullying, or emotional abuse) in American workplaces is a relatively recent development. The results from the first major study in the United States were released by Northwestern National Life Insurance Company in 1993. In 2000, the United States Hostile Workplace Study was released. And then, in 2007, both the American Workplace Survey and the U.S. Workplace Bullying Survey were released.

Significant findings reported in these four studies on psychological aggression and the most relevant to this book include:

1. Between 13-19 percent of employees in the United States are harassed during any given twelve-month period.

2. Victims of harassment report experiencing two times the rate of stress-related conditions (e.g., depression, anger, insomnia, headaches, and ulcers) compared to those who were not.

3. Targets of bullying are twenty times more likely to have reduced productivity and were ten times more likely to leave their jobs, compared to those who did not report experiencing workplace harassment.

4. Targets of bullying are exposed to bullying behaviors on the average of 16.5 months with 42 percent of the targets reporting the bullying behaviors lasting eighteen months.

5. Of those targets who indicated that they were bullied, 77 percent did not qualify under the law as illegal discrimination.

6. Of those targets who reported the bullying to their employer, 62 percent indicated that the problem became worse or the employer did nothing.

7. Forty-five percent of bullied targets reported stress levels that affected their health (i.e., psychological or physical complications) and 33 percent of them suffer more than one year.

Physical Aggression in the Workplace: Its Prevalence and Impact

I discuss the prevalence and impact of physical aggression in the workplace in this section. Under the heading of non-fatal acts of physical violence, I present the relevant statistical findings of two pertinent surveys, which are: the Northwestern Study and the National Survey of Workplace Health and Safety. The general statistics for each survey can be found in Appendix A, including the sources or types of perpetrators involved in physical aggression.

I also explore the specter of workplace homicide in this section, especially "insider" (coworker, or former coworker) workplace homicide. I referenced the statistical findings relevant to this section from government reports. In Appendix A, I provide a more complete review and presentation of statistics for the focus on workplace homicide.

Non-Fatal Acts of Physical Aggression in the Workplace

The significant findings reported in the two studies for non-fatal acts of physical aggression, most relevant to this book, include:

1. The prevalence and frequency of non-fatal physical violence reported at work for the previous twelve months for one of the studies was <u>3 percent</u>. Based on that year's total workforce, as estimated by the authors, it was projected that <u>approximately 2.2 million employees were the recipients of aggressive physical acts.</u>

2. The prevalence and frequency of non-fatal physical violence reported at work for the previous twelve months in another study was <u>6 percent</u>. Projecting the number of employees affected, based on that year, as estimated by the Bureau of Census, <u>approximately seven million employees were the recipients of aggressive physical acts.</u>

Physical Aggression in the Workplace: The Specter of Workplace Homicide

Significant findings reported in government reports for workplace homicide and the most relevant to this book include:

1. From 1980 to 1989 workplace homicide was the <u>third leading cause of death in the workplace</u>.[21] During the span of these ten years, 7,600 or 12 percent of all fatalities in the workplace were deemed a result of occupational homicides. The findings from the study did <u>not</u> show, however, what percentage of the occupational homicides were related to current or former employees.

2. Workplace homicides from 2005 to 2006 were the <u>fourth leading cause of death in the workplace</u>[22] behind fatalities caused on the highways, falls, or injury by workplace objects. Workplace homicide had seen an annual decline since 2003, declining 9 percent from 2005 to 2006, or from 567 to 516.[23]

3. Estimates for the annual average of workplace homicide where a coworker or former employee perpetrated the crime ranged from 6 percent to 15 percent.

In the first section of this chapter, I evaluated and presented findings from four national studies on psychological aggression in the workplace. In the second section, I presented findings of two national studies on non-fatal physical acts of violence and findings from government reports on workplace violence. These findings support the conclusion that psychological and physical aggression in the workplace are epidemic in the United States. In an attempt to understand the context of workplace violence for psychological and physical aggression, many factors need to be taken into consideration. For that reason, they are discussed below.

Factors of Workplace Violence

In examining workplace violence involving psychological aggression, four categories of factors implicated in bullying are discussed, namely, a) political, b) social and economic, c) organizational, and d) individual. In examining factors involved in physical aggression, the focus is limited to factors involved in "insider" (former or current employee) workplace homicide. Factors implicated in insider workplace homicide include the four categories of factors noted for psychological aggression, plus two additional factors: the media factor and the availability of guns factor.

The factors of workplace violence I considered in this discussion are by no means inclusive. They are, however, some of the most cited in the professional literature on the topic. Although the examination is brief, my hope is that readers unfamiliar with factors involved in workplace violence will arrive at a better appreciation for the reasons violence occurs in the workplace, particularly workplace murder and suicide.

This examination provides the context to the discussion of workplace violence within the Postal Service in the final section of this chapter and Appendix B.

Factors of Workplace Bullying

Political Factors

No discussion on bullying is complete without the discussion of how public policy influences the prevalence and impact of workplace bullying. When good paying jobs are outsourced to foreign countries, workers left to compete in a leaner workforce will experience more frequent bullying. When government policy is directed at weakening unions and is successful, employees become bullied more frequently. Further, when regulatory constraints to protect the interests of employees are non-existent or are weakened, employees will experience more frequent bullying. If government policy does not legally protect workers from psychological aggression directed by the employer, its prevalence will not be curbed or adequately dealt with. In chapter eleven, I provided requirements and recommendations to address these issues.

Social and Economic Factors

The greater the degree of emotional abuse or bullying that occurs in the society or culture at large influences how we treat one another in the workplace. If one is raised in a broken family, experiences a high degree of racism, experiences a higher degree of emotional abuse from family members, or has lived in poverty, these factors may influence the degree of bullying in the workplace, especially at the hands of those with the most power—the "bosses."

In the past twenty to thirty years, with the emergence of a globalized economy, relentless competitive pressures have negatively impacted the workplace environments for millions of workers. During this timeframe there have been unprecedented downsizings, restructurings, and mergers of companies, resulting in "pressurized work environments" for the affected workers.

These pressurized workplace environments have been and are triggers for bullying or emotional abuse. In addition to the "pressurized work environments" resulting from the effects of a globalized economy, there are not any meaningful laws or legal restraints at the federal and state level to effectively deal with the suffering and pain caused by bullying. In chapter eleven, in my open letter to Congress, this issue is addressed further.

Organizational Factors

As mentioned previously, pressurized work environments are significantly created by the impact of the global economy on organizations. The organizational cultures of many large- and medium-sized corporations in the United States have dramatically changed as a result of these global forces of competition. In fact, many studies show that the extent of bullying and pressurized environments is more prevalent in larger organizations where these changes occur more frequently.

These pressurized environments create the context for increased levels of stress, job insecurity, ineffective communications, decreased concern for employees' well-being, increased union and management tensions, *increased employee demands, and less autonomy*. Increased employee demands (i.e., heavier workloads and fewer resources) are usually the result of fewer employees in the organization, while less autonomy is most notable in the context of reduced employee involvement in decision-making and increases in electronic monitoring. In chapters seven through nine and appendices C-E, I explore and discuss these issues in the context of the postal culture.

Significant organizational factors that create the context for increased bullying in the workplace include autocratic leadership, rigid organizational structures, ineffective work design, ineffective role models (i.e., superiors who don't "walk the talk"), ineffective bonus or pay systems, and highly inflexible administrative processes and managerial policies.

These organizational factors play out in the workplace by first negatively impacting the managers and supervisors directly responsible for day-to-day operations. That is, they are given very high or unreasonable expectations for short-term results from their "bosses" and experience, in many cases, bullying from these "bosses." The supervisors and managers then cascade this pressure to the rank and file employees and, in too many cases, bully them in their attempts to achieve goal-driven results. In chapters ten and eleven, many of these issues are discussed in the context of how the Postal Service can shift from an unsafe and unhealthy organization to a healthy and safe one.

Individual Factors

Several studies have been conducted to shed light on what workplace bullies have in common. In one study, many of the bullies described themselves in comparison to others as anxious in social situations, low in social competence self-esteem, and highly aggressive. In another study, active bullies were found to have a higher sense of disregard for others and to have low self-esteem stability. In short, although studies showed that bullies were more competitive, assertive, and confrontational, there was an implication that they also lacked empathy for others. This prompted one author to title his book *Snakes in Suits24* and identified some bullies as clinical psychopaths.

Factors of Employee-Directed Homicide

Political Factors

Like psychological aggression, public policy influences the degree of physical aggression in the workplace, including employee-directed homicide. When the frequency and severity of bullying increases in the workplace, the greater is the potential for employee-directed homicide. Accordingly, when there is a lack of commitment for state and federal government representatives to create and enforce a public policy to protect the rights of employees, a greater likelihood for workplace violence exists.

Social and Economic Factors

Family structure and its dynamics shape individual members of our society, including our schools and cultural heritage. As indicated previously in the brief discussion of factors involved in bullying in the workplace, these social factors may also play a role in workplace homicide. Further, as previously discussed with bullying, economic factors related to the global economy and its impact on downsizing, restructuring, and mergers may play a role in workplace homicide.

Organizational Factors

Both individual bullying (i.e., stemming from "bosses") and organizational bullying (i.e., stemming from organizational practices) eventually can be a trigger or factor of workplace homicide. This is especially true regarding the over-control of employees and abusive supervision.

The role of organizational factors in workplace homicide needs to be given careful and full consideration; its role in workplace tragedies should not be underestimated.

The authors of the book *Ticking Bombs* stated it this way: "[N]o discussion of workplace violence would be balanced unless we focused some attention on what could be psychologically unfriendly companies, where employees are controlled through a culture of suppression and fear."[25]

It is important to note that factors of bullying or emotional abuse can and do lead to workplace suicides. In chapter eight, the impact of both individual bullying, organizational bullying, and the subsequent suicide of several postal employees are discussed from an insider's perspective.

Individual Factors

Many individual factors have been cited as triggers of workplace homicide, especially when viewed as a cluster of factors. The most common clinical factors provided are substance abuse, paranoid states (e.g., paranoia, delusional), psychotic disorders, major depressive disorders, and personality disorders. On the other hand, some of the more descriptive factors provided include a history of violence, fascination with weapons or lethal violence, concern about losing job, low self-esteem, pathological blamer, sense of outrage for perceived unfairness or injustices, a loner—socially isolated from others—and a low tolerance for criticism.

Media Factors

As a result of twenty-four-seven news and their continual replaying acts of horrific violence committed in the workplace and schools, some researchers have indicated that this phenomenon eventually may be a trigger for an individual who is "on the brink" of committing a homicidal act of violence in the workplace to actually carry it out.

In the book *The Copycat Effect*,[26] the author argues that some acts of workplace homicide are influenced by the media blitz environment in which we live. In this endeavor, the author presents a credible, fact-based presentation on the influence of the media on the occurrences of tragedies, ranging from shootings in schools, workplaces, suicide clusters, sniper incidences, to mass suicides in cults. In coverage of workplace shootings in his book, the author presents an entire chapter titled "Going Postal"[27] where he discusses some of the postal shootings from 1983 through 2001. The chapter investigates the copycat effect and the possible influence of extensive media coverage on prior workplace shootings.

Availability of Guns Factor

The easy availability of guns provides for an increased opportunity for workplace murder, especially multiple murders. As noted in Appendix B, many of the weapons used in the postal shootings were highly sophisticated weapons. In a significant number of the shootings, the perpetrator had multiple weapons, including assault weapons. Some of the perpetrators had a long history of mental problems, but still were able to obtain guns legally to carry out their deadly deeds.

Workplace Tragedies in the Postal Service

In presenting the history of workplace tragedies from 1983 to 2006, my sources included materials from the USPS violence prevention program, textbook and research articles, congressional reports, and Internet sites related to workplace violence. In Appendix B, I discuss each workplace tragedy, including the name of the perpetrator and the year of the tragic event.

From 1983 to 2006, there were seventeen workplace tragedies in the USPS. These workplace tragedies focused on employee-directed homicides (including suicides) by current and former employees. I define employee-directed homicide as *an act of murder of others or self by a current employee or former employee. The murder has a clear nexus to the workplace and is perpetrated against another employee(s) or self, in response to political, social, economic, organizational, individual, media, or the availability of guns factors.*

From 1985-1998, there were nine other incidences of postal workplace tragedies in USPS. Some of these tragedies received notoriety and press, while others did not. Unlike the previously mentioned seventeen workplace tragedies, there were no noteworthy links to organizational factors. There was, however, one suicide (discussed in Appendix B) that strongly appeared to involve organizational factors, but its occurrence was off postal premises.

In my review of a myriad of documents and credible anecdotal information regarding the twenty-six cases discussed in Appendix B, I attempted to report the cases in a balanced perspective, demonstrating the various factors involved in these postal tragedies. As previously discussed, factors involved in employee-directed homicide include political, social and economic, organizational, individual, media factors, and the availability of guns factor.

As a result of reviewing the seventeen workplace tragedies from 1983 to 2006, there were indications that virtually all the incidences were connected with both organizational and individual factors. Less clear are the relationships between these incidences and social and economic factors. In chapter eight, the relationship between incidences of workplace suicides and the organizational culture of the USPS is discussed. In chapter ten, steps to improve the workplace culture of USPS are delineated. If implemented, these guidelines will likely reduce workplace violence, including employee-directed homicide.

The potential influence of media factors in workplace tragedies was also previously discussed. It is interesting to note that of the seventeen postal tragedies from 1983 to 2006, two occurred in 1983 and three occurred in 2006. Taking in account all of the twenty-six postal tragedies (seventeen in this section and nine in the following section), the timeline ranges from: two in 1983, two in 1985, two in 1988, two in 1989, two in 1991, two in 1993, four in 1995, two in 1996, two in 1997, and three in 2006. These multiple years of postal tragedies don't prove that media factors were involved, but do provide statistical support that media events may influence the frequency of these tragedies. It supports the work of Loren Coleman in his book *The Copycat Effect: How the Media and Popular Culture Trigger Mayhem in Tomorrow's Headlines.*

Concluding Comment

In analyzing situations of workplace bullying or workplace homicide, it is critical to take an inclusive perspective, a perspective that takes in account political, social, and economic, organizational, and individual factors when bullying occurs, and the inclusion of media factors and the availability of guns factor when workplace homicide occurs. By taking an inclusive perspective, we not only gain a better understanding of why a particular incidence of workplace violence may have occurred, but we are also in a better position to take preventative measures in reducing the likelihood of it in the future.

In 2000, the highly publicized Califano Report[28] was released. However, since many of the report findings are a comparison between the national workforce and the U.S. Postal Service on measures for psychological aggression and physical aggression, the findings are discussed principally in chapter four.

CHAPTER THREE

Making the Case: "Going Postal" a Myth?

In this chapter, I discuss past attempts to frame the notion of "going postal" as a myth, primarily in the context of reports by the Centers for Disease Control (CDC) and the United States Postal Service Commission on a Safe and Secure Workplace.[29] I review the public relations efforts by the U.S. Postal Service to frame the notion of "going postal" as a myth. I conclude the chapter by providing a brief review of consultants and others in the popular and professional literature who essentially echoed the public relations efforts by the Postal Service.

"Going Postal" is a Myth and Bad Rap

Since the USPS's sponsoring of the first National Symposium of Workplace Violence with private and government participants in December 1993, the *St. Petersburg Times*[30] has been credited with popularizing the pejorative term "going postal." In response to this characterization, reports released by the Centers for Disease Control[31] (CDC) in 1993 and 1994 and the United States Postal Service Commission on a Safe and Secure Workplace Report in 2000 indicated that "going postal" was a myth and a bad rap. Below, I present two studies from the CDC, the second of which is supportive of this argument and was released to all major media outlets.

National Institute for Occupational Safety and Health Study Reports

In 1993, the National Institute for Occupational Safety and Health (NIOSH), a branch of the Centers for Disease Control (CDC),[32] released an in-depth study where it reported that **from 1983 to 1989** the USPS had experienced thirty-four work-related homicides at eleven post offices. The important point underscored in the study was that twenty of these work-related homicides were committed by a current or former employee, fourteen of which were committed in one incident.

Just several months later, on August 19, 1994, the CDC released to the major media outlets a report titled *Occupational Injury Deaths of Postal Workers—United States, 1980-1989*,[33] hereafter referred to as the CDC Report. *The major finding stated in this report, based on the timeframe **from 1980 to 1989**, was that neither the Postal Service industry nor postal occupations were at higher risk for workplace homicide.*

Before I provide the chief findings from the commission report below, it is important to note there were four separate postal tragedies **from 1991 to 1993** where ten more postal employees were killed at the hands of current or former employees. Two of these postal tragedies occurred on the same day, May 6, 1993. These tragedies are chronicled in Appendix B, including the tragedies from 1983-1989.

Report of United States Postal Service Commission On A Safe And Secure Workplace

On August 31, 2000, the *Report of United States Postal Service Commission On A Safe And Secure Workplace*[34] was officially released at a press conference held at the USPS's national headquarters in Washington, D.C. Joseph Califano, Jr. was the chairman of the Commission on a Safe and Secure Workplace and the signatory of the commission report, a report said to have cost the Postal Service over 4 million dollars. For the sake of brevity, the report hereafter in this book is referred to as the Califano Report.

The Califano Report was an intensive and comprehensive report commissioned and financed by the USPS for the expressed purpose of making the organization a safer one for its employees. The commission as part of its mission conducted onsite visits at postal installations, held three hundred fifty focus groups with rank and file employees, and interviewed more than three hundred postal management and union officials, at postal headquarters and in the field.

The commission also conducted a detailed examination of the USPS's postal policies and practices, chronicled postal workplace homicide from 1986 to 1999, and reviewed the USPS's violence prevention program. A critical component of the Califano Report was the **surveying** of twenty thousand postal employees. The survey involved six groups of employees, including city carriers, APWU employees, rural carriers, postmasters, and "other management."

As a result of their fact finding and surveying of employees, the Califano Report arrived at what was referred to as two bottom line conclusions about workplace violence and the USPS. The first major conclusion of the Califano Report was that "*[g]oing posta' is a myth, a bad rap.* Postal workers are no more likely to physically assault, sexually harass, or verbally abuse their coworkers than employees in the national workforce."[35]

The second major conclusion underscored in the Califano Report was that "[p]ostal employees are only a third as likely as those in the national workforce to be victims of homicide at work."[36] In support of this conclusion, the Califano Report[37] referenced a statistic from a NIOSH report (**1992-1998**) where it was reported that, annually, postal employees were only ***one-third as likely to be a victim of workplace homicide*** compared to the national workforce. It is important to note that the statistic from this report differed dramatically compared to the statistic in the CDC Report of 1994, which showed that the likelihood of being a victim of workplace homicide was **close to equal between the USPS and the national workforce for the years 1983 to 1989**. The relevancy of the statistics used and comparisons noted herein are discussed in greater detail in chapter four.

Public Relations Efforts by the Postal Service

The USPS received a bonanza of media attention and positive public relations with the release of the CDC Report in 1994 and the Califano Report in 2000. The sponsoring of the first National Symposium of Workplace Violence in 1993 contributed to the positive image of the USPS as an active participant in dealing with the issue of workplace violence. Over the past fourteen years, the USPS has used the CDC and Califano reports as "proof positive" that the notion of "going postal" is a myth and a bad rap. Several examples are explored below, starting with the earliest one in 1997.

A 1997 article in *Postal Life*,[38] a national newsletter from the USPS, makes reference to the conclusion of consultants, saying that the notion of USPS employees as violent is an unfair stereotype. Interestingly, the title of the article is "Going Postal Myth or Reality." In the article, reference is made to the CDC Report of 1994 in support of the argument that the USPS is a less dangerous place to work than the private sector.

In a 1998 USPS publication[39] titled *A Violence-Free Workplace*, a manual that typically has been provided at postal workplace violence prevention training sessions, the

USPS indicated that the organization is safe compared to the private industry. It goes beyond that statement by including the following quote taken from U.S. Department of Labor, Bureau of Labor Statistics (1996): "Postal work is one of the safest occupations in the job pool. Postal workers are not even a blip on the Department of Labor's scale of occupational fatalities, no matter how the statistics are compiled by job-related accident or homicide."[40] As indicated previously, these types of statistics and their relevancy are discussed in chapter four.

In the Postal Inspection Service's "Annual Report of Investigation,"[41] released in 2000, it specifically cited two key findings in the Califano Report, which were that *postal employees are only one-third as likely to be a victim of workplace homicide compared to the national workforce and that "going postal" is a myth and a bad rap.* Similarly, a communication to the press from the Public Affairs and Communications Department,[42] dated January 31, 2006, titled *USPS Commission on a Safe and Secure Workplace*, echoed these two key findings.

Private Consultants with Vested Interest

For brevity's sake only three examples are provided below regarding consultants echoing and ostensibly being part of the Postal Service's public relations efforts. Over the years, consultants with an "invested interest" have enjoined the USPS's public relations attempts to frame the notion of "going postal" as a myth. For example, Dr. Dennis Johnson was highly supportive of helping the Postal Service's public relations efforts to promote the argument that "going postal" was a myth and a bad rap. Dr. Johnson, a clinical psychologist, provided extensive consulting services on behalf of the USPS in the 1990s, including analyzing threat correspondences from postal employees and contributions to the development of the USPS's threat assessment team guidelines.

In an interview with Dr. Johnson, placed on the Howland Group website,[43] the interviewer asked about the phrase "going postal" and what has contributed to this image. Dr. Johnson responded by stating that the CDC, in one of their reports, indicated that the USPS did not even show up as one of the eighteen most dangerous positions. After a follow-up question was asked about thirty-five postal homicides committed by postal employees seeking revenge in the 1980s, he did not address the issue in the context of "going postal," but instead spoke in general terms about categories of work-related homicides.

Two national mediators, Rendon and Dougherty, who have provided extensive mediation services to the USPS, wrote an article titled "Going Postal: A New Definition and Model for Employment ADR."[44] In this article, the authors stated that the USPS had received some bad press in the 1990s about workplace violence despite actually being at or below the national average for workplace violence. In another article, titled "Avoiding Aggressive Behavior at Work,"[45] dated December 16, 2006, the consultants with Anderson and Anderson emphasized that the USPS had a proactive workplace violence program and that the Postal Service had instituted an anger management program. The authors claimed, without offering any credible evidence, that the USPS had made a remarkable change in morale as a result of this program. In support of the Postal Service's public relations efforts to frame the notion of "going postal" as a myth, the authors stated:

> For many years, the United States Postal Service was considered to be an organization in which employees exhibited problems managing anger in the workplace. In fact, the phrase "going postal" was commonly used to describe the behavior of problem employees at work. It is interesting to note that the United States Postal Service is now considered one of the safest large organizations in the nation to work.[46]

Interestingly, the consulting firm of Anderson and Anderson, on their website, indicated that they have provided consulting services to the USPS since February 29, 2004.

Popular and Professional Press

In popular and professional literature there have been numerous articles where the notion of "going postal" was described as misleading or closer to a myth than a reality. Below I provide three examples from the popular and professional literature. The notion of popular press is loosely defined here as information available on the Internet.

In an article presented by Paul Temple titled "Real Danger and 'Postal' Mythology,"[47] he cites statistics provided in the Califano Report and then concludes that "the math tells us it isn't fair that postal workers have become poster children for workplace violence" where he makes notes of CDC reports. Similarly, in the book *Violence on the Job: Identifying Risks and Developing Solutions* (1996) authors VandenBos and Bulatao state:

> The U.S. Postal Service, despite all the media hype on particular workplace homicides in its facilities, is far from being a high risk environment for occupational fatalities. Relative to other work settings, the Postal Service is in fact a "safe" workplace environment—the occupational fatality rate of postal workers is only 37% of the rate for all workers combined.[48]

Interestingly, the last chapter[49] of the above-mentioned book was written by a former USPS manager of the Employee Assistance Program (EAP), along with Dr. Dennis Johnson[i] and another contract employee with the EAP. As a final example of the professional press taking aim at the notion of "going postal," in the book *Understanding Workplace Violence: A guide for managers and employees*, Paludi states:

> Myth 2: The Post Office is the worst place for workplace violence. Reality: The phrase "going postal" implies that postal workers frequently kill people at work. Of course, there have been some tragic episodes of this, but the Post Office is hardly the most dangerous place to work, and in many ways it is relatively safe.[50]

In this chapter, I provided conclusions from both CDC and Califano reports stating that the USPS is a safe work environment compared to the national workforce and that going postal is a myth. I presented the public relations efforts by the USPS in its campaign to frame the notion of going postal as a myth, including the role of consultants and the popular and professional literature providing credence to this position. In chapter four, I critically analyze the relevancy, accuracy, and ethical stance of these conclusions.

---

i   See excerpts taken from aforementioned interview with Dr. Johnson.

CHAPTER FOUR
Let's Examine the Record: "Going Postal" a Reality?

In chapter three, the Postal Service and the Califano commission both used Centers of Disease Control (CDC) reports to bolster the claim that the USPS was a safe place to work and to frame the notion of "going postal" as a myth. In this chapter, I re-examine the 1994 CDC Report[51] and Califano Report[52], noting discrepancies in key findings and conclusions. In the broad re-examination of these reports, I discuss two germane professional articles and a congressional report.

Closer Look at the CDC Report

In the CDC report of August 19, 1994, as part of an ***editorial note***, it specifically stated that "[a]lthough the occupational rate for the Postal Service industry is similar to the national rate for all industries, coworkers appear to be disproportionately responsible for homicides that occur in the Postal Service."[53] This editorial note is in stark contrast with the ***opening sentence*** in the nationally released media bulletin:

> Extensive media coverage of work-related homicides at U.S. Postal
> Service facilities raised the concern about whether postal workers are
> at increased risk for work-related homicide, particularly from those
> committed by disgruntled coworkers. Based on national surveillance
> data, neither the Postal Service industry nor postal occupations are
> among the groups at increased risk for work-related homicide.[54]

One has to wonder if the CDC released this entire report, including the editorial note, to the press on August 21, 1994, or just page one of the document. Although the facts provided in the report support that the USPS is a safer place to work compared to many other industries, it is imperative to consider more specifically what this means. In a 1995 NIOSH Alert Bulletin,[55] it noted that *high-risk workplaces* for homicide include establishments such as taxi cabs, liquor stores, gas stations, and grocery stores. Similarly, the bulletin noted that *high-risk occupations* for homicide include taxicab drivers/chauffeurs, law enforcement officers, hotel clerks, and gas station workers.

When looking at these facts in the broader context, it does not support the conclusion by the Califano Report or the USPS that the notion of "going postal" is a myth. The commonly held understanding of the term "going postal" by the general public is a disgruntled employee acting out violently, usually in the form of homicide, toward bosses or coworkers in the workplace. Historically, it has been a commonly held understanding by the general public that postal employees are disproportionately involved in employee-directed homicides.

Accordingly, in order to make a valid determination about the notion of "going postal," it is a reasonable requirement that the category of postal employee-directed homicide only be compared with other industry employee-directed homicide.[ii] It is clear that taxicab drivers are not shooting their bosses or coworkers. They are being shot in the act of robbery. So the question becomes: Why would the CDC release a report that is very misleading or appears very misleading to the press and public? The answer to this question follows.

In her book *Crisis Communications*,[56] Kathleen Banks frequently quotes Roy Betts, as a result of her interview with him in 1995. During this timeframe, Roy Betts was the media relations representative for the USPS, who reported to Frank Brennan, the manager of media relations, who in turn reported to Larry Speakes, Corporate Relations Vice-President and a former member of the Reagan administration. During this timeframe, Larry Speakes directly reported to Marvin Runyon, the Postmaster General.

Roy Betts is quoted in *Case: U.S. Postal Service and Workplace Violence* regarding the Postal Service's collaboration with the CDC on their report of August 19, 1994. Mr. Betts was quoted as follows: "We were aware that people from employee relations had been working with the CDC on the study."[57]

Banks further states that the CDC released the subject report to the Associated Press and that positive stories about the USPS were reported in many of the major newspapers in the country. In the conclusion of her case study of the USPS's public

---

ii   The categories, sources, or types of workplace violence are discussed in Appendix A.

relations campaign on workplace violence, she attributed the following statement to Roy Betts: "The whole idea of 'going postal' is a myth. To us, 'going postal' means delivering billions of cards, letters, and packages on time. That's going postal."[58] As previously stated, taxicab drivers are not shooting their bosses or coworkers. It is current or former coworkers that are doing the shootings.

Looked at from this vantage point, the statistics from the CDC report[59] for the years 1992 to1998 showed that the homicide rate for taxi drivers was one hundred fifty times higher than letter carriers. Clearly, this is an irrelevant comparison in terms of either supporting or refuting the notion that "going postal" is a myth, a bad rap. In this context, only the focus on the frequency rate for employee-directed homicide is relevant. Below, I examine two scholarly articles and a congressional report with this focus in mind.

In the article titled "Firing back: The Growing Threat of Workplace Homicide,"[60] Fox notes that the vast majority of homicides in the workplace involve intruders (i.e., outsiders) in the act of robberies of taxicab drivers and convenience store clerks, rather than the vengeful acts of angry and disgruntled employees. He goes on to say that the USPS has more than a fair share of these violent tragedies where employees are trying to *get even* with their supervisors or employers.

Similarly, in the article titled "Labor and Politics in the U.S. Postal Service,"[61] Baxter points out that the postal homicides at postal facilities are unique in that the killings are directed at fellow employees, their bosses, and themselves. He indicates that these types of incidences point to the ways in which the organizational culture may trigger certain individuals to commit these acts of violence.

In a joint hearing of the United States Congress[62] in its review of violence in the U.S. Postal Service, NIOSH estimates were cited as part of the record for the 1980s *where it is noted that during this timeframe 13 percent of the employee-directed homicides occurred at postal facilities by current or former employees, where less than three-quarters of 1 percent of the total full-time civilian labor force was employed*.

Closer Look at the Califano Report

The examination of the Califano Report is critical because it has been an integral part of the Postal Service's public relations efforts to support that the notion of "going postal" is a myth. The enormity of the report is revealed by how the national media reacted to it, especially national newspapers and magazines. If you Google "going postal as a myth," for example, there are still archived articles from the national media emphasizing the major conclusions and findings of the report.

After fully examining the facts provided in the articles and the report above, statistically the USPS is by far a more dangerous place to work when compared to other industries and occupations as a whole in terms of employee-directed homicide. Viewed in this context, the **second significant conclusion** of the Califano Report that "[p]ostal employees are only a third as likely as those in the national workforce to be victims of homicide at work"[63] is meaningless and arguably disingenuous.

In reading the Califano Report with this conclusion in mind, the authors seem to completely avoid addressing the issue as to *why* there is a disproportionate number of employee-directed homicides at postal installations in the timeframe that they examined, from **1986 to 1999**. A statement on page two of the Califano Report does not absolve the members of being misleading or biased in how the report was presented and what was emphasized or not emphasized in the report.

For example, on page two in the report it states: "It is impossible to compare with any precision the likelihood of a postal employee being killed by a coworker or a non-coworker with that of an employee in the national workforce."[64] Although this is factually true, it is still useful to make comparisons based on information that is available. The aforementioned statement, along with the other facts discussed previously, gives credence to the inference that the members of the Califano Report were purposely trying to place the USPS in a more positive light.

I critically analyzed the second conclusion of the Califano Report first because it is the most relevant regarding what is generally meant by the notion of "going postal"—namely, homicide(s) committed in the workplace by a disgruntled former or current postal employee. It was the **first conclusion** in the report, however, that actually was linked to the notion of going postal.

More specifically, the authors state the first conclusion as: "Going postal is a myth, a bad rap. Postal workers are no more likely to physically assault, sexually harass, or verbally abuse their coworkers than employees in the national workforce."[65] This conclusion does not address the issue of employee-directed homicide. Aside from this omission, the examination below begins with the first conclusion of the Califano Report, within the context of what we learned in chapters one and two and regarding psychological aggression and non-fatal physical violence. In this examination, discrepancies in the report's survey methodology and the reported findings are discussed.

A significant criticism of the Califano Report was that fully developed sampling weights were not satisfactorily used to account for differences in probability for selection, non-response, and post-stratification to known populations.[66] Despite this criticism, I review the Califano findings that supposedly support the conclusion that postal employees are no more likely to **physically assault or verbally abuse** their coworkers than employees in the national workforce. I will first analyze the reported findings for verbal abuse, followed by an examination of findings pertaining to physical assault.

Psychological Aggression Findings

Before I begin this discussion, it is relevant to delineate the items that made up the category of verbal abuse in the Califano survey.[67] The items in the category of verbal abuse include: 1) tried to provoke arguments, 2) called you names or put you down in front of others, 3) made you feel inadequate, 4) shouted or swore at you, 5) frightened you, and 6) made intimidating or threatening gestures at you.

The Califano Report showed that for the previous twelve months, for **outsiders and co-workers combined**, the frequency of verbal abuse for the USPS compared to the national sample was 36 percent vs. 33 percent.[68] Accordingly, this finding demonstrated that the frequency of verbal abuse found in the USPS was 3 percent higher. However, when reviewing the findings of the Califano Report for the previous twelve months for **only coworkers**, the frequency rate for the USPS compared to the national sample was 30 percent vs. 25 percent,[69] indicating that the frequency of verbal abuse found in the USPS was 5 percent higher.

Unlike some of the national studies I examined in chapter two regarding harassment and bullying, this study did not take a systematic look at the repetitiveness of verbal abuse or its impact on employees' health and well-being. It also did not make a judgment in terms of the behaviors associated with verbal abuse rising to the level of harassment or bullying. The frequency of verbal abuse, therefore, in this study was considerably higher compared to the studies that looked at harassment or bullying in the workplace over a twelve-month period. For example, as reported in Appendix A, the Northwestern Study[70] found the frequency of harassment at 19 percent for the national population during the previous twelve months, while the frequency estimate from the U.S. Workplace Bullying Survey[71] was around 13 percent.

It is difficult to understand why the Califano study did not provide separate findings, like some of the studies reviewed in Appendix A, regarding the source of the behavior in terms of coworkers or bosses. Rather than using the term "coworker," as noted in the study, it would have been less misleading if the authors used the term "insider." Why? Because in this study **"coworkers"**[72] included all of the following employees: 1) supervisor or manager, 2) someone who reports to you, and 3) other employees. By charting and presenting the results with craft employees and management officials rolled up together, one has to wonder if this was by design to place the USPS in a more favorable light. This is especially remarkable in that the more specific findings were readily available to report and comment upon. For example, verbal abuse attributed to employees by their postal supervisors/managers compared to supervisors/managers from the national sample was: **61.8 percent for the USPS sample vs. 48.2 percent for the national sample**—a very remarkable difference of 13.6 percent.[73]

From whatever vantage point you view the Califano Report's conclusion that USPS's employees are no more likely to verbally abuse their coworkers than employees in the national workforce, the report's own findings do not support this conclusion. Of course, 5 percent is not significantly higher, but it is significant.

When you compare the difference between the USPS and the national sample regarding verbal abuse and the category of supervisor/manager, the difference of **13.6 percent is a highly remarkable difference**. In view of the inaccurate conclusion provided in the Califano Report regarding verbal abuse and the data used to support it, it seems highly likely that the Califano commission purposely skewed their own findings to place the USPS in a more favorable light.

Physical Aggression Findings

The Califano Report findings regarding the prevalence of physical assaults in the workplace were within the range of the findings from two national studies noted in chapter two and Appendix A. For example, in the Northwestern study[74] physical assaults were reported occurring at a 3 percent rate in the previous twelve months, while the National Survey of Workplace Health and Safety[75] reported an overall frequency rate of 6 percent in that timeframe. The reported frequency in the Califano

Report, when combining the categories of outsiders and coworkers, was 5 percent for the Postal Service and 5 percent for the national sample.

Before I review additional findings of the Califano Report regarding physical assault, it is first relevant to list the items used to make up the category of physical abuse used in the survey.[76] The items used were: 1) thrown something at you that could hurt you, 2) pushed, grabbed, kicked you, etc., 3) hit you with an object, 4) beat you up, 5) threatened you with a gun, knife, or other weapon, 6) used a gun, knife, or other weapon on you, and 7) raped you or attempted to rape you.

As stated previously, the Califano Report showed that for the previous twelve months for **outsiders and coworkers combined**: the frequency of physical assault for the USPS compared to the national sample was: 5 percent vs. 5 percent.[77] Thus the results showed that the frequency of physical assault found in the USPS was equal to that of the national sample. However, when reviewing the findings of the Califano Report for the previous twelve months for **only coworkers**, the frequency rate for the USPS compared to the national sample was 4 percent vs. 3 percent,[78] indicating that the frequency of physical assault found in the USPS was 1 percent higher.

Comparable to what was discussed with verbal abuse previously, the category used for "**coworker**" for physical attack in the study include three sub-categories,[79] namely: 1) supervisor or manager, 2) someone who reports to you, and 3) other employees. Accordingly, the findings arrived at and compared between postal employees and the national sample are seriously flawed and are dramatically misleading.

For example, in looking at the comparison for "supervisor/manager" committing a physical assault on employees under their purview, the reported frequency rate was **19.9 percent** for the USPS vs. **15.3 percent** for the national sample, **a difference of 4.6 percent**. More dramatic and startling, when comparing the frequency of "other employees" committing physical assault, the frequency was **73.8 percent** for the USPS vs. **46.5 percent** for the national sample, **a remarkable difference of 27.3 percent**. These findings (i.e., data frequencies) can be found at Table C.1, Q34 in the report.[80]

As noted previously, a significant criticism of the Califano Report was that fully developed **sampling weights** were not used to satisfactorily account for differences in probability for selection, non-response, and post-stratification to known populations. Suffice to say, at this point, because of methodological concerns with how the data was calculated in this study and how the information was presented with respect to comparing the frequency of physical assault between the USPS and a national sample, the conclusion that postal employees are no more likely to physically assault their coworkers than employees in the national workforce has to be rejected outright. As noted with the presentation of findings for verbal abuse in the Califano Report, it similarly can be concluded that the findings for physical assault in the study strongly appear to be skewed in order to place the USPS in a more favorable light.

Concluding Remarks

In taking a closer look at the record presented herein, it became very clear that the arguments by the USPS, CDC, Califano Report, and invested consultants to frame the notion of "going postal" as a myth is not supported by the overwhelming evidence to the contrary. It can be cogently argued that the term "going postal" is demeaning and inflammatory; however, this is not a valid reason to paint a false narrative. The observation or conclusion, however, that the USPS's work environments have been a factor involved in some of its employee-directed homicides and that the occurrence of these types of homicides are far more frequent in the Postal Service compared to other organizations is supported by the record. The overwhelming empirical evidence supports that this notion is both accurate and fair.

There are two old adages that are relevant to the last two chapters: 1) the truth lies somewhere in between, and 2) the devil is in the details. In the broader context of these two chapters, it is unmistakable: The devil is in the details.

CHAPTER FIVE
A Closer Look: The Postal Service's Violence Prevention Efforts

In this chapter, I review the implementation of a comprehensive workplace violence prevention program by the Postal Service. Since I played an important role in the development of several key parts of this program, it is relevant that the discussion begin with a brief history of my professional career with the USPS. After discussing my various professional roles in the USPS, important events that influenced the USPS's violence prevention program are highlighted, including the influence of the General Accounting Office (GAO) and congressional committee reports in response to concerns about workplace tragedies in the Postal Service and its culture.

In the last section of the chapter, I critically examine specific workplace violence prevention strategies emphasized by the USPS, including: 1) selection, 2) security, 3) communication of policy, 4) environment and culture, 5) employee support, and 6) separation. In examining these specific strategies, where appropriate, my role and experience are highlighted.

Brief History of Professional Career with USPS

From 1982 through 1986, I served as a union steward with the American Postal Workers Union (APWU) in Southern California. During this timeframe, I served as the APWU Vice-President and President of a small local branch in San Diego County. Beginning in September 1986 and ending in November 1993, I worked as an Employee Assistance Program (EAP) coordinator/supervisor. During this timeframe, I held positions in the EAP at a management sectional center (MSC) and two postal divisions.

As an EAP representative, counseling and support services were provided to both craft and management employees and their family members. Specific counseling services provided included dealing with issues ranging from alcohol and drugs, marriage and family issues, work and life stress, legal and financial concerns, and anger management. I provided training for supervisor/managers on key aspects of the EAP and how to deal with employees who were having difficulties in the work-place. I collaborated with postal unions to help benefit all employees by developing zero tolerance policies and joint statements of support to combat violence in the workplace.

During the 1992-1993 postal restructuring, I was selected as an internal consultant (i.e., workplace improvement analyst) to deal with workplace violence and work-place climate issues at a postal district. In this position, I analyzed workplace issues, provided consultation to the leadership on how to improve the workplace climate, and gave feedback and coaching services to district leaders, including two of the lead executives of the district. I provided a detailed analysis of the district's Voice of Employee (VOE) survey each quarter and mediations, retention studies, and work-place climate assessments were conducted. I provided recommendations on change management, and I utilized various assessments tools to improve managerial com-munication and leadership skills. Additionally, I had a central role in the develop-ment of the national threat assessment team (TAT) guidelines and zero tolerance policy statements and procedures. Effective January 3, 2007, I retired from the USPS after thirteen years in this position.

Events Leading up to the Postal Service's Violent Prevention Program

Prior to the development and implementation of the USPS's violent prevention pro-gram, there were eleven postal tragedies from 1983 to 1991[iii]. During this timeframe, there were four major reports from the GAO[81] (i.e., 1986, 1988, 1989, and 1990) and a 1991 congressional committee report,[82] titled *A Post Office Tragedy: The Shooting at Royal Oak*. The GAO reports assessed the postal culture. The congressional report examined aspects of the postal culture, including the specific events leading up to the shooting at the Royal Oak postal facility by Thomas McIlvane.

Shortly after the Royal Oak shooting in 1991, the USPS formed a Violence in the Workplace Committee, consisting of representatives from major union organiza-tions, management associations, and high-ranking postal management officials. A

---

iii   As noted in Appendix B.

national twenty-four-hour hotline was set up for employees to voice concerns about their workplace, including threats and assaults.

In 1990, in the capacity as an EAP representative, I developed a joint statement of support document on behalf of union organizations, management associations, and management sectional center (MSC) leaders, where it was agreed that all would co-operate in the prevention of workplace violence. To the best of my understanding, this was the first such agreement between postal unions, management associations, and the USPS. Shortly after the most recent postal tragedy at the Royal Oak postal facility, while detailed to a position at postal headquarters in December 1991, I submitted as noted in Appendix B a copy of this joint statement to the attention of Joe Mahon, former senior vice-president of labor relations, at postal headquarters.

In February 1992, the USPS and the union organizations and management associations signed a "Joint Statement on Violence and Behavior". All major union organizations entered into the agreement, with the exception of the American Postal Workers Union. After several drafts, Vincent Sombrotto, former president of the National Association of Letter Carriers, was subsequently credited as authoring the final document.

From 1993 to 1997, there were ten more postal tragedies,[iv] two of which occurred on the same day, in 1993. As a result of the prior tragedies and these more recent ones, the GAO conducted investigations in 1992, 1994, and 1997. The GAO reports[83] of 1994 and 1997 investigations were in-depth studies on the USPS's culture, including its labor/management relations. Both the 1994 and 1997 GAO reports resulted from congressional leaders' requests, due to concerns stemming from the congressional joint hearing[84] in 1993, titled *Joint Hearing to Review Violence in the U.S. Postal Service*, including the scale of postal shootings over the previous decade.

After the shootings in 1993, the USPS conducted focus groups throughout the USPS. Most of the reviews were facilitated by outside contractors. I conducted a review in a major Northern California mail processing facility. As a result of these two shootings, it spurred the USPS to create a new position to help with violence prevention and with organizational change and workplace climate issues. Initially, the position was titled EAP Coordinator and later changed to Workplace Improvement Analyst. Beginning in November 2007, the position title was changed to Workplace Environment Analyst.

---

iv   As noted in Appendix B.

The new position of workplace improvement analyst coincided with the massive restructuring of the USPS in 1992-1993, which is discussed in more detail in chapter six. In the beginning, there were eighty-five workplace improvement analysts selected, one for each postal district. In 1994, some postal districts began developing zero tolerance policies and action plans to deal with threats and assaults in the workplace.

From 1994 to 1997, the USPS developed the basic components of their violence prevention program, including the development and implementation of the "Threat Assessment Team Guide" and six-point violence prevention strategy. In 1996, I was selected by postal headquarters to a national task force to develop the USPS's "Threat Assessment Team Guide" for its eighty-five postal districts and played a key role in its development. Incorporated in the "Threat Assessment Team Guide" is the USPS's six-point violence prevention strategy; I review this document below.

Critical Examination of the Postal Service's Six-Point Violence Prevention Strategy

1. **Selection:** Hire the right people for the right job in the first place.

The strategy "selection" focuses on conducting pointed interviews, thorough background checks on new hires, pre-employment drug testing, and continuation of the ninety-day probationary period for new employees. In my last ten years with the USPS as a workplace improvement analyst, the organization had done a fairly credible job in implementing this specific strategy at my postal district. Prior to the mid-1990s, there was ample anecdotal and documentary evidence that showed employees were still being hired without background checks.

Historically, officials had felt pressured to hire employees quickly in order to make short-term performance goals. Documentary evidence noted in the Califano Report[85] showed that several of the postal tragedies may have been averted if background checks were more effective.

2. **Security:** Ensure appropriate safeguards for people and property.

In late 1991 through 1993, part of this strategy was addressed by setting up a twenty-four-hour postal hotline to report work climate issues, threats, and assaults. This hotline was later discontinued and an Office of the Inspector General (OIG)

800 number was substituted for this purpose. Beginning in 1997, the OIG became primarily responsible for oversight of the USPS violence prevention program, while the inspection service continued with its role of investigating threats and assaults in the workplace. In its early history, the OIG conducted a significant number of audits regarding the USPS's workplace violence program, including specific strategies related to the program.[v]

In 1993 congressional testimony,[86] the APWU proposed the installation of video cameras and silent alarms, increasing the number of security staff at offices with a high risk of outside violence, and monitoring employee parking lots. However, no significant physical security was provided in the USPS's facilities prior to the events of September 11 and the subsequent anthrax deaths in 2001.

Fortunately, today the majority of large postal facilities have extensive security measures in place; however, physical security is not necessarily sufficient, especially in light of the easy access to guns by people with severe mental disorders. For example, Jennifer San Marco[vi] was noted as having severe mental disorders and she forcibly entered a postal facility with a gun she legally purchased.

The Califano Report[87] recommended the establishment of a communication system for letter carriers on delivery routes, especially in high crime and remote areas. This is a worthy recommendation, but it has not been implemented.

3. **Communication of Policy:** Consistently communicate and enforce postal policy regarding violent and inappropriate behavior.

This strategy emphasizes communicating and enforcing a clear and direct zero tolerance policy regarding threats and assaults. It also emphasizes the reporting and recording of serious inappropriate behaviors, including threats and assaults.

Although a zero tolerance policy had been developed in most postal districts since 1994, it generally was not communicated annually to employees and effectively enforced. Many of the serious threats and assaults were not recorded at many of the postal districts. The inspection service is charged with recording *credible threats* and assaults, but sometimes this does not happen. If the information is not reported to

---

v   Additional information on the OIG and its impact on security and the postal culture are detailed in Appendix E

vi   See Appendix B.

them, it cannot be recorded. This is especially true in some districts that historically did not have an active threat assessment team.

Neither the USPS headquarters nor its eight area offices provided ongoing monitoring of the above-noted critical gaps. As a serious consequence of this lack of oversight, a postal district close to the one where I had worked rarely communicated a zero policy to its employees. This was allowed to occur over a ten-year period, leaving serious inappropriate behaviors, including threats and assaults, unenforced and unrecorded.

4. **Environment and Culture:** Create a work setting and maintain an atmosphere that is perceived to be fair and free from unlawful and inappropriate behavior.

Below I review the factors or emphases the USPS provided to achieve this particular strategy, including well-trained supervisors/managers and threat assessment teams. Other relevant factors or emphases provided by the USPS to achieve this strategy include labor/management relations, employee communications, and participation.[vii]

Well-Trained Supervisors and Managers

When discussing the notion of well-trained supervisors, the USPS touts the Associate Supervisors Program (ASP) as one of its pinnacle achievements. The USPS has also developed numerous programs for corporate succession for its middle and senior management employees. Clearly, it is a sound business strategy to plan and develop managers for future critical positions, especially in view of a massive departure of seasoned veterans from the "baby boomer" generation. Sadly, these training or succession programs in the USPS have not significantly impacted the work setting in terms of creating and fostering a fair and respectful work atmosphere, as perceived by rank and file employees.

As a corollary duty to my job as an internal consultant, I reviewed promotion applications and interviewed hundreds of candidates for the Associate Supervisors Program (ASP), from 2004 through 2007, at my postal district. The program was fairly successful in preparing the candidates for targeted mail processing or delivery operations positions. The training program prepared them technically in terms of managing mail processing or delivery operations within the USPS; however, training targeted

---

vii   These factors are examined primarily in chapter seven, and a more detailed analysis of the USPS's culture is presented in chapters six through nine and Appendices C-E.

to improve interpersonal skills and trustworthy leadership rarely was practiced in the work setting.

Upon their arrival at the mail processing or delivery units as supervisors, they were expected to behave contrary to the human relations training they received by their higher-level supervisors. One of the common themes I heard from graduates of the ASP regarding "instructions" by their higher-level supervisors went something like this: Your classroom experience was one thing; now you must adjust to the *real world* on the workroom floor.

The USPS is to be commended for preparing its supervisors and managers for future technical tasks and back filling of critical positions. Very little change transpired, however, toward creating a more respectful work climate as a result of training targeted to improve interpersonal or leadership skills of management personnel. Over the last three years of my employment as an internal consultant, the work environment steadily eroded in terms of how employees were treated in the workplace.[viii]

Threat Assessment Teams

In 1998, the development and implementation of threat assessment teams in the USPS was a remarkable achievement. The TAT[88] was designed primarily to identify potential perpetrators, assess risk of violence, and recommend plans to reduce the potential for violent actions. The composition of the TAT included representatives from human resources, postal operations, and the inspection service. The workplace improvement analyst played a key role on the team in most postal districts.

At my postal district, I had a highly significant role in the TAT, including the arranging for quarterly meetings, documenting significant meetings, developing risk abatement plans, and ongoing collaboration with the inspection service. I usually became aware of a threat or an assault before other TAT members, and when this occurred, I would initiate TAT meetings. It is important to note that I was formally recognized for my duties and role as a TAT member by the inspector-in-charge of an area that spanned three postal districts.

Historically, one significant problem with TAT membership at the vast majority of postal districts has been the lack of involvement of the unions in the process. Another significant problem was that the roles of certain members of the team

---

viii   This observation is examined in detail in Part 4.

changed several times from 1998 to 2007. Because of TAT "turf battles" among members of human resources, postal operations, and the inspection service, team functioning was far from optimal in carrying out its primary duty at some postal districts. More specifically, the responsibilities of the team to reduce threats and implement risk abatement plans were compromised because of these issues. Compounding this problem of TAT functioning, a significant number of postal districts did not have regular TAT meetings to deal with threats and assaults in the workplace. Several OIG audits and postal headquarter audits support this observation.[ix]

5. **Employee Support:** Ensure that managers, supervisors, and employees are aware of the resources available to assist them in dealing with the problems of work and daily living.

In the restructuring of the USPS in 1992-1993, its internal Employee Assistance Program (EAP) was contracted out; the transition was a disaster. For example, a significant number of postal districts closed their internal EAP offices before new contractors were hired to provide counseling services. At a critical time in USPS history, EAP counselors were not available to assist postal employees. In the 1993 congressional hearing,[89] criticism of the new external EAP provider was noted by one of the postal management associations.

Besides the very poor implementation process to change from an internally based program to an externally contracted one, the learning curve for the outside EAP representatives was a long and time-consuming effort. The USPS has a unique culture, and it took many of these new EAP representatives up to two years to understand how postal culture influences employee behavior. For a number of years many of the outside EAP representatives behaved as if they did not serve the USPS, but instead served their contracting company. This was actually encouraged by Federal Occupational Health officials (the third party for the contractors and the USPS), and one contracting company in particular, during the transitional years.

In the last six to eight years, however, the Employee Assistance Program (EAP) has done a good job in providing counseling services to postal employees, especially recently. Beginning in 2005, an EAP committee in each district was formed to provide support, guidance, and oversight of the EAP. The committee consists of representatives from union organizations and postal management. Interestingly, this was a recommendation made in the Califano Report.[90] Unlike the lack of monitoring

---

ix   Relevant findings from these audits and some specific examples of turf battles in the TAT, based on my own personal experience, are highlighted in chapter eight.

of zero tolerance policies and the TAT noted above, postal headquarters had been doing a good job of monitoring the responsibilities of the districts' committee on a quarterly basis prior to my retirement.

6.**Separation:**When separation becomes necessary, handle the process professionally, including assessing inappropriate behavior and potentially violent circumstances.

As part of this strategy, the Postal Service developed a publication[91] to deal with the sensitive issues of separation or removal from postal employment. The implementation of a "Peaceful Parting" initiative was a critical, two-part recommendation in the Califano Report.[92] It included that the USPS expand its pilot training program "Separation: A Peaceful Parting" nationwide, incorporating lessons from the pilot phase. It recommended that the postal unions develop systematic and sensitive procedures and train those responsible for notifying grievants when a termination has been upheld in arbitration. One of the justifications the Califano Report used in proffering the above-noted recommendations was based significantly on the fact that two postal tragedies were immediately triggered when postal employees found out they lost their arbitration cases to keep their jobs.[x]

The main point is that the removal of an employee or the process that may lead up to the eventual removal of an employee needs to be handled in a respectful and sensitive manner. The authors of *Ticking Time Bombs* summed it up this way:

> For some people, the job is more than just what they do, it becomes who they are; it gives them identity and purpose. To some rational, normal people, losing their job is just the same as losing their identity … Work, to most of us, is not a place to earn a paycheck and leave, it gives us social interaction, satisfaction, and for some, a reason to even get out of bed in the morning. Faced with no job, or even the prospect of job loss, some people find their coping mechanisms sadly lacking.[93]

Interestingly, one particular book on workplace violence is titled *When Work Equals Life*.[94] This title complements what is conveyed in the above-noted passage. It behooves management officials, who have the responsibility of removing employ-

---

x   For example, as noted in Appendix B, the postal tragedies committed by Thomas McIlvane in 1991 and Charles Jennings in 1996.

ees from their jobs, to recognize that separation from employment can be highly traumatic and usually engenders serious consequences for the employee, the employee's family members, and the organization. Management officials need to be aware that demonstrating a caring attitude and respect for employees during the removal process reduces the likelihood that an employee will later seek revenge on the organization and its members. This acknowledgment and practice can proactively prevent a workplace tragedy.

During August 2000, in a presentation by Suzanne Milton,[95] former manager of workplace environment improvement, she indicated that there were four pilot sites for the Peaceful Parting initiative and that standard operation procedures (SOP) would later be implemented nationally. I was very hopeful when this information was initially disseminated; however, the initiative was never expanded nationally. As indicated previously, this was a recommendation in the Califano Report to expand this initiative nationally within the USPS.

As one of their most important strategies, in my opinion, the USPS has done very little to actually implement the Peaceful Parting initiative. The reasons for this are complex, but the most obvious reason is that the USPS is strongly resistant toward implementing initiatives that could potentially challenge the paramilitary culture of its organizational structure. Historically and currently, labor relations in the USPS have served to buffer any real attempts to change these dynamics; this point will be discussed in Part 4. To the best of my knowledge, postal unions have not taken a proactive stance to fulfill the Califano Report's[96] recommendation to devise systematic and sensitive procedures along with training to those responsible for notifying grievants that their terminations had been upheld in arbitration.

In this chapter, I examined the USPS violence prevention program and its related core strategies. To the USPS's credit, it has developed an excellent violence prevention plan to deal with violence in the workplace for both psychological workplace aggression and physical workplace aggression. The problem with the program is that its six core strategies were not fully implemented or fully executed, especially the Peaceful Parting initiative. In Part 4, it is shown that this lack of commitment to follow through is related to the USPS's emphasis on top-down controls and paramilitary approaches to solving its organizational issues.

CHAPTER SIX
Building Blocks of the Postal Culture

In this chapter, I briefly discuss the early history of the Postal Service from 1775 to the 1950s. In the next section, I examine significant events and changes in the Postal Service from the 1950s to 1992. In this examination, I give special attention to the far-reaching 1970 Postal Reorganization Act[97] and the subsequent realignments, re-structurings, and downsizings that transpired after its passage.[xi] In the final section of the chapter, I conclude with a brief commentary on the philosophy of scientific management and the significant changes in top leadership positions, beginning in 1998.

Early History

The first Postmaster General of the Postal Department was Benjamin Franklin, in 1775. He was selected under the Second Continental Congress, which was empowered to establish post offices and postal roads. It is interesting and perhaps telling that the word "general" in the title "postmaster general" may suggest something impor-tant about how postal work was conducted and how employees were treated and thought about in these earlier times. The title has an unmistakable military "ring" to it. The conveyance of dominance and top-down control becomes more suggestive by the juxtaposition of the word "general" in relation to the word "post(master)."

Prior to the Postal Reorganization Act of 1970, postmasters across the country were political appointees. The term "postmaster" has an unusual etymology and this

---

xi   In Appendix C, for the reader who is interested, I examine important events over the last ten years in the Postal Service as they relate to the building blocks of the postal culture. In this presenta-tion, the Postal Service's six strategic plans, the Presidential Commission Report of 2003, and the 2006 Postal Accountability and Enhancement Act are examined.

makes one wonder if the deepest roots of the postal culture are somehow tied to the importance of protecting, securing, and preserving the "sanctity" of the mail. For example, it has been suggested that the term ***postmaster*** evolved from the following historical context:

> In ancient times the kings, emperors, rulers, zamindars or the feudal lords protected their land through the intelligence services of specially trained police or military agencies and courier services to convey and obtain information through runners, messengers and even through pigeons. The chief of the secret service, known as the **post-master** (emphasis added), maintained the lines of communication.[98]

Most of the individuals appointed as postmasters by presidents during the timeframe of the Postal Department (i.e.,1800s-1970), including the Postmaster General and other high-ranking postal officials, had no mail processing or delivery operation experience prior to their appointments. Many of these political appointees had no vested interest in the long-term viability of the Post Office Department (hereafter referred to as POD) or their patrons, as they were called prior to 1970.

During the long history of the POD, employee wages, safety, benefits, and treatment were deplorable. From World War I to the 1950s, postal workers' pay was sometimes frozen and cut back. President Eisenhower even vetoed four postal salary bills. By the 1960s, conditions were so deplorable the POD's employee turnover rate was 25 percent a year, which in turn put pressure on postmasters and their line of command to become more autocratic and abusive toward employees in order to get the mail delivered.

Welfare payments were higher than postal wages during this timeframe, and, in some cases, postal workers worked two to three jobs to survive financially. Significantly because of these conditions, in 1966 an estimated ten million pieces of mail piled up in Chicago mail processing centers. Because of the leadership structure of the POD (i.e., political appointees having no vested interest), the below poverty postal wages, the demeaning and disrespectful treatment of its employees in the workplace, and huge budget deficits, the POD became unable to provide reliable service to its patrons.

It was within this overall context that the business community, especially advertisers and publishers, worked behind the scenes with government policy makers (i.e.,

Washington politicians) to start a process so that the POD could be privatized and pushed for the implementation of new, revolutionary technology to automate mail processing operations. One of the chief recommendations of the 1968 Presidential Commission Report[99] was a need for a greater use of technology to automate mail processing operations.

In 1969, less than four months into his term, Richard Nixon set in motion a plan to create a self-supporting "Postal Corporation." Many of the postal unions were highly suspicious that this postal reform could lead to the privatization of the POD. They were outraged with the stated objective of the postal reform plan to strip away civil service benefits and protections. Adding fuel to the fire, Congress failed to act on the commission's recommendation to provide the same collective bargaining rights to postal unions that were afforded to private-sector workers.

On March 18, 1970, postal employees went on strike, and eventually over two hundred thousand employees refused to go to work. In the interim, the National Guard was called to "serve" at post facilities in a futile attempt to process and deliver the nation's mail. After eight days, the strike was settled and postal employees got immediate increases in their pay and amnesty for strikers. Additionally, postal reform was set into motion with the new Congress.

In short, beginning in the late 1960s, there were dramatic pressures both internally and externally impacting the POD. Pressures from business customers, especially advertisers and publishers, unions, and the advent of revolutionary changes in technology, spurred the POD to become more flexible and efficient in its operations. The pressures from business customers and their alliance with politicians to privatize the POD have remained unabated to the current day.[xii]

Significant Historical Events and Changes from 1971-1992

The Postal Reorganization Act

The Postal Reorganization Act,[100] hereafter referred to as the Act, went into effect on July 1, 1971. This comprehensive postal reform created the context for the newly formed Postal Service, hereafter referred to as the USPS. This sweeping act required the newly formed USPS to finance its operations and capital needs from its own

---

xii   These pressures and their negative impact on the postal culture are examined in chapters seven through nine and Appendices C-E.

revenues and securities. In other words, the USPS was required to behave and operate more like a business rather than a government agency. This was a critical component of the postal reform measure, because before the Act was implemented, the old POD had budget deficits for one hundred thirty-one of its one hundred sixty years operation, some of which were highly significant.

The Act represented an agreement with the interest of the postal unions, high-profile mailers, and national elected officials to create a more efficient, economical, and productive mail processing and delivery system for the nation's mailings. It eliminated political appointees to postmaster positions at post offices throughout the country.

The Act allowed for the creation of a postal corporation, where nine members are elected by the President with the advice and consent of Congress. As a result, the POD was transformed into a semi-independent federal agency. Currently, these nine members of the Board of Governors select the Postmaster General and the Assistant Postmaster General, and they then become members of the board. Since the Act has been enacted, there have been eleven postmaster generals at the helm of the USPS.

The USPS's Board of Governors is similar to the board of directors of a private corporation in their function; its directors generally have a strong business background. Historically, they have had the requisite business background to evaluate the efficiency and productivity of the USPS in the light of economic criteria and to manage it more like a private business.

The purpose of the Board of Governors, as required by the Act and as decision-makers for the USPS, is to ensure that the USPS is self-sufficient and that it functions without budget deficits and federal subsides. Using these criteria, the USPS has been a success over the last several decades. From 1942 to 1971, the POD deficit was 19 billion dollars, while from 1972 to 2007, the USPS deficit was 0.6 billion dollars.[101] The Act forever changed the manner in which the new USPS conducted its operations. Baxter stated it this way:

> A new management coalition was recruited from the mass production sector of private industry. The corporate form of governance displaced electoral with bureaucratic politics in the technical core of the organization. A new structure of authority was enacted to

direct, monitor, and evaluate employee performance, manage inter-
actions with customers, and transform the organizational rhetoric
and myths that bind members to the organization.[102]

The primary seal of approval from the business community perspective was that the Act created a postal rate commission to regulate postal rate increases, requested by the USPS, regarding business mailings in particular and all its customers in general. The victory or seal approval from the postal unions was the official right to bargain for collective agreements with the USPS on matters of wages, benefits, and a grievance process for discipline, work hours, overtime, safety, and other workplace conditions.

The Act permitted for interest arbitration when the postal unions and the USPS could not reach agreement on new contracts or contractual disputes. A key provision of the Act was that the USPS would be required to provide compensation to postal workers that was comparable to the private sector

After the Act was enacted, there were three major restructurings that occurred in the USPS reflecting its priority to function more like a business. Shortly after passage of the Act, Postmaster General Elmer Klassen (1972-1974) oversaw a top-down restructuring of the USPS, without any significant involvement from the postal unions or rank and file workers—a trend that has continued through several more major reorganization and downsizing efforts, to this day. In July 2008, the Government Accounting Office (GAO) issued a report[103] on the Postal Service's contracting plans, and one of the key criticisms was that input from the major stakeholders was not sought.

In 1986, the USPS's management structure was realigned to improve service for postal customers, especially business mailers. As a result of the realignment, lines of authority were shortened and task forces were increasingly used to monitor efficiencies and other targets. This was one of the recommendations of the 1968 Presidential Commission,[104] commonly known as the Kappel Report.

In 1992, Postmaster General Marvin Runyon, nicknamed "Carvin Marvin" for his previous stewardship role with the Tennessee Valley Authority (TVA) as the chairman of the board, was hired to effect the largest restructuring in USPS history. In an interview, Runyon once noted that the reason he went to TVA was to prove that he could run a government agency as effectively as a private business, and he claimed to have done the same with the USPS.[xiii]

Under the Runyon 1992-1993 restructuring of the USPS, many layers of management were eliminated based on the premises that the organization was too top heavy with managers. Local divisions did not have enough decision-approving authority and bold action was necessary to improve mail processing, delivery services, and reduction of operating costs.[105] In describing the purpose and effects of these changes (i.e., USPS restructuring and downsizing efforts), which included changes in job design, performance monitoring, and costs reductions after the passage of the Act, Baxter wrote:

> Automation and downsizing of the post office since 1986 are associated with increased pressure on line managers and upper management to privatize the post office ... The discourse and practice of domination in the post office involving **scientific management** (emphasis added) of job approach to efficiency, competition among managers, and pressure on craft employees to achieve productivity goals frequently engender confrontation, intimidation, and acts of resistance that violate norms of social control.[106]

Baxter used the term scientific management to explain the approach used by the USPS to achieve its overall budget and service goals. The notion of scientific management is a concept or approach to managing employees, in contrast to a human relations approach to the management of employees, where employees are expected to do what they are told and have no significant input in their job design or how work is accomplished.

In chapter eight, I provide a more detailed presentation of the management philosophy known as scientific management, in the context of the impact it has had on the overall postal culture. Suffice to say, at this point, this philosophy and the subsequent dramatic changes to the postal organization have *contributed* to the development of toxic workplace environments and workplace tragedies in the USPS. Baxter captured these observations in the following:

---

xiii   Prior to Runyon's departure in 1998, a five-year strategic plan was implemented in the USPS, which is presented in Appendix C.

> Managerial strategies designed to reduce labor costs during a pe-
> riod of rapid change have certainly contributed to employee para-
> noia and perceptions of harassment. These issues have had tragic
> consequences. It is hoped that efforts of postal managers to pro-
> mote two-way communication and worker participation will mend
> this dangerous climate.[107]

In support of these observations, during the turbulent years of postal restructuring, realignment, and downsizing (i.e., from 1972-1992), the USPS had a multitude of rage murders and suicides in its workplaces. Within this timeframe, as noted in Appendix B, there were twelve workplace tragedies and two more in 1993, which included homicide and suicides at postal installations by former or current postal employees.

The timing of these tragedies supports the notion, as highlighted in chapters two and three, that economic and organizational factors are triggers to these types of tragedies. Reports from psychologists providing post-crisis follow-up services, congressional and Government Accounting Office inquires, commission reports, and anecdotal accounts all support the notion of the relationship with the turbulent changes in the USPS and subsequent workplace tragedies.

It is also important to note that, as it pertains to building blocks of the postal culture, beginning in 1998 there was a dramatic change in leadership positions. For example, in 1998, William Henderson, the new Postmaster General, selected a chief operating officer with a well-known and documented history of micromanagement practices and poor human relations skills. In my opinion, he selected individuals who mirrored his management style and lack of human relations skills for Area Vice-Presidents positions.

The Area Vice-Presidents then selected individuals who had poor or marginal human relations skills and an autocratic management style for district managers, and so on, down the line. It was during this timeframe that USPS's culture worsened. These selections of high-ranking postal officials eventually markedly increased employee fear, stress, anger, and turmoil in the workplace, having the overall effect of creating more toxic work environments within postal installations throughout the nation.[xiv]

In this chapter, a historical context to the postal culture was provided by highlighting important events, particularly from the 1960s to 1992. Special attention was paid to the 1970 Postal Reorganization Act and the subsequent realignments,

---

xiv   These observations are supported in Appendix D and chapters eight and nine.

restructurings, and downsizings that transpired after its passage. I provided a brief commentary regarding the philosophy of scientific management and highly significant changes in leadership positions beginning in 1998.

For additional background as it relates to the building blocks of postal culture, the reader may find it beneficial to read Appendices C-E. These appendices provide a more detailed and comprehensive examination of developments in the last ten to fifteen years. The reader may find it beneficial to read them prior to reading chapter seven. Below I provide a brief synopsis of each appendix.

In Appendix C, I assess the impact of USPS's seven strategic plans on postal culture from 1998 to 2013. I also assess the impact of congressional oversight and accountability on postal culture, especially in the context of the 2006 Postal Accountability and Enhancement Act and subsequent clashes between union and management organizations and the USPS on how some parts of the Postal Reorganization Act were or were not being implemented.

In Appendix D, I examine the role of the USPS's Board of Governors, the four postal unions, and the three management associations in the context of how they have impacted the postal culture, especially in the last fifteen to twenty years. Finally in Appendix E, I examine both the United States Postal Inspection Service and the United States Postal Inspector General Office (OIG) in the context of how they have impacted the postal culture, especially since 2003.

CHAPTER SEVEN
A Paramilitary, Authoritarian Postal Culture?

This chapter is divided in three broad sections: In section one, I revisit and assess the Kappel Report[108] as it pertains to the postal culture. In section two, I analyze important reviews of the postal culture, including reports by the Government Accounting Office (GAO), congressional committees, and the Califano Report. In section three, I examine the organizational culture of the USPS as it relates to its primary, core values.

I provide the relevant findings and conclusions of this review at both the beginning of the chapter and at the end. Hopefully this will enable the reader to maintain focus on what I consider the most important and relevant factors about the postal culture. I then provide a prompt "answer" to the overarching question: Is it accurate and fair to conclude that the Postal Service is a paramilitary, authoritarian organization?

Significant Findings and Conclusions

Significant Findings

The USPS has had a long history of very troubled work sites. These troubled work sites have been viewed in numerous reports as lacking a management commitment to treat employees with respect, dignity, and fairness. Postal management has traditionally viewed employees in the context of "scientific management," a school of management coined in the early 1900s by Fredrick Taylor. In his perspective or school of management, Taylor viewed employees' participation and input in decision-making as an impediment to productivity and efficiency. He believed that all work methods and practices ought to be standardized, focusing heavily on measurements and continual monitoring of both the processes and employees.

It is in the spirit of scientific management we can better understand the **core values** of the USPS. An organization's core or bedrock values are its most fundamental values. They determine in large measure how an organization will treat its employees while in pursuit of achieving organizational goals.

In examining USPS's early history of postal culture, its strategic plans, the role of the Board of Governors, the role of the USPS Office of Inspector General, and reports by Kappel, the GAO, congressional committees, and the Califano commission[xv], the following core values became evident:

1. Achievement of corporate, strategic goals such as organizational productivity, customer service efficiency, and revenue generation needs to take high precedence over employee satisfaction, dignity, and respect.

2. The end justifies the means; that is, do whatever is necessary to reach organizational goals.

3. Command and authority structure needs to be rigid and hierarchical, as opposed to flexible, adaptable, and participative.

4. Employees are viewed as replaceable and their production output needs to be highly measured and monitored.

In short, the core values embedded within the postal culture can be characterized as simply supporting the end justifies the means, and lacking in consideration for employee welfare, respect, or dignity. It employs outcome-driven, bottom-line approaches and doing whatever is necessary to reach organizational goals.

The shared meanings and perspectives on how to accomplish strategic goals relating to both USPS's bedrock values and organizational structure are highly visible in the autocratic management style of senior management, middle management, and first-line management. The impact of these autocratic management styles has had serious consequences at postal work sites throughout the country in the form of widespread tensions, anger, turmoil, and fear.[xvi]

---

xv   As noted in chapter six, Appendices C-E, and parts 1-2 of this chapter.

xvi   The noted consequences resulting from autocratic management styles are documented in Appendices C-E, chapter six, and sections 1-2 of this chapter.

Conclusions

The core values embedded in the USPS's organizational culture and its alignment to its organizational structure has engendered a paramilitary, authoritarian postal culture. It is a culture that promotes unilateral, top-down approaches to manage its employees and their workload. This bottom-line mentality is highly visible in postal facilities where autocratic management styles are too often characterized by use of fear, harassment, bullying, or intimidation to achieve service, financial, and productivity goals. These management styles are frequently rewarded by promotions, annual merit raises, or cash awards for achievement of corporate goals.

Consequences of the unilateral, top-down approaches employed by the USPS include widespread fear, anger, stress, and turmoil, for both craft and management employees alike. Because of the concerted efforts by the USPS's Board of Governors to contract out core postal operations, these negative consequences have escalated in the last several years. Also, since these management approaches are systemic in the USPS, many postal facilities have toxic work environments and can thereby be a catalyst or trigger for serious acts of workplace violence, including homicide and suicide.

Based on my review of a myriad of reports, studies, and investigations regarding the USPS culture, coupled with my experience as an insider, it is an inescapable conclusion that the USPS is a highly paramilitary, authoritarian organization.

Kappel Report

As indicated in chapter six, in 1968, a presidential commission issued a report titled *Towards Postal Excellence*.[109] This report commonly has been referred to as the Kappel Report, after the commission's chairman. The Kappel Report was the first major report to underscore the existence of rigid autocratic management styles and frequent poor employee relations within the USPS. For example, in the report it was stated that "[s]upervision tends to be strongly authoritarian … and there are frequently bad relations between worker and boss."[110]

The concerns noted in the Kappel Report about authoritarian management styles and strained employees relations were an important focus of congressional committees and the Government Accounting Office (GAO) during the 1980s and 1990s, especially in light of the multitude of postal workplace tragedies during this timeframe. I analyze the findings of these investigations, reports, and reviews below.

GAO and Congressional Reports from 1986-1992

From 1986 to 1992, five significant GAO reports[111] were provided to congressional committees regarding the workplace environment and culture of the USPS. In what follows, I will highlight relevant findings from these documents as they pertain to a harsh postal culture. In this section, I also examine the congressional report of 1992[112] titled *A Post Office Tragedy: The Shooting at Royal Oak*.

December 1986 GAO Report

In the December 1986 GAO report[113] titled *USPS Employee-Management Relations at the Evansville, Indiana, Post Office*, the chief findings were: a) three employees were fired without having their performance adequately documented, b) two employees were fired after on-the-job injuries, and c) three employees who had prior military service were fired without notification of their appeal rights under the Merit System Protection Board. Despite these findings, one of the conclusions of the report was that the workplace climate had improved subsequent to their initial 1980 review.

March 1988 GAO Report

In March 1988, GAO issued a report[114] titled *United States Postal Service Employee-Management Relations and Customer Services at the Simi Valley, California Post Office*. This GAO report was a follow-up to see if there were improvements made at the facility. In this report, the GAO referenced the chief findings of a 1986 GAO report on this facility in 1986, which were: a) a majority of the employees interviewed indicated that they were being harassed and treated with disrespect by their supervisors, b) union grievances were not handled properly, and c) employee-management channels had broken down. The report concluded that significant improvements were made since November 1986.

October 1989 GAO Report

The GAO issued another significant report in October 1989[115] titled *United States Postal Service Improved Labor/Management Relations at the Oklahoma City Post Office*. Similar to the March 1988 GAO report previously discussed, this report indicated that there was marked improvement in the workplace environment after the August 1986 tragedy, where letter carrier Patrick Henry Sherrill killed fourteen of his coworkers, wounded six others, and then committed suicide at one of the postal facilities in the Oklahoma Division.[xvii]

Interestingly, in an interview with the current Oklahoma Division manager at the time of the subject GAO investigation, he reportedly told the GAO officials that the relations between labor and management had been poor for at least sixteen years, and in 1986, it even worsened when new postal management became more rigorous in enforcing policies and practices. This new emphasis on "enforcement" led to increases in disciplinary actions and interference with the unions' legitimate union activity, a condition that the GAO referred to as ***endemic strife***[116] in their report. The GAO reported that conditions became so bad during this timeframe that discipline and grievances were indiscriminate.

One of the GAO conclusions noted in this 1989 report is particularly interesting and telling. Why? Because even after the horrific Oklahoma murderous rampage committed by Patrick Sherill, postal management did not even slightly change the workplace conditions in the Oklahoma post offices. Instead, conditions worsened until the GAO began its inquires as a result of prompting from congressional committees.

It is telling because the GAO was probably all too aware of how postal facilities with poor workplace climates may improve in the short term, but in the long term it generally was different. The lesson here is that continual oversight and accountability are necessary in order to ensure that workplace improvements are maintained, especially when the negative or toxic workplace conditions have had a long history.

In response to this report, Anthony Frank, Postmaster General, in a memo to a GAO official dated September 12, 1989, strongly suggested throughout that the local unions were high contributors to the previous negative workplace conditions. He indicated in this letter that management's implementation of procedural changes in 1986 and early 1987 to ensure compliance with previously unenforced postal regulations were appropriate.[117] Rather than any acknowledgement by Mr. Frank of the existence of an autocratic or paramilitary management approach to achieve organizational goals within the USPS, the "blame" was pointed elsewhere and rationalizations were provided. Ostensibly, he was more concerned with the image of the Postal Service rather than addressing the real issues.

---

xvii   An in-depth account of this postal tragedy can be found in Appendix B.

June 1992 Congressional Report

On June 15, 1992, the Congressional Committee on Post Office and Civil Service's investigative report,[118] titled *A Post Office Tragedy: The Shooting at Royal Oak*, was published. As noted in Appendix B, on November 14, 1991, Thomas McIlvane fatally shot four postal workers and then himself.

It is important to point out that this congressional committee's inquiry relied heavily on an April 1990 GAO report,[119] as well as Senator Carl Levin's file,[120] which was based on a two-month investigation conducted by staff members from the office of Senator Carl Levin and hereafter is referred to as the Levin Memorandum. The Levin Memorandum was written only **two months prior** to the Royal Oak's postal tragedy. Despite the involvement of his staff in issues and concerns about serious labor-management problems within the Royal Oak MSC, they were never addressed by postal management. In the June 1992 congressional report, a passage from the Levin Memorandum was noted in the record. It stated:

> It was found by GAO that the USPS's management style caused tension between its employees and their union. This tension was blamed for heart attacks suffered by three employees and numerous physical confrontations by supervisors. Many of these supervisors have been brought to Royal Oak by Mr. Prescilla. The GAO report also found that in a two-year period the Indianapolis division issued 2,700 disciplinary actions against a workforce of 4,000 [emphasis added] ... [T]hese patterns are taking place in this region since the arrival of Dan Prescilla as MSC Postmaster (which was a promotion).[121]

Interestingly, one of the supervisors who was transferred and promoted to Royal Oaks from Indianapolis was Thomas McIlvane's supervisor. In testimony referenced in the 1992 congressional report from a supervisor at Royal Oaks, it was noted: "In an interview with one supervisor at Royal Oaks, it was reported that some supervisors purposely tried to 'set up certain letter carriers, one of whom was McIlvane, to make examples of them.'"[122] An overarching conclusion from the Levin Memorandum was the use of excessive discipline and the existence of harsh work conditions throughout the Royal Oak MSC. For example, it stated:

All the materials here show an intent on the part of MSC management to manage through the use of threat, fear, intimidation, demotions, involuntary detail and sometimes physical confrontations … Mr. Prescilla not only alienated the postal unions in his MSC, he also alienated the management associations. For example, one high-ranking management association leader for the supervisors wrote a very critical article in the association's magazine's with regard to the management style in Royal Oak. Also, at a Postmaster Association meeting in June 1991, at their national convention, a resolution passed criticizing Prescilla … During Prescilla's tenure, serious customer services were curtailed and mail was delayed to improve on work hour usage, which resulted in rampant customer complaints.[123]

In the 1992 congressional report, it indicated that after a meeting between Senator Levin's staff and Mr. Prescilla's boss, John Horne, the Detroit Division postmaster, Mr. Horne showed no concern about the serious issues occurring in Royal Oak. It was reported[124] that he continued to publicly express his support of Mr. Prescilla, even one month before the Royal Oak tragedy.

The most chilling findings and conclusions of the 1992 congressional report were the uncaring and insensitive responses from postal headquarters prior to the Royal Oak tragedy and shortly after it occurred. The Levin Memorandum was given to the postal headquarters' staff prior to the tragedy, but in testimony to the congressional committee it was reported that their response was that "They did not review any labor relations problems because labor/management relations are considered a regional manner."[125] Despite this official declaration, the report cited that the regional office was instructed by postal headquarters not to review the labor relations problems. Ostensibly a case of classic finger-pointing.

This reported callous attitude and posture by the Postal Service was summed up in the report as follows: "Thus, prior to the killings, no one reviewed the labor/management climate at Royal Oak—in spite of Senator's Levin's file, the NAPS resolution, informational picketing, increased number of grievances and adverse press articles."[126]

The most disturbing statement was presented in a memorandum by Anthony Frank, Postmaster General, to Senator Levin, dated November, 19, 1991, <u>five days after the</u>

postal massacre at Royal Oaks. In this memorandum, he submitted a plan of action to address concerns noted in the Levin Memorandum. Mr. Frank listed three actions where he would address the "human relations climate at the MSC."[127] This on its face is not problematic; what is disconcerting, however, was the uncaring, insensitive attitude displayed throughout the memorandum. In a dismissive posture in the memorandum, Postmaster General Frank stated:

> You should also be aware that there are two processes through which employees may address dissatisfaction with management actions or alleged discriminatory treatment at any time. Employees who are dissatisfied with management action may file a grievance under the grievance-arbitration procedures established by the National Agreement with the postal unions … Also, an individual who believes that he or she had been discriminated against on the basis of race, color, sex, religion, national origin, or physical or mental handicap may seek a resolution through the Equal Employment Opportunity Complaint process.[128]

Clearly, Mr. Frank did not address the core issues pertaining to, arguably, a well-documented case of a harsh, toxic workplace. Instead, he simply deflected the issues by pointing to avenues of employee redress.

September 1992 GAO Report

The September 1992 GAO report[129] titled *Royal Oak Tragedy* was a response to the previously discussed congressional inquiry and report. The purpose of this GAO review was to ascertain if the management practices identified in the congressional report prior to the tragedy were proactively addressed after the shooting. The report cited findings from a comprehensive Postal Inspection Service report. The Postal Inspection report showed that budget hours savings prior to the Royal Oak tragedy was achieved at the expense of customer service and tight management of letter carriers' time in the office and on the street.

The GAO report confirmed this finding in their investigation and thereby provided credence to congressional committee members' well-founded concerns about events and concerns prior to the shootings.[130] The GAO, however, concluded that the USPS had finally taken positive steps to reverse the toxic workplace conditions that existed prior to and up to the date of the Royal Oak massacre. Steps that, arguably, were necessary before the tragedy occurred, especially in light of the Levin Memorandum.

1993 Joint Hearings to Review Violence in the USPS

In August and October 1993, a congressional committee and two sub-committees[131] with oversight authority held joint hearings with the stakeholders of the USPS. The chief purpose of these joint hearings was to review postal violence and violence prevention steps taken by the USPS. It is important to note that in 1992 Roy Barnes shot himself in front of coworkers on the workroom floor. In May 1993, there were two more workplace tragedies on the same date, in which Lawrence Jaison and Mark Hilbun killed coworkers in postal facilities. Prior to these joint hearings, there had been fifteen workplace tragedies leaving many dead or injured. These events are chronicled in Appendix B and were the impetus for the joint congressional hearings.

At the congressional joint hearings, the factors that may have contributed to the numerous workplace tragedies in the USPS since 1983 were examined, including stressful working conditions. Stakeholders who testified at these hearings included the postmaster general, postal union leaders, and postal management association leaders. Marvin Runyon, Postmaster General, testified that the USPS had been taking affirmative steps to improve the workplace environment.

He pointed out that all executives in the USPS would be provided 360-degree feedback, where they are evaluated anonymously by their boss, peers, and direct reports. He testified that this initiative would cascade throughout the ranks of management personnel in the USPS. As a result of this 360-degree feedback process, he indicated this would impact upward mobility and demotions because not having or not improving in the area of "people skills" would be a determining factor in promotions or demotions. However, the USPS only continued with this 360-degree feedback initiative for two years and it never cascaded to middle and first-line management.

Mr. Runyon touted the use of the "Employee Opinion Survey" (EOS) as a useful tool in assessing and improving the workplace climate. He testified that executives would receive one-third of their performance-based compensation as a result of improvement in the EOS index score. This survey was abandoned several years later because of uproar from the postal unions. Remarkably, a labor advocate for the USPS misused the results of the survey during binding-arbitration hearings, where he emphasized that the survey showed that a sizable majority of postal employees were satisfied with their pay and benefits. A new survey called the Voice of the Employee (VOE) was later implemented by the USPS in 1997.

In his testimony, Mr. Runyon stated that after the two workplace tragedies in May of that year, focus groups were held all over the country. When asked for the documentation of these meetings, his answer was that "[f]ocus groups were conducted on a local basis with no requirement to report back to headquarters regarding results."[132]

In the district I worked at during this time, however, I was informed that it was a requirement that all focus groups meetings be documented and sent to the area office. I personally took notes at a focus group meeting at a major mail and processing facility during this time, submitting a report to the area office. *It is my opinion that the USPS did not want to share this information with the congressional committee because, despite the testimony to the contrary, one of the major themes pinpointed from the focus groups would have been complaints about the existence of a highly autocratic and paramilitary management style in postal facilities throughout the USPS.*

In response to one question from a Congressman regarding keeping employees informed on changes in the USPS, Mr. Runyon replied:

> There has been a significant change in our commitment to involve employees in the workplace decisions that will affect them. There are a number of important efforts underway to ensure that employees who will be affected by route adjustments and automation equipment are properly informed as to how it might personally affect them.[133]

I personally find this incredulous because this issue is still relevant and has never been fully addressed. Employees have routinely been reassigned to new jobs with little planning or communications and kept in the dark about relevant issues. On numerous occasions, I have seen route adjustments conducted without any involvement from letter carriers. Only since 2007 has this issue begun to be addressed by a joint task force comprised of members from the National Association of Letter Carriers (NALC) and the USPS. Finally, in November 2008 an interim agreement was reached on how to address route adjustment issues.

Two Comprehensive GAO Reviews of the USPS

In March 1992, prompted by the Royal Oak tragedy, congressional oversight committee members requested that the GAO conduct a full-scale review of the USPS's labor-management relations, including the current status of these relations, past efforts to improve relations, and opportunities for further improvements. Subsequent to this request, in 1994, the GAO submitted a 156-page report[134] titled *U.S. Postal Service Labor-Management Problems Persist on the Workroom Floor*. As a follow-up to this report, in October 1997, the GAO released its 111-page report[135] titled *U.S. Postal Service—Little Progress Made in Addressing Persistent Labor-Management Problems*. Below I review both the 1994 and 1997 GAO reports.

March 1994 GAO Report

In this 1994 report, Marvin Runyon was quoted as follows: "Autocratic management is out."[136] The report noted Mr. Runyon indicated that employee empowerment was one of the key elements of his agenda as postmaster general. As the reader will clearly see in this review and subsequent reviews, autocratic management has not been rooted out in terms of how employees are managed in their day-to-day performance, nor has employee empowerment taken root. The findings from the October 1997 GAO report, as well as other reports and personal accounts, provide support that employee empowerment in the USPS has dramatically diminished over time.

Based on interviews with employees in postal management, postal unions, and management associations in mail processing plants and post offices throughout the country, the GAO reported[137] that these employees generally characterized the USPS's workplace culture as: 1) having highly structured work rules, 2) having an autocratic management style, and 3) historically with work conditions that contributed to the violent episodes at postal facilities since 1983.

Efforts to Change its Corporate Culture

The 1994 GAO Report noted that the USPS articulated three actions to change its corporate culture, including: 1) restructure the organization, 2) establish a national leadership team, and 3) modify performance management incentive systems. The restructuring of the organization actually created more stress and hardened the postal culture. Over thirty thousand management positions were eliminated from August 1992 to November 1992, many of which were critical middle management positions.

The elimination of these positions in the 1992 restructuring placed increased workloads on the first-line management, resulting in increased levels of stress for all field operations personnel. This initiative over the years led to a harsher postal culture. In the last three to four years, **complement management** has become the major buzzword—a clarion call to eliminate as many positions as possible. For example, complement management committees at each district are heavily pressured by area offices and headquarters officers to cut positions. Not cutting positions, even when it is wise not to so, is a career decision for many executives.

It is important to note that in early March 2008, members of postal headquarters began conference calls to district managers requesting that first-line supervisor positions be reduced by two thousand four hundred nationwide.[138] Shortly thereafter, a hiring freeze was initiated throughout the USPS. These events have increased the stress levels at many postal facilities where resources and workload requirements were already highly problematic for field supervisors, managers, and postmasters.

The streamlining of management positions in the 1993 restructuring, combined with increased workload and less resources for field management personnel in the past ten years (especially in the last three to four years), eventually served to degrade the corporate or organizational culture of the USPS. The second action, the establishment of a national leadership team, which touted to improve the culture of the USPS, was short-lived.

Only for a short period of time after the 1993 restructuring were the major postal unions and management associations permitted to attend and participate at top-level corporate meetings. Historically, the postal unions and management associations were not viewed as relevant stakeholders regarding information sharing or input at any level within the organization, and this viewpoint still prevails.

The third action heralded by the USPS, as noted in the 1994 GAO Report, was its emphasis on a new performance management incentive system where officers and executives would be rewarded for "people skills" as a means to improve the organizational culture. This new focus emphasized treating employees respectfully and fostering teamwork as opposed to the "old system," with its emphasis on budget, productivity, and controlling sick leave and injury rates.

This new incentive system was limited to improvement in the "Employee Opinion Survey" scores and the 360-degree feedback process, both of which were discussed previously. Suffice to say, their impact or emphasis on changing organizational culture were insignificant or short-lived.

Shortly after the 1992 restructuring, there was more of an emphasis and focus on improving employee relations, but its emphasis only lasted three to four years. During this timeframe, there was increased emphasis on customer service targets and decreased emphasis on budget. Thereafter, especially in recent years, the emphasis on fostering people skills and healthy workplace environments was greatly deemphasized in favor of high workload expectations, budget reductions, revenue generation, performance improvements, and improved service in a myriad of categories.

In summary, none of the three actions touted in the 1994 GAO report by the USPS came to fruition. One of the overall conclusions of the report was that, for the most part, the USPS did not implement changes below the national level and executive management levels in the field. Consequently, labor and management relations at many postal facilities continued to be highly adversarial and employees were caught in the proverbial middle.

October 1997 GAO Report

The 1997 GAO report, as mentioned previously, was a follow-up to the 1994 GAO report. One of the major conclusions of this report was: "[L]ittle progress has been made in improving the persistent labor-management relations problems that had, in many instances, resulted from autocratic management styles." [139] The report also indicated that many of the initiatives espoused by the USPS as a means to improve its organizational culture never were fully implemented or they were discontinued.

One specific failure regarding improvement in relations between the USPS and National Association of Letter Carriers (NALC) was "delivery redesign." Both sides agreed that the current system fostered too many tensions between supervisors and letter carriers on the workroom floor and on the postal routes. In the 1994 GAO report, it was noted that the labor-management relations between the USPS and the NALC could be vastly improved if they jointly strived to create a "delivery redesign" system, similar to the rural carriers. However, according to NALC officials, the USPS repeatedly rejected its invitations to work together for achieving a workable system.

What became clear is that both sides ended up far apart on the development of a new delivery system and formed separate teams to study the issue. To this date, no agreement has been reached and the tensions and stress between supervisors and letter carriers continue to remain a very volatile and serious issue. As a result of the national agreement between the two parties and a 2008 "Memorandum of Understanding," as discussed in detail in Appendix D, there may be some hope that they can develop a system viewed by both parties as fair and workable.

Another specific failure to the dismay of the NALC, which was not fully addressed in the GAO report, was the unilateral termination of the Employee Involvement program in 1996 by the USPS. This program began in 1982 with the promise of alleviating the adversarial relationship between postal unions and postal management. The NALC contends that this action purposely coincided with the NALC opposition to the USPS unilateral implementation of a new letter carrier redesign system. NALC viewed the termination of the EI as a clear sign from the USPS it was moving from a position of jointness and cooperation to a position of domination and confrontation.

I vividly remember the ramification of these issues with the USPS as an internal consultant. I agree with the conclusion that, commencing with the unilateral termination of the EI program in 1996, the USPS started an unmistakable campaign of domination and confrontation with the NALC. This conclusion is discussed in detail in chapter eight and Appendix D with regard to the issues of both delivery redesign and EI.[xviii]

In response to the 1997 GAO report, Marvin Runyon, Postmaster General, was in agreement with the finding that progress in the relations between postal management and the unions was limited, isolated, and unimpressive. He indicated that he favored an independent commission comprised of a national, impartial academic body to study the USPS, which was previously proposed in a congressional bill. A postal-funded commission eventually was formed and its report is discussed below.

August 2000 Report of United States USPS Commission on a Safe Workplace

In chapters three and four, I reviewed many of the findings of this commission report[140] as they pertained to violence in the workplace. In the previous examination,

---

xviii Also, in Appendix D, the unique concerns from other postal unions and the management organizations are investigated as they relate to the organizational culture of the USPS and the previously discussed congressional and GAO reports, including more recent reports.

the report was referred to as the Califano Report and I will continue to do so. The Califano Report, besides focusing on violence in the workplace within the USPS, as compared to the national workforce, assessed the USPS's organizational culture and its violence prevention strategies. In the foregoing, some of the more salient observations, findings, and conclusions in the report are discussed.

Two Survey Dimensions: Positive Attitude Toward Management and Autonomy

As part of the Califano study, they surveyed twenty thousand postal employees and then compared the results to the national workforce as a whole. Two important dimensions of the survey were *"positive attitude toward management"* (seven items) and *"autonomy"* (four items).[141]

Regarding the dimension *"positive attitude toward management"* used in the Califano survey, postal employees had a less favorable attitude on all seven items compared to the national workforce. Overall postal employees scored only **58 percent favorable rating compared to the national workforce score of 79 percent**[142] on this dimension.

On the specific item, *"I have confidence in the fairness and honesty of management,"* **postal employees scored 37 percent favorably while the national workforce scored 60 percent favorably**.[143] Broken down by postal unions, the favorable rating on this particular item was as follows: city letter carriers 32 percent, APWU 32 percent, rural carriers, 58 percent, and mail handlers 25 percent. The rural carriers generally have been content with their work environment in that historically they have been more empowered in carrying out their assigned duties. Sadly, this has changed significantly in the past several years. Collectively the favorable rating for the two management categories on this item was at 59 percent.

As for the dimension *"autonomy"* used in the Califano survey, postal employees had a less favorable attitude on all four items compared to the national workforce. Overall, postal employees scored only a **39 percent favorable rating compared to the national workforce score of 77 percent,**[144] nearly half as likely to have positive perceptions on this dimension.

On the specific item, "I have very little freedom to decide how I do my work," **postal employees scored 23 percent favorably while the national workforce scored 48 percent favorably**.[145] Of the six job categories, the highest agreement to this statement was the city carriers at **62 percent.** This score makes sense in that, historically, letter carriers have been micromanaged more than any other craft or postal management job categories.

Although the Califano Report goes the "extra mile" in its attempt to place the USPS in the best possible light, especially in its cover letter to the Postmaster General, several of their observations or comments strongly contradict this positive assessment. It is important to highlight these points in order to show the continuity of a postal culture that uses rigid, autocratic management styles to achieve bottom-line results. Below, I provide two excerpts in the Califano Report that essentially validate the concerns of previous GAO reports, especially the 1994 and 1997 reports.

> In interviews and focus groups, supervisors' and managers' behavior came up repeatedly as a focus when we asked about workplace violence. Thus, a complex picture emerges, of an organization in which management styles are changing but in which "old-style" management is still prevalent and highly salient in influencing the work climate and perceptions.[146]

> Postal Service employees have more negative views of managers than do employees in the national workforce … Arbitrators who handle postal grievance cases commented, "Supervisors … don't have the proper training to manage so they become militaristic," and "Employees are regularly spoken down to— not privately, they do it publicly. The norm is the employee is embarrassed, ridiculed in the presence of other employees." Managers commented, "Maybe 30 percent of managers are good communicators, 70 percent are still from the old school," and "We need to break the paradigm of what a leader is.[147]

In chapter four, specific findings and conclusions in the Califano Report were highlighted, findings and conclusions that strongly appeared either deceptive or very misleading. In the previous examination of the dimensions of "positive attitude toward management" and "autonomy," the main problem is that the significant findings related to these two dimensions were not considered important enough to be emphasized either in the cover letter of the report or in the beginning of the report. A reasonable conclusion that can be drawn from this omission is that the authors' intention was to provide "positive headlines" for the USPS's public relations campaign.

Organizational Culture of the USPS

In order to understand the postal culture, we need to first look at what are the relevant parts of a culture. Subject matter experts generally agree that the main parts of a culture include: 1) ethical core or bedrock values, as to what really matters and what is important, 2) shared meanings and perspective on how things are to be accomplished, 3) shared stories, 4) rituals (i.e., routines, customs, and traditions), and 5) codes or expectations (i.e., norms) for ways of behaving.

These five factors, when viewed in the context of a business or company, are frequently referred to as <u>organizational culture</u>. One management scholar cogently describes the development of an organizational culture as follows: "Organization culture evolves from myriad sources, including the organization's history, its patterns of successes and failures, its founders, its policies and practices."[148] For these reasons, I examined the building blocks of the postal culture in great detail.[xix]

Of the five parts of the USPS organizational culture, I only examine two below, namely: *bedrock values and shared meanings* and *perspectives on how things are to be accomplished.* In this examination, I placed heavy emphasis on top management's role in the creation and sustaining of these two factors. I consider the other three factors of postal culture, including shared stories, rituals, and codes or expectations for ways of behaving in the next chapters.

Bedrock Values

An organization's core or bedrock values are its most fundamental values and they determine, in large measure, how an organization will treat its employees in achieving organizational goals. As a result of examining the building blocks of the postal culture,[xx] the following core values became evident:

---

xix   See chapter 6, sections 1 and 2 of this chapter, and Appendices C-E.

xx   See USPS's early history (chapter six), its strategic plans (Appendix C), impact of board of governors on postal culture (Appendix D), impact of OIG on postal culture (Appendix E), and reports by Kappel, GAO, congressional committees, and Califano commission, (sections 1-2 of this chapter)

1. Achievement of goals such as organizational productivity, customer service efficiency, and revenue generation needs to take high precedence over employee satisfaction, dignity, and respect. The end justifies the means; that is, do whatever is necessary to reach organizational goals.

2. Command structure needs to be rigid and hierarchical as opposed to flexible, adaptable, and participative.

3. Employees are viewed as replaceable and their production output needs to be highly measured and monitored.

In looking at the core values of the USPS, it is clear that they have adopted, as the means of achieving organizational goals, the tenets of scientific management as opposed to the human relations approach to management. The scientific management tenets conclude that the manager does the thinking and the employee does the labor. Furthermore, all aspects of the employees' labor needs to be rigorously and uniformly timed and measured.

In sum, based on my examination, it became clear that the core values embedded within the postal culture can be characterized as supporting the end justifies the means: lack of consideration for employee welfare, respect, and dignity; a bottom-line driven approach, and to do whatever is necessary to reach organizational goals.

Shared Meanings and Perspectives on How to Accomplish Strategic Goals

The notion of shared meanings and perspectives in the context of how to accomplish strategic goals in the USPS is primarily related to its core values. The USPS's recent strategic plans, coupled with its continual attempts to slowly and deliberately privatize its core operations, have had a very negative impact on a preexisting harsh postal culture These actions are reflective of its bedrock values. For example, the Board of Governors approved strategic plans from 1998 to 2008 are reflective of views that employees' welfare is secondary to achieving organizational goals, that a rigid and hierarchal command structure is necessary, and that employees' work needs to be highly measured and monitored.

The shared meanings and perspectives emanating from the USPS's bedrock values are reflective of its organizational structure. The formal decision-making framework where job tasks are divided, grouped, and coordinated is accomplished in a top-down command approach. It is in this light that we can see the results of the top-down command approach in terms of workplace anger, stress, fear, and turmoil.

More specifically, the shared meanings and perspectives on how to accomplish strategic goals as they relate to both the USPS's bedrock values and organizational structure are clearly seen in the autocratic management styles of higher management, middle management, and first-line management. The results of these autocratic management styles are well documented throughout Part 4 of this book. In this extensive review of the postal record, reports of intimidation, harassment, bullying, unilateral decision-making, and high monitoring of employees were frequently noted as highly problematic.

Concluding Remarks

In this chapter, the bedrock values of the USPS and their relationship to shared meanings and perspectives by postal management on how to accomplish strategic goals were identified and discussed. The impact of these values, shared meanings, and perspectives were briefly discussed in terms of how they influenced management styles in particular and the postal culture overall.

Based on the identification of the major themes, as they pertain to the building blocks of postal culture and how they play out in many of the postal facilities nationwide, the overall conclusion is that the USPS has a culture that can be described as paramilitary or authoritarian. It is a culture that promotes a unilateral, top-down approach to managing its employees and their workload.

This bottom-line mentality is highly visible in postal facilities where autocratic management styles are too often characterized by use of fear, harassment, bullying, or intimidation in order to achieve service, financial, and productivity goals. These management styles are frequently rewarded by promotions, merit increases, training opportunities, or cash awards for achievement of corporate goals. Real life examples of the impact of this postal culture on its employees are provided in the next two chapters.

CHAPTER EIGHT
Postal Culture from An Insider's Perspective

In this chapter, I present my relevant experiences in the USPS from 1973 to 2007, which point to a harsh, authoritarian culture. Because of space requirements, the chronicling of experiences in my craft positions are relatively brief, while the chronicling of experiences in postal management are more detailed. The reporting of these lived experiences serves to validate the conclusion that there exists, in agreement with the ample evidence examined and presented throughout many of the chapters of this book and its appendices, a harsh postal culture.

Stated differently, my personal experiences, as I report in this chapter, are in agreement with the conclusion that the postal culture fosters a management style at all levels of the organization that is oppressive, autocratic, and uncaring. This claim is in agreement with the documentary, quantitative, qualitative, and anecdotal evidence I reviewed from congressional hearings and investigations,[149] GAO reports,[150] postal commission reports,[151] USPS strategic plans,[152] and from the literature in the workplace violence field.

As mentioned in chapter six, the effects of postal management's unilateral, top-down approaches that play out on the workroom floor are reflective of the bedrock values embedded in the postal culture and lead to workplace bullying, harassment, and emotional abuse.[xxi] Suffice to indicate at this point, bullying and emotional abuse are used interchangeably in this chapter and they are generally defined as having a longer duration than harassment.

Career Highlights with the USPS

xxi   The notions of bullying, harassment, and emotional abuse in the workplace are defined and discussed in chapter two.

My career with the USPS began in 1973 as a letter carrier at a Southern California postal facility. From 1974 to 1986, I held postal clerk positions at five different postal facilities in Southern California. Duties at these offices included mail delivery, mail processing, letter sorting machine (LSM) operator, special delivery messenger, expediter, and responsibility for handling and distribution of accountables (i.e., registers, certifieds, and CODs) to letter carriers.

From 1986 to 2007, I held management positions at one management sectional center (MSCs), one division, and two district offices, one of which was a division prior to the 1993 restructuring. Three of the four positions, from September 1986 to October 1994, were as an Employee Assistance Program (EAP) representative. The last position I held, from October 1994 to January 2007, was as a Workplace Improvement Analyst, an internal consultant.[xxii]

Craft Positions

City Letter Carrier

In 1973, my first career position with the USPS as a letter carrier at a city delivery station was a real "eye-opener." Employees told me that the postmaster was well known at all levels of the organization, including postal headquarters, because of his reported bullying of city letter carriers. They said that higher-level managers did not care and condoned his management style.

They indicated that numerous city letter carriers had been fired based on trumped-up charges and had their paychecks delayed for weeks if they filed grievances or other complaints. I was told that numerous employees had quit because of poor treatment, inability to take their daily breaks—including lunch breaks—and because they had the longest routes in the country. Several letter carriers told me on one occasion that some of the letter carriers at the station, while at a private affair and off postal premises, beat up the postmaster bad enough that it required him to be hospitalized. I was informed that when he came back to the station, he carried out the same tactics of intimidation and bullying.

My first training experience at that station was on an auxiliary route, which normally required an experienced letter carrier about four to five hours to complete daily. In addition to carrying the auxiliary route, I was required to deliver special deliveries

---

xxii   These positions and the associated duties are discussed in chapter five.

and to make a morning collection. After about four days on the route, I was told by my supervisor that the postmaster thought that I was too slow. I was already skipping all my so-called "entitled" breaks during the day.

Accordingly, in order to finish the route more quickly, I cut through customers' yards to save time on my deliveries and, when practical, I literally ran from delivery point to delivery point and back to the postal vehicle. The postmaster was then very pleased with my performance. My reward for finishing the route in three hours or less was to learn the clerk scheme in the office for all twenty city delivery routes. In other words, I was given additional duties and a heavier workload.

Postal Clerk #1

Since I was in my early twenties and I did not have a family to support, I decided to quit the letter carrier position and applied at another postal facility as a clerk. Within several months, because I had received positive recommendations from postal management at my previous job location, I was hired as a clerk and later qualified on the letter sorting machine (LSM). This was a relatively new, semi-automated system to sort mail by zip code and letter carrier routes within a defined zip code.

While employed at this mail processing postal facility, there was an incident with two postal police agents and a coworker was assaulted. The circumstances included that two coworkers and I left the facility to go to lunch and, while leaving, we apparently made too much "noise." After returning to the facility, one of the postal police agents read an excerpt from a postal manual about employee conduct, stating employees needed to refrain from creating an unpleasant work environment.

One of my coworkers apparently was not attentive while the postal police agent read this excerpt so the agent told him that he did not like his attitude. My coworker smartly responded back, "You mean you can see my attitude?" The postal police agent became violent. He hit his gun in his holster several times with his hand and then ran toward and tackled my coworker to the ground. After he calmed down, he told us to go back to the work area.

My coworker was highly distressed and scared as a result of this verbal and physical assault. When I got back to the mail processing area in the facility, I informed a tour manager what had occurred. After a follow-up meeting with him several days later, he said it was just a misunderstanding and I needed to let it go. I was outraged that this could happen in a postal facility, without any consequences, for someone who clearly assaulted an employee while on duty.

Postal Clerk #2

At this Southern California main post office, I was a distribution clerk from 1978 to 1982. There were approximately seventy-four city delivery routes at the station. In 1980, the postmaster selected his second-in-command for the vacant manager, customer services position. Supervisors at the office disclosed to me that this manager was more or less forced on the postmaster from a higher level manager.

The new manager, who I will call John hereafter, was a rather tall and large person who liked to use his stature and presence to intimidate and harass the employees in the office. He had little respect for personal boundaries and would hide behind city letter carrier cases ostensibly to "monitor" their work. City letter carriers reported that he would hide behind bushes or cars while they were delivering their routes. He even illegally posted a memorandum on employee bulletin boards, falsely stating that he was the official Equal Employment Opportunity officer for our facility.

Within several months, John created a toxic workplace environment[xxiii] in our postal facility. On one occasion, while I was distributing mail to the city letter carriers' cases, I noticed that he issued a letter of warning for unsatisfactory performance to over two-thirds of the city letter carriers in the facility.

The letters of warnings were placed on the desk of the letter carriers' cases and the charges noted for unsatisfactory performance were identical. This egregious public action showed that John not only disrespected their due process rights, but also discounted their right to privacy. His motive ostensibly was to instill fear and thereby achieve higher productivity from them. He was successful in his goal. Productivity goals were exceeded; however, a toxic work environment was created in the process.

Fortunately for the employees at this postal facility, John was promoted to another postal facility less than a year from his arrival at our unit. I was told later he eventually was promoted several more times, and the last position was an executive marketing position at a large postal division. Reliable sources indicated to me that, several

---

xxiii A toxic workplace environment is defined as a workplace where there is a high incidence of stress-related illnesses.

years after receiving the last position, he was removed from his position because of several sexual harassment claims.

Postal Clerk #3

In 1982, I transferred to a main post office as a part-time regular clerk in order to complete my graduate studies. At this office, I held the position of branch Vice-President of the APWU, and later as the President.

While I was working the box mail at this facility about six o'clock in the morning, there was a power failure and the emergency lighting came on, providing light about 20 percent of the original capacity. I recalled reading in a recent APWU citywide bulletin that management did not have the right to direct employees to work under such a condition because it posed a safety hazard.

Accordingly, I directed the clerks in the building to stop working to the chagrin of the floor supervisor, hereafter known as George. When I walked by George, he grabbed my arm, pulled me toward him, and then ordered that I go back to work. While looking at him in a state of disbelief, he then ordered me to the break room, where I sat for about thirty to forty-five minutes until the power came on.

Shortly after the foregoing events, the postmaster called me to his office and I was provided the opportunity to explain what had occurred while in the presence of George. As a result of the meeting with the postmaster, George apologized to me. The postmaster asked if I wanted to pursue the matter any further and, fortunately for the supervisor, I agreed to accept his apology and not pursue a formal investigation. Legally, George's physically aggressive actions constituted an assault. The postmaster later disclosed to me in private that the USPS did not have to follow OSHA guidelines; I respectfully disagreed.

It is important to note that in my last craft position as a distribution clerk at a main post office the work environment was good. The postmaster did an excellent job of buffering the negative effects of the postal culture within the confines of his postal facilities. Fortunately, there are many other postmasters, managers, and supervisors throughout the country that act as a "buffer" to the postal culture. <u>They are the unsung heroes of the Postal Service, absorbing the "heat" of a very harsh postal culture in order to protect their employees</u>.

Management Positions

Employee Assistance Program (EAP) Coordinator

From 1986 to 1990, I worked at a management sectional center (MSC) as an EAP coordinator. The workplace environment at many of the postal facilities, both city delivery offices and mail processing plants, were toxic for many of their employees. The relationship between postal management and the unions and management association were often strained and combative.

When I first reported to the MSC in this position, at least six city letter carriers were on leave, without pay, pending removal from the USPS. I was told by my "boss," the director of employee and labor relations, hereafter known as Mike, that the workers would probably win their job backs through the arbitration process. However, unless they agreed to a "last chance agreement" before their scheduled arbitration (which could take up to six months), they would suffer dramatic consequences. For example, some of these employees scheduled for arbitration were in the process of losing their homes, suffered from marriage and family problems, and were highly stressed and depressed. Several postal managers informed me they served as examples to the other employees of what could and would happen if they did not comply with what was expected by postal management.

At the main mail processing plant at this MSC, I was aware of one supervisor who referred to the employees under his purview as his "animals." When an employee became too vocal or strident at this mail processing plant, the postal management team would collectively monitor the employee and make his or her life "a living hell." One of the mail processing managers shared with me that they would work together in this manner in order to "keep the peace."

In my four years at this MSC, Mike angrily yelled at me when he was upset. However, I was not singled out. He yelled frequently at all his staff members, with the exception of his female secretary. Aside from this working environment, I received two far-exceeds expectations on my annual merits from Mike. It is also important to note that the lead executive, during my tenure at the MSC, frequently and publicly yelled at his subordinates and berated them publicly.

While at this MSC, discipline was very high at a significant number of postal facilities. Employee sick leave usage was monitored closely and some employees were disciplined unfairly for its legitimate use. There was an inordinate amount of discipline for vehicle accidents. Employees were sometimes unfairly referred to me, as the EAP representative, for non-fault vehicle accidents and legitimate use of sick leave. On one occasion, at a city delivery station, a supervisor taped EAP referral forms onto city delivery letter cases with the individual's name written on them. This event contributed to strained relationships between these employees and their supervisors and between the union and local management.

In 1990, before my promotion to another EAP position, I developed what presumably was the first joint statement of support for the prevention of violence in the USPS; all major unions and management associations throughout the MSC were signatories. As a sign of their trust and support, all the major postal unions in the largest city in the MSC actively endorsed and promoted the EAP.

EAP Supervisor #1

In the summer of 1990, I was promoted to EAP supervisor of a postal division. In my eighteen-month tenure in this position, I was treated disparagingly by my immediate manager. My manager's friend worked in the EAP office as an EAP specialist and reported to me. This dynamic created high turmoil and stress, and it was a central reason why I transferred to another postal division. Below are some major concerns I had with postal management at this division.

Before arriving at this division, it was reported to me that the current division manager was being relieved of his duties in a couple of weeks because of his involvement in unauthorized purchases. He was later detailed to postal headquarters on special projects. On one occasion, I met with this division manager to discuss a sensitive issue and he yelled and screamed at me for at least one minute. He never did apologize. This behavior, as I sadly came to learn, was routinely accepted and condoned as part of the postal culture.

One year later, I was invited to a meeting with the director of human resources, without being provided a reason. I was chastised publicly at the meeting for previously advising one of the EAP specialists not to release information to a labor relations representative unless he first secured a release from the EAP client. The director belligerently informed me that management was entitled to this information and that I would comply.

I never did comply and this issue was not pursued any further; however, I received a low rating for the very first time in my postal career on my annual merit. These types of privacy violations were too often accepted and tolerated in the postal culture. Fortunately, it only occurred once during my tenure as an EAP representative. The contracting out of EAP services to private contractors in 1993 eliminated these types of privacy violations and other violations.

As a result of my encounter with the director of human resources, I discussed these privacy concerns with a high-ranking EAP official at postal headquarters. He indicated that, of course, I handled the situation correctly. In a previous discussion with this official, he disclosed to me that the Postal Inspection Service had access to the electronic EAP information system, which identified EAP clients in terms of assessed problems, including alcohol and drug problems. A related, alleged privacy violation is discussed below in the next postal division I worked at as an EAP supervisor.

Another major issue at this division during my tenure dealt with the excessing of several hundred mail processing positions from the day shift to a new mail processing facility that was fifty miles away. Most assignments were split days off and on the late afternoon shift or the night shift. Before the official notification of excessing was announced, employees on the day shift were informed only of general changes through their local unions.

Postal management did not communicate to employees that a major excessing plan was underway. The first official notification was through a posting on employee bulletin boards. The notification listed the affected employees in the facility, indicating when they were required to report to the new facility and their new hours and days off. It was so upsetting for some of the employees that they were escorted off the workroom floor by postal police. Some were sobbing and crying loudly while others were cursing profusely. Sadly, this is just another distressing example of how the postal culture plays out on the workroom floor.

EAP Supervisor #2

In 1991, I transferred to another postal division as an EAP supervisor. In my tenure, there were not many serious issues that came to my attention. The main concern, reflective of the postal culture, was the explosive and demeaning temper of the plant manager. He routinely yelled at and angrily berated his staff, union officials, and craft employees with impunity. He was subsequently promoted to a higher level executive position during the major postal restructuring in 1993.

One very serious breach reported to me by one of the EAP specialists during my tenure at this division was the violation of privacy regarding confidential EAP records. This EAP specialist disclosed that a previous EAP supervisor, who had retired several years earlier, actually shared confidential files with Postal Inspectors. Specifically, it was disclosed to me that the records of employees that were identified as having drug problems were flagged by a former EAP supervisor and then provided to Postal Inspectors.

The EAP specialist disclosed these records to Postal Inspectors and eventually helped them with a major drug bust at the division's main mail processing facility. Subsequently, the former EAP supervisor and Postal Inspectors involved in this "sting" were rewarded by postal management with certificates of appreciation and cash awards. Before the implementation of the externally based EAP, what is reported to have happened at this California district also occurred at other districts and MSCs across the nation.[xxiv]

In my role as an EAP representative with USPS I was frequently left "out of the loop" regarding workplace climate issues occurring at specific postal facilities. It was not until I was selected for the newly created position of workplace improvement analyst at a postal district that I routinely became aware of workplace climate issues at specific postal facilities.

Workplace Improvement Analyst (WIA)

During the 1992-1993 postal restructuring, I was selected as an internal consultant (i.e., workplace improvement analyst) to deal with workplace violence and workplace climate issues at a postal district.[xxv] The impetus for creating this new position was related to the numerous postal workplace shootings in the 1980s and the early 1990s. According to the information shared with me from a postal headquarters official, immediately after the two workplace shootings on May 5, 1993, several postal executives and an outside consultant convened to develop a job description to address workplace violence and its prevention, change management, and the postal culture.

---

xxiv It is important to remind the reader that these issues became moot with the advent of external EAP providers in 1993.

xxv   In chapter six, an account of the duties and responsibilities I engaged in as a workplace improvement analyst is provided.

Accordingly, workplace violence and its prevention, change management, and the postal culture are discussed below in the context of unilateral, top-down management approaches. Although these factors are arbitrarily separated for the purpose of this discussion, they are in fact interrelated. The troubling issues that emanate from them are artifacts of the USPS's deeply embedded core values.

Workplace Violence and its Prevention

As indicated previously in chapter five, as a member of a task force, I actively participated and contributed to the development of threat assessment team (TAT) guidelines for all postal districts within the USPS. In these guidelines, the workplace improvement analyst, in tandem with other district postal officials and the inspection service, were scripted to play a central role in the assessment of threats and their abatement.

In my district, the TAT met at least quarterly, as required, and on an ad-hoc basis when a serious threat or assault had occurred. Many districts, however, did not meet regularly as required and did so with impunity. This concern and related concerns are discussed in chapter ten.

On one occasion, at a meeting with TAT members, we discussed an alarming correspondence I received from a postmaster. The correspondence indicated that two employees informed the postmaster that a coworker was having thoughts about killing him. I later met and talked with this troubled employee, hereafter known as David, after conducting a workplace climate assessment at his postal facility.

In my meeting with David, he admitted that he was having homicidal thoughts about killing the postmaster and IRS agents. He told me in detail how the postmaster micromanaged his duties, repeatedly spoke to him disrespectfully, did not give him appropriate resources to get the job done, and continually violated the contract to work him out of schedule. A significant number of employees in the unit agreed that David had been bullied by the postmaster for several years. As a result of my interview with David, he agreed to call me if he continued to have homicidal thoughts and to continue with his therapy with the Veterans Administration. He gave me permission to call him periodically, either at work or at home.

After my meeting with David, the TAT met and it was decided that a Postal Inspector, hereafter named Marvin, and I would go back to the office together to meet with the two employees who initially notified the postmaster of the threat and David. To the surprise of Marvin, when the two of us met with David, he admitted to having homicidal thoughts in the past about the postmaster. As a result of the meeting, some time off work was arranged for David so he could better manage the stresses in his life. The postmaster committed to me and to his "boss" that he would be more considerate in his dealings with David, especially in light of his "mental state."

I continued to follow up with David over the next four to five months and he told me that things had improved initially, but were slowly deteriorating back to how he was treated in the past. Later, I received a call from one of David's coworkers, who informed me that David purchased an AK-47 assault weapon and that he was very concerned about what he might do. I immediately called David and, when asked, he told me that he purchased the weapon with thoughts of killing the postmaster. He told me that he had trouble sleeping at night because of these thoughts. Fortunately, I was able to talk David into turning over the assault rifle to his coworker/friend.

Shortly after these recent events, a TAT meeting was held and it was agreed that Marvin and I would meet with David. Marvin subsequently took possession of the AK-47 rifle from David's coworker. Sadly, I spoke with a few of David's coworkers and they confirmed that the postmaster continued to bully and treat him poorly. In my professional opinion, this is just another blatant example of a management official not being held accountable for unacceptable, psychological violence.

After the meeting with David, I convinced him to voluntarily admit himself into an inpatient treatment program at a VA hospital and to file for disability retirement. He subsequently completed inpatient treatment and was accepted for disability retirement. It is important to note that prior to his admission for inpatient treatment, a VA psychiatrist and counselor both indicated that David suffered from homicidal and suicidal ideation. A leading expert in the violence prevention field, who was providing training of our TAT team in the area of violence prevention during this timeframe, indicated that because of my follow-up and prompt attention, it was likely that I prevented a workplace homicide.

On a positive note, for the last eighteen months of my tenure with the USPS, I collaborated with another Postal Inspector regarding potentially dangerous employees, and he was always very professional and a tribute to his profession. It is important to note that I received a letter from the inspector-in-charge from a large Postal

Inspection Division, along with a plaque, as a tribute of my collaboration with them and my efforts in the violence prevention field.

Aside from the amicable and collaborative relationships I had with the vast majority of Postal Inspection Service officials during my tenure as an internal consultant, especially the last eighteen months prior to my retirement, the TAT did not function as envisioned. A prime example is that the input from the managers of human resources and labor relations on TAT issues were too determinate. More specifically, they became increasingly reluctant to send potentially dangerous employees to a psychiatric-fitness-for-duty. Conversely, they became increasingly more likely to recommend and ensure excessive disciplinary action was taken, including removal, against potentially dangerous employees, even when it appeared likely that the action would not be sustained by an administrative judge or arbitrator. These combined actions, especially the callous lack of concern toward these employees and lack of a team approach to deal with all the issues, eventually could have served to trigger a workplace tragedy.

As noted in the foregoing, these combined actions heavily support the need for the Postal Service to fully implement the 1997 Peaceful Parting initiative, a plan for supervisors and managers to deal with employees being removed from the Postal Service in a respectful and collaborative manner. However, as discussed in chapter five, it was never implemented nationwide. This, sadly, is another prime example of a lack of follow-through by postal management, which is consistent with its rigid adherence to top-down control approaches to deal with serious issues

It is also important to note that after I retired from the Postal Service, there was nobody to step in to conduct credible follow-up and monitoring of potentially violent employees in my district. In my thirteen-year career as the workplace improvement analyst, I successfully encouraged and assisted approximately eight to ten potentially dangerous employees in their application for disability retirement. Of these employees who were medically retired, all had chronic and serious psychological disabilities. Some had serious alcohol or drug problems.

Change Management

There were a significant number of realignments, restructurings, elimination of positions, and excessing of employees from one postal unit to another in my postal career. In the vast majority of these change management initiatives, one of which was previously mentioned, these changes were implemented without sufficient fore-thought, absence of input from important stakeholders, poor communication of a plan to employees, and sometimes no real attempt at all to manage the transitions in a manner that showed concern for the welfare and well-being of its employees.

In chapter seven, I indicated that ***complement management*** had become the major buzzword or a clarion call to eliminate as many postal positions as possible. Complement management committees at each district were heavily leaned on by area office executives and headquarters officers to cut positions. Not cutting positions, even when it was wise not to, was a career decision for many postal executives. When the Postal Service's change management practices are viewed from this specific context and the overall context of the postal culture, the failures and negative fallout of these practices, as discussed in the foregoing and below, become comprehensible.

From 2003 to 2006, several hundred employees were excessed from various postal units to other postal units in my district, especially in the mail processing function. The vast majority of the excessing implemented during this timeframe was done very poorly. Some employees were moved more than once and some were moved more than several hundred miles from their originating facility. Those employees who were moved more than several hundred miles were eventually placed back at their originating postal units because of management's violations of the national agreement between the USPS and the NALC.

In late 2004 or early 2005, I proposed a change management initiative to address the negative impact of complement management on employees within my district. It was a proposal to create a change impact team (CIT) for dealing with issues of coordination, communications, and implementation of excessing decisions. The proposal was given less than lukewarm approval by my supervisor, the manager of human resources, and the district manager.

The CIT was structured to function as a separate committee and collaborator with the complement management committee on the previously discussed issues, including improved relations with the postal unions to deal with these issues. Over a three-month period, the CIT held about six to seven meetings. I developed plans to address these issues and they were presented to my supervisor and the district manger. However, these two postal representatives clearly did not support the mission or goals of the CIT. For that reason, I made a decision with the team's agreement to dissolve it.

Although the proposed district CIT clearly did not have the capacity to address the larger systemic issue emanating from area and headquarters officials to expedite the elimination of positions by attrition, it would have been able to address how certain aspects of excessing of employees was implemented locally and help "smooth" the transitions of these employees into their new positions. It would have had the potential to improve the working relationship between labor and management and reduce the likelihood of employee mistrust, loss of commitment, and feeling devalued as an employee. In my opinion, the central reason why the CIT was sabotaged in my district was because of the lack of commitment and integrity of local leadership to buffer the fallout of harsh top-down expectations to reduce complement levels, without the full consideration of its operational or ethical impacts.

I am reminded of two anomalies in the context of management at my former district responding proactively regarding the reduction of complement. One was the result of a national agreement with the USPS and the APWU, while the other was strictly a headquarters' initiative. The agreement between the USPS and the APWU dealt with the displacement of craft employees at remote bar encoding centers (RBEC)[xxvi], and the other initiative involved the displacement of human resources personnel at the district.

When RBEC was shut down in my district, the communications and implementation of this initiative was done collaboratively and successfully by the APWU and the USPS. The process was highly considerate of employees' dignity and proactive regarding their need for reliable information and updates. To help with their transitions, both local management and the APWU ensured that the EAP was readily available to assist them.

The reduction of human resources personnel positions at the district level involved transitioning their duties and responsibilities to a national call center, including retirements, health benefits transactions, and a host of other personnel-related duties under the umbrella of human resources. During a two-year implementation period, affected employees were cross trained in different operations and successfully placed into new positions locally.

Communications were trustworthy and there were frequent updates communicated to all affected employees. Again, like the RBEC site example, the process was considerate of the affected employees and their transitions. These two bright examples

---

xxvi The development and implementation process for the displacement of employees at the RBEC process is discussed in Appendix D.

of change management need to be a consistent business strategy in the USPS, not an anomaly.

Toxic Workplace Environments

In my role as an internal consultant, there were four major tools to assess the workplace environments at specific postal facilities and the overall workplace environment for the district, including climate assessments, focus groups, VOE survey, and hot spot lists. The first three tools were maintained and utilized at the district level and the fourth tool was maintained by postal headquarters. In the thirteen years at my district, I conducted over one hundred fifty climate assessments and over sixty focus groups.

In comparison to focus groups, climate assessments were more time-consuming to conduct, but provided both quantitative and qualitative data for specific worksites. Focus groups provided rich qualitative data on what actions, from the employees' perspective, would best improve their overall workplace climate.

The VOE survey provided specific data on individual postal facilities and the district, including quality of supervisor communications, supervisor treatment of employees with dignity and respect, and other useful workplace indicators. Specific "hot spots" were chiefly identified by headquarters staff, based on employee complaints to congressional members, OIG, postal unions, and postal management associations and employee petitions to headquarters.

The findings and conclusions of climate assessments that I conducted in my district invariably supported serious employees concerns. Besides systemic issues, these concerns were identified as stemming from one or more sources, including: one or more rank and file employees creating a negative workplace atmosphere, a union official(s) creating unnecessary turmoil in the workplace, or a stressful workplace environment fostered by the prevailing management style in the unit.

Aside from the ubiquitous impact of systemic issues stemming from the postal culture, in the vast majority of climate assessments, the findings and conclusions supported that a negative prevailing management style was the chief contributor to creating a stressful and/or toxic workplace environment. Sadly, most of the facilities identified with harsh management styles fostered these types of environments. Many higher-level managers at the district level rarely took immediate corrective action. Some continued to give unequivocal support to the management staff at these facilities and most did not follow up consistently to ensure that employee concerns had been satisfactorily addressed.

In my thirteen years as the WIA, I interviewed over two thousand city letter carriers and several hundred clerks, rural carriers, mailhandlers, management and union officials, maintenance employees, and employees in other craft positions. The ensuing discussion, however, is primarily limited to the city letter craft and postal management. I examine systemic issues emanating from top-down control approaches.

Beginning in 1996, the workplace environment at city delivery facilities began to markedly decline. The diminutive but meaningful input and participation that city letter carriers had in their workplace ended that year with the unilateral discontinuance of employee involvement by the Postal Service.

This action was followed by increased pressure on city letter carriers, resulting from implementation of new monitoring devices to track performance and methods to increase performance. It was in this timeframe that the egregious "Street Management" PowerPoint training program was rolled out to the field, a training program that eventually became required training for mid-level managers at city delivery carrier units throughout the USPS. Below are five "cartoon slides" taken from this PowerPoint presentation.

After conducting a climate assessment at a facility in 1997, I was provided this particular "Street Management" presentation from a postmaster. The climate assessment primarily dealt with city letter carriers in his office who outlined concerns in a petition.

The petition suggested and the climate assessment validated that the workplace was highly stressful because of the management style of the supervisor and the condoning of the style by the postmaster. During my exit interview with the postmaster, he said that his supervisor was just enforcing the training policy that came from the district and subsequently gave me a copy of it. He said the operations manager from the district who presented the training appeared very embarrassed by its content. I later confirmed with this operations manager that he was required to present the training and it was difficult because of the offensive slides.

Interestingly, two years later, I was informed by this same operations manager that the area office was requiring a similar training for field postal management at all postal districts, which included the same offensive and degrading slides. I asked him if there was a way to identify where the training presentation originated from. He responded by right clicking on the ppt icon on his computer and then clicking on properties, which eventually identified the author and the location. The location was postal headquarters and the author was identified as a headquarters' employee. As a result of my meeting with the district manager on this required training, he decided it would be presented but **without** the offensive and dehumanizing slides.

In the late 1990s, changes in methods and practices regarding how city letter carriers were managed in the office and street served to increase hostile or toxic workplace environments throughout the USPS in general and within my district in particular. In 2003, with the introduction of the Delivery Operation Information System (DOIS)[xxvii], even more workplace sites became either hostile or toxic. These impacts are discussed below in the context of two city delivery facilities within my district.

Mirroring the reality throughout the USPS, city letter carriers in my district were treated less fairly, given less respect, micromanaged more often, and intimidated, harassed, and bullied more frequently compared to other employee crafts. One prime example of this lack of respect is the long-standing practice of not providing air conditioning in city letter carrier vehicles, regardless what part of the country they delivered mail. It was not uncommon in my district, which was not the hottest climate in the country during the summer by any means, for some employees to suffer heat stroke during the summer months.

xxvii More specific information on DOIS is incorporated in Appendix D.

It is important to note that in thirteen years at my district there were at least ten suicides brought to my attention. Contrary to the Califano Report on postal suicides, the USPS, at least in my district, did not track the suicides of its employees. Accordingly, the comparison of postal suicide rates with outside industry suicide rates noted in the report cannot be considered a valid comparison. Based on what I learned subsequent to some of the suicides in my district, at least three of the ten involved organizational factors as "triggers" to the event. One of these tragedies is discussed in the following scenario.

1. City Delivery Station

This particular examination focuses on a postal facility that has a *hostile* workplace environment in contrast to a toxic one. Although in this facility city letter carriers' performance was highly monitored, emotional abuse or bullying was not part of the management style employed by the facility management team. Like management teams throughout city delivery facilities in our district, the management team at this facility had very little latitude on how the letter carriers' workload would be assessed and monitored. The prevailing attitude or systemic bias pushed down from the highest level of postal management was that achieving the numbers was more important than giving due consideration to the dignity, safety, and welfare of its employees.

With the arrival of a new manager, extra attention was placed on improving city delivery productivity at the station, resulting in increased monitoring and disciplinary actions. City letter carriers were pressured to complete their office and street duties in less time than what was expected before the arrival of the new manager.

One city letter carrier, hereafter known as Mark, reacted violently to this added pressure and committed suicide. Tragically, while still on his delivery route, he closed himself into the back of his postal vehicle and shot himself in the head. Several months before this shooting, a clerk from the same office shot himself in his privately owned truck. A short time before these two suicides, a city letter carrier working in the same city killed himself shortly after resigning from the USPS. The employee ostensibly resigned because of ongoing harassment and intimidation from local management and mid-level management in the city.

As a result of Mark's suicide while on duty, the district manager and I interviewed employees at his postal facility. What we heard was both very sad and telling. Mark was described as quiet and hardworking, but continually worried about the possibility of losing his job. This was in spite of his overall good performance and good postal record. Several of his coworkers indicated he brought a bottle to carry on the route to urinate in because he was afraid to use the time to stop at a gas station or convenience store while on his route.

Coworkers indicated that Mark routinely skipped his designated breaks, including his lunch break. They complained of the daily pressures on them from local management, pressures they blamed on their district's policies. Of special significance, the city letter carriers at the facility informed the district manager and me that the day before Mark committed suicide they were strongly instructed to improve their performance. We later confirmed that the facility supervisor had notified the city letter carriers, in writing, the day before Mark committed suicide, essentially conveying that performance needed to improve—no excuses.

Based on the information from the foregoing sources, the overall picture of Mark was that he was oversensitive. He took "everything to heart." Ostensibly, he wanted others to know why he committed suicide. He was found dead in his postal jeep with a self-inflicted gunshot to his head, splattering blood on dozens of letters. Next to him reportedly was a handwritten letter where he stated that he could not take his job anymore.

This third suicide in the city had a chilling effect on craft and management employees alike. Some management employees, knowing differently deep down, pushed the idea that this employee's personal problems were the cause of his suicide, not wanting to acknowledge that the postal culture and its eventual impact on workplace environments likely had an ominous role in Mark's death.

It is important to note that in my tenure as an internal consultant there were a number of postal facilities that had very low Voice of Employee (VOE) survey scores. However, in many cases these facilities were not given the special attention needed to address employee concerns identified in the surveys. They were rationalized by some postal managers as a reflection of employees not happy with accountability requirements of the local management staff and union antagonism.

One particular station received the lowest or near lowest VOE survey score in the country in relation to comparable facilities and approximate number of employees. Despite several workplace climate assessments indicating that there was a toxic workplace environment for city letter carriers, very low VOE survey scores, employee petitions, several unfair labor complaints with the National Labor Relations Board, the postmaster was shielded by higher management for nearly a year.

It is important to note that the hot list initiative[xxviii] did not always work as intended because of pressure from district officials and perhaps at higher levels within the organization. In making this point, I review the process steps involved in the initiative and discuss what reportedly happened twice at another postal district.

At one large city, as a result of an employee petition, the entire city was reportedly placed on the hot list by postal headquarters, triggering a notification to the area office and finally to the district. It was further reported to me by an employee at the area office that the district WIA, as a result of the city's placement on the hot list, was directed to conduct a workplace climate assessment to identify if the issues in the city were systemic or individual in their origin.

The WIA conducted a climate assessment and subsequently identified the issues and concerns as individual in their origin. Sadly, the district manager, as reported to me from an official in the area office, directed the WIA to rewrite the climate assessment report and indicate that the workplace environment issues were systemic in their origin. This district manager, as reported by this area employee, directed this same WIA to re-write another climate assessment report from individual to systemic regarding another facility that was placed on headquarters' hot list. Accordingly, the concerns of the employees at these facilities were never addressed and the workplace conditions worsened.

2. Postal Management District-Wide

In the first section of this examination, I provide the context or the early history of events that served to foster a toxic work environment for the management employees in my district. In the second section, I explore the highly fear-based practices directed by the district manager and many of the direct reports toward supervisors, managers, and postmasters domiciled in field facilities. In chapter nine, I analyze the negative effects of this toxic work environment on the mental and physical health of these field supervisors, managers, and postmasters.

From 2000 to 2006, the Area Vice-President, hereafter known as Bill, responding to the pressure from postal headquarters, reportedly fostered higher tensions, turmoil,

---

xxviii   The hot list was an initiative designed to identify and address troubled work sites.

and fear throughout the districts under his purview. Bill had the reputation of frequently and publicly belittling employees in postal management, especially at area office review meetings at the districts.

One of the most egregious examples of how this "played out" is noted below. It provides a wide-ranging insight to what is tolerated and allowed to occur with impunity for high-ranking postal management officials in the USPS. It provides a picture of what is considered as an acceptable management style to be modeled by postal officials throughout the area office and the districts under its purview.

At an area office review meeting at a postal district, Bill reportedly arranged for postal managers at one of the largest cities in the district to "play" his version of the "Weakest Link." In arranging for this "contest," Bill reportedly selected the five operations managers as participants who were direct reports to the local postmaster. Each worker was placed at separate podiums in front of over a hundred district officials and later videotaped. Bill played the part as the MC. He asked the participants complex postal operations questions, some of which had several parts.

All the participants did poorly in the contest and Bill reportedly was very disrespectful and belittling toward them throughout. At the end of the contest, Bill reportedly summarily dismissed the participants and concluded by saying, "Now we know what is wrong with this city's performance; it's middle management." It was reported to me that these managers felt highly humiliated and violated in this toxic game of shaming.

In the subsequent discussion, I provide my experiences with an individual hereafter known at Chris. Prior to my retirement, Chris was promoted to district manager in my district. First, however, it is important to point out that from 2002 to 2007 there were six district managers in my district, including three officers-in-charge. The frequent changing of district managers weakened any semblance of a harmonious workplace environment, especially for field postal management. There were some serious workplace climate issues that resulted from the policies and methods of two of Chris' predecessors, but they pale in comparison to what transpired.

My history precedes Chris' selection as district manager. In 2001, at a facility where Chris was the postmaster of a large city, the facility was placed on headquarters' hot list. Numerous disciplinary actions were taken against city letter carriers, resulting in numerous grievances and EEO complaints. Employees at the facility sent petitions to the district office, congressional representatives, OIG, and to area office management and union officials.

Because of the serious issues and concerns stemming from the subject facility, I was asked by the area office human resources analyst, hereafter known as Sharon, to conduct a joint climate assessment. It is important to note that this subject facility was not in my district. Chris had previously painted my counterpart as biased and unprofessional and did not want him to be part of any assessment.

Several years later, one of Chris' direct reports confided that Chris had bragged to him that a workplace improvement analyst—referencing my counterpart—was prevented from entering the subject postal facility. Sadly, shortly after the joint climate assessment was conducted, the WIA in this district had a complete mental breakdown and filed for disability retirement. His claim was accepted. Based on my observations and numerous conversations with this WIA and his predecessors, a highly toxic work environment had existed, without abatement, for at least five years in his district.

After conducting the climate assessment at the subject facility and a subsequent conversation with a supervisor who had worked previously under Chris at the facility, it was my professional opinion that a toxic workplace environment existed primarily because of the harsh management style of Chris. This supervisor, hereafter referred to as Wayne, told me that at times Chris would stand by him on the workroom floor and direct him to take disciplinary actions on specific city letter carriers.

In one conversation, Wayne reported that Chris had pointed to the letter carriers on the workroom floor and told him that they were the "enemies." He reported that Chris would type numerous letters of warnings, without any input from him, and then order him to give them to the city letter carriers. Wayne indicated that because of the enormous toxic stress in the office, he passed out on the workroom floor. He stated that he was later rushed to the hospital from the postal facility, via ambulance, with a bleeding ulcer.

Within a couple of weeks of sending the climate assessment report to the district manager and manager, postal operations, Sharon and I met with these officials to discuss an action plan for improvement of Chris' facility. Shortly after this meeting, it was disclosed to me that Bill, the Area Vice-President, arranged for Chris to come to the area office, on detail, in a higher-level position. Less than a year later, Chris was promoted to this position, and about two years later, was promoted by Bill to an executive position at the area office. Several years later, Bill promoted Chris again as my district manager.

Within a very short period time from Chris' arrival at my district, it was transformed into a toxic environment for many of its supervisors, managers, and postmasters.

I began receiving numerous complaints about negative workplace climate conditions and stress-related problems from many of these postal officials. For that reason, I conducted a climate assessment including a review of relevant disciplinary records, memoranda, and e-mail messages.

After completing this assessment, I developed a formal report, which was sent to the area manager of human resources. Since he did not respond in a timely manner, I sent a copy to the relatively new Area Vice-President, hereafter known as Paul, and to the Assistant Postmaster General. In my memorandum, I requested that they pass the report on to the Postmaster General on my behalf, since correspondences directed to him frequently were sent back to the field office.

Paul, in my opinion like Bill, subscribed to the same mentality of achieving bottom-line results no matter what. Paul's written word of achieving results by treating people fairly and respectfully, in my professional opinion, did not match what was happening at my postal district or at other districts since I retired. Sadly, the same can be argued about the Assistant Postmaster General and the current Postmaster General. For these officials, it strongly appears that bottom-line results, without due consideration for its impact on employees, is expected from those under their purview.

Since I did not get a response to my climate assessment report from these postal officials and the results of my meeting with the area manager of human resources were unsatisfactory, I sent a cover letter and copies of my report to the OIG director, human capital, and OIG auditor-in-charge of the human capital team with copies to a U.S. senator, President, NAPS, and the President of NAPUS. To the best of my knowledge, there was no follow-up inquiry or investigation conducted after I retired from the USPS.

In the above-referenced report, the findings included:

1. The vast majority of the target employees with stress-related illnesses or health problems report working fifty to seventy hours per week.

2. High micromanagement from the district manager or by many members of the district's staff is coupled with no forgiveness when failure is the result of system issues beyond the management official's control.

3. The use of fear and intimidation tactics is constant in attempt to achieve high results, especially in the area of customer service.

4. Discipline and direct or implied threats of corrective action are common-place.

These findings are rigorously and diligently supported throughout this sixty-one page climate assessment. Sadly, based on feedback from postal officials in this district after I retired, no action was taken to correct these serious conditions. Instead, the feedback I have received states that the workplace environment has worsened for postal management.

Interestingly and tellingly, subsequent to my workplace climate assessment report, several of the direct reports of Chris who were identified as contributing to the toxic workplace environment for postal management have been promoted to postal executives positions. Chris was eventually promoted to a higher-level executive position, subsequent to the report and my retirement.

Based on this review and my extensive investigation of the postal culture, it encourages a top-down mentality that communicates by its actions or inactions that it is an acceptable practice to achieve results through harassment or bullying. In my district, this was tolerated and condoned by high-ranking officials at the area office and postal headquarters. The OIG,[xxix] as third appendage of postal management, has also turned a blind eye to this psychological violence.

Summary and Concluding Remarks

In this chapter, I presented my relevant experiences in the USPS from 1973 to 2007, which point to a harsh, authoritarian culture. The chronicling of these experiences serve to validate the conclusion that there exists, in agreement with the ample evidence examined and presented throughout many of the chapters of this book and its appendices, a harsh postal culture.

Accordingly, my personal experiences, as reported in this chapter, are in agreement with the conclusion that the postal culture fosters a management style at all levels of the organization that is oppressive, autocratic, and uncaring. This claim is in agreement with the documentary, quantitative, qualitative, and anecdotal evidence I reviewed from congressional hearings and investigations, GAO reports, postal commission reports, USPS strategic plans, and from the literature in the workplace violence field.

---

xxix The role of the OIG contributing to a negative postal culture is chronicled in Appendix E.

CHAPTER NINE
Impact of Postal Culture on Postal Employees, Families, and Organization

The impact of the postal culture on postal employees, families, and the organization has been dramatic and horrific, especially in the last three decades. The violent manifestations of its impact[xxx] were previously discussed in the context of workplace violence, both psychological and physical.

In the first section of this chapter, I review the contributions of occupational health psychology to our understanding of workplace stress and its impact. In the next section, I briefly discuss how the postal culture contributes to job strain and how it negatively affects its employees' health and well-being. I review scholarly studies that investigated the impact of job strain on employees' health.

Furthermore, in the second section, I chronicle the impact of job strain on the health and well-being of postal employees. The chronicling of this relationship is based on the climate assessment I conducted and discussed in the previous chapter. Specifically, I provide excerpts from some of my interviews from this assessment and a profile listing specific health concerns and consequences of these health concerns.

In the third section, I examine the impact of the postal culture on employees' families and the organization. This examination is based on my personal and professional experiences from 1986 to 2007 with the USPS as an EAP representative and as an internal consultant. In discussing the impact of the postal culture on the organization, the specific organizational outcomes that I discuss in this section include: 1) retention, 2) absenteeism and loss productivity, 3) management turnover and loss productivity, and 4) violence and reputation.

---

xxx   See chapters three and four and Appendix B.

Contributions of Occupational Health Psychology

In order to understand how chronic job stress or toxic stress levels negatively impacts the aforementioned areas, it is instructive to first consider contributions made in the field of occupational health psychology (OHP). It has been less than two decades since occupational health psychology became recognized as a separate discipline in the field of psychology.

This recognition as a new discipline stems from the collaborative work of the American Psychological Association and the National Institute on Occupational Safety and Health.[153] For example, together in the 1990s, their joint efforts led to four international conferences on occupational stress and health, including a new journal titled the *Journal of Occupational Health Psychology*.

Occupational health psychology is committed to improve the quality of work life and to protect and promote the safety, health, and well-being of employees. Stated differently, its primary focus is to prevent psychological and physical illnesses and injuries resulting from high levels of occupational stress. An important area of focus in the OHP field is the identification of factors within organizational structures that *foster* employees' health and well-being and also correlate with positive business and customer objectives, including high retention, reduced accidents and absenteeism, increased revenues and productivity, and premier customer services.

Similarly, another important area of focus in the OHP field is the identification of factors in organizational structures that *compromise* employees' health and well-being, thereby leading to employee health-related problems such as cardiovascular disease and mental health problems including depressive and anxiety disorders. Some other important OHP areas of focus include workplace violence, work-home spillover, downsizing, workplace safety, and accident prevention. As a result of these other areas of focus, there is a recognition and a body of evidence in the OHP field supporting the notion that work characteristics and higher level organizational factors facilitate work stress and lead to negative outcomes for employees, their families, and the organization.

In the 1970s, one of the most influential work characteristics models in the emerging field of OHP was the job demand-control (DC) theory.[154] Simply stated, this work characteristics model predicts that chronic job strain results when workers have high job demands (i.e., high workload requirements) and low control (i.e., low decision authority and low skill level).

In the 1980s, a third factor, **support** (i.e., worksite social support), was incorporated in the model as a means to better understand occupational stress from the work characteristics model and, conversely, employees' well-being from the work characteristics model. The shorthand for this extended three-factor model is commonly referred to as DCS.[155]

Looking through the prism of the DCS model, the highest incidences of occupational stress and associated negative outcomes (i.e., diminishing of employee health/well-being) result from jobs that include high *demand*, low *control*, and low *support*. It is also important to note that the DCS model predicts that, when there is a mix of high work demands, low control, and high support, support acts as a buffer to the job strain/stress potential. In effect, high support has shown to mitigate the development of workplace stress symptoms and a toxic workplace.

Job Strain and its Impact on Postal Employees Health and Well-Being

The *toxic mix* of increased job demands, low job control, and low social support has serious health consequences.[xxxi] Based on my extensive review of the postal culture, the evidence is unequivocal that employees in many of the postal facilities throughout the USPS can be characterized as having high job demands, low job control, and low social support, especially with regard to field postal management and city letter carriers. The evidence supports that these conditions have become increasingly problematic (i.e., increased job stress levels) for postal employees in the last ten to twelve years, especially the last three years, and they were influenced by changes in the broader economic and political context.

Clearly, my interest in this *toxic mix* (high job demands, low job control, and low social support) focuses on the conditions of the USPS employees. Since I documented a toxic mix and its associated negative health outcomes for postal management in a workplace climate assessment as noted in chapter eight, the discussion below is limited to this subgroup of employees. This workplace climate assessment, in my role as an internal consultant, documented the horrific negative impact of a toxic workplace environment on the physical and mental health of postal employees. Before I begin this discussion, however, I review several important studies on negative health outcomes resulting from job strain/stress.

---

xxxi This toxic mix was highlighted in context of employee stress, turmoil, and low morale in chapters seven and eight and Appendices C-E.

Significant Studies on Job Stress/Strain and Health Outcomes

As indicated previously, there is credible research evidence that a significant relationship exists between a stressful work environment and the health and well-being of employees. The relationship between job **stress/strain** and health has been well documented in the literature.

In their review of the literature on this topic, Veldhoven concluded: "[J]ob demands (especially time pressure) are primarily associated with job strain (e.g., fatigue, emotional exhaustion, psychosomatic complaints)."[156] The effects of this relationship include headaches, sleep disturbances, cardiovascular disease—including high or elevated blood pressure—difficulty in concentrating, upset stomach, absenteeism, depression, and anxiety. My interviews with employees, as presented later in this discussion, clearly support research findings that a significant relationship exists between high stress/strain and all these negative outcomes.

Sleep disturbance is one common deleterious manifestation of the relationship between job **stress/strain** and health. Research has shown that high demands and low social support from coworkers and supervisors were associated with sleep disturbances and fatigue at work.[157] The most salient finding in this longitudinal study with seven hundred participants regarding the relationship between job strain and sleep disturbance was that "an excessive commitment toward work intrudes on an individual's sleep."[158] My interviews with employees, as presented below, clearly support the relationship between high stress/strain and sleep disturbance.

Another common, deleterious manifestation of the relationship between job **stress/strain** and health is high or elevated blood pressure. A prospective study (10,308 participants) conducted by Kuper[159] supports this conclusion. For example, the main finding from this study was that the combined effect of high job demands and low decision making were positively associated with coronary heart disease. Also, a prospective study (8,395 participants) conducted by Guimont[160] showed that cumulative job strain was significantly related to increases in systolic blood pressure. My interviews with employees, as provided below, clearly support the relationship between high stress/strain and high or elevated blood pressure.

In summary, I provided this very brief review of the literature to underscore the conclusion that there is an unequivocal connection between job stress/strain and the health and well-being of employees. In support of this conclusion, below I provide excerpts taken from the more than fifty interviews conducted with field postal management.

Interviews with Supervisor, Customer Services, Manager, Customer Services, and Postmasters Level 17-24

Prior to my retirement and as a result of the toxic workplace environment created at my postal district, I documented key events and interviews with the affected postal employees to substantiate that this environment existed: Over seventy-five interviews were conducted with *field postal management*. The employee complement for this target population, according to the District Complement Committee chairperson, was about three hundred employees. Of these seventy-five interviews, over fifty employees reported health disturbances, which they attributed to management practices and policies.

Below I provide excerpts from some of my interviews with the subject employees and a profile listing specific health concerns and consequences of these health concerns. These brief narratives provide support that a toxic mix of stress has negatively impacted their health and well-being. In some of the narratives, the notation *1st time* is used to underscore that an employee had never experienced this health issue prior to the dramatic increase in workplace stress. Similarly, in the profile chart that follows, *1st time* indicates that this is the first time an employee had experienced the identified health concern.

1. Excerpts Taken from Climate Assessment: Reported Health Concerns

a. Reports suffering from panic attacks. Chest Pains 1st time—Went to emergency room hospital from work. He stayed in hospital for two days for observation. Later, he had a heart attack and a stent was placed in his artery because of 90 percent blockage. Other stress-related complaints noted were frequent heartburn and sleep disturbance, with night sweats and rolling and tossing.

b. Went to emergency hospital after work because of heart concerns. Within the next couple days, she had a stroke and was rushed to the emergency hospital room. Several months prior to the stroke, she reported having migraine headaches and periodic sleep disturbance, not able to sleep. Weeks before the stroke she was having night sweats.

c. On sick leave for two months because of stress-related illness, including a bleeding ulcer and headaches. Voluntarily transferred from a supervisor position to a custodian position.

d. Rushed to hospital emergency room from home with an anxiety attack and high blood pressure. He also reports ongoing sleep disturbances.

e. Yesterday **1ˢᵗ time** placed on blood pressure medication. He reports ongoing sleep disturbance for past eight months, depressive symptoms, and racing heart beat. He is working very long hours.

f. Reports to have been on **anti-depressant/anti-anxiety RX** for the past three months, along with panic attacks, nausea, crying spells, fatigue and tossing at night, and work stress dreams. Night sweats last two weeks. She is trying to downgrade to lower level position. Starts professional counseling next week. Left a station manager's meeting and she went to the medical unit; her blood pressure was too high.

g. Last thirty days on blood pressure medication for the **1st time**. Last sixty days, she reports gaining fifteen pounds, night sweats, depression, tossing at night, heartburn, crying spells, and professional counseling. **RX for depression**. She is working long hours.

h. She reports elevated blood pressure for the past several months. In last twelve months waking up many times during the course of the night. Five months ago was diagnosed with 40 percent blockage in one of her arteries. Reports heartburn for the past six to eight months, at work and at night. Five months ago, she reports hospitalization because of suspected broken blood vessels in her eye. She reports working sixty-seventy hours a week. On one occasion, she had to leave work because her face was swelling up.

i. Had a stent put in because of artery blockage. Put on **blood pressure RX and cholesterol RX 1ˢᵗ time**. She reports now taking ten different medications re-lated to heart. Reports eighteen pound loss in the past eight months. Has sleep disturbances, waking up three to four times during night.

j. Reports leaving work in the morning and going for an emergency appointment with her treating physician. She reports that her blood pressure reading at the doctor's office was 220/180. She is now on **blood pressure RX for the 1ˢᵗ time.**

k. Reports elevated blood pressure lasting one and a half years. Reports sleep disturbance, including night sweats. Anxiety attacks, with the most recent one this morning. Has had heartburn at night and during the day. For the last month, throwing up at night at least once a week. Reported loss of concentra-tion, working long hours, depressive symptoms, anxiety symptoms, shortness of breath, empty feeling, and wanting to run out of the office.

l. Reports angioplasty is scheduled. After work, went to the emergency room hospital because of shortness of breath and heaviness on his chest. Reports to have been taking blood pressure medication for the last couple of years. Re-ports sleep disturbances and tossing for the past year and night sweats for the past six months, occurring about once a week. Reports symptoms of depres-sion, nausea, and panic attacks over the last six months. He describes the panic attacks as racing heart, heaviness on chest, and feeling like wanting to run out of the building.

m. Reports that his doctor wanted to put him on blood pressure medication three months ago. In the last six months, he reports the following symptoms: 1) loss of appetite, 2) tossing at night, trouble sleeping because he was thinking about work, 3) night sweats a couple of times, 4) sense of dread, tired, 5) wife indicated that he is distant, 6) heartburn at night and during the day. It wakes him up, feels like he is going to have a heart attack. He reports, "I have no life."

n. He reports the following symptoms in the last three to four months: elevated blood pressure, diarrhea, sleep disturbances—both tossing and sweats, and heartburn. Taking medication for heartburn past several months.

o. Last week, after work, went into emergency hospital because of double vision. Last two months she has been experiencing the following symptoms: headaches, night sweats, rolling and tossing at night, and muscle cramps in legs, neck, and shoulder.

p. He reports headaches in last couple of weeks. Diarrhea once a month for the past nine to ten months. On several occasions, in the last couple of months, he has had night sweats. Anxiety attacks in the past nine to ten months. Heartburn for the past ten months, which includes throwing up. Has sought professional counseling through the EAP.

q. Placed on blood pressure **RX for 1st time**. While on another assignment, he reported experiencing the following symptoms: diarrhea, sleep disturbances—including night sweats—heartburn, and anxiety attacks once a week, loss of appetite, and depressed mood.

r. He reports the following symptoms: started blood pressure **RX for 1st time** about four months ago, headaches about two times a week for the past eight to ten months, and sleep disturbance for the past eight to ten months. Reports a sense of dread about his job situation.

s. He was taken to the emergency hospital from home, wherein he was admitted for bleeding ulcers and was operated on. Employee reports that he has suffered from headaches in the past ten months, and on the average, has had trouble sleeping two to three times per week.

2. Profile of Employee Reported Health Concerns and Consequences

HEART ATTACKS	2
ANGIOPLASTY	3
STROKES	2
SLEEP DISTURBANCES W/O NIGHT SWEATS	18
SLEEP DISTURBANCES W/ NIGHT SWEATS	20
ELEVATED BLOOD PRESSURE	15
BLOOD PRESSURE MEDICATIONS 1st TIME	11
DEPRESSION OR SIGNIFICANTLY DEPRESSED MOOD	19
ANXIETY ATTACKS	8
TRIPS TO EMERGENCY HOSPITAL FROM WORK	4
TRIPS TO EMERGENCY HOSPITAL OTHER THAN FROM WORK	10
URGENT TRIPS TO PRIMARY PHYSICIAN	3
THE NUMBER OF TRIPS TO EMERGENCY HOSPITAL OR URGENT TRIPS TO PRIMARY PHYSICIAN RELATED TO ELEVATED OR VERY LOW BLOOD PRESSURE	6
EMPLOYEES TAKING OFF WORK MORE THAN <u>THREE MONTHS</u> BECAUSE OF STRESS-RELATED CONCERNS	2
EMPLOYEE TAKING OFF WORK MORE THAN <u>TWO MONTHS</u> BECAUSE OF STRESS-RELATED CONCERNS	3

An important question to ask at this point is: How can a stressful work environment become *toxic* in a short period of time for a significant number of employees? The answer to this question in great part can be best understood in light of the DCS model previously discussed. Aside from the new district manager and many of the direct reports increasing demands and control over these employees, these two factors are not totally responsible for the toxic workplace environment that ensued.

The chief factor for the rapid emergence of this toxic workplace environment was the dramatic *decrease* in support received from the district office and from many of the district manager's direct reports. The standard position or posture toward these employees was that there was *no acceptable reason* for not meeting business or customer requirements, which was followed by numerous audits, telecoms, and threatening correspondences when there were "failures." Accordingly, in this scenario, the *low support* for these employees translated into violations of their dignity, lack of trust, emotional abuse or bullying, fear of losing their jobs, and, of course, serious health problems.

Impact of Postal Culture on Employees' Families and the Organization

As mentioned previously, besides occupational health psychology's focus on how work characteristics can negatively affect employees' health and well-being, it also has studied the impact of an unhealthy workplace environment and its negative spillover to the *employees' family* and its relationship to *organizational outcomes*. The discussion that follows in these two areas is viewed primarily in the context of my twenty years of experience as an EAP representative and as an internal consultant with the USPS.

Impact of Postal Culture on Employees' Families

The most dramatic impact an unhealthy or toxic workplace environment can have on employees' families is the loss of their loved ones because of a workplace tragedy, for example an employee's loss of life resulting from a workplace shooting or suicide. Suffice to say, I have personally witnessed the impact of these acts of violence on postal families. This is not to say by any means that all postal workplace shootings or suicides were the result of an unhealthy workplace environment. It is fair to conclude, however, based on the evidence presented in this book, that too many of these workplace tragedies were in part facilitated or triggered by organizational factors. This in no way diminishes the responsibility of employees who committed these acts of violence, but it does help explain why some felt compelled to take such dramatic and horrific actions.

Fortunately, I was not a witness to someone dying on the job because of a toxic workplace environment. In the excerpts noted previously, clearly someone could have had a fatal heart attack, stroke, or other sudden death syndrome as a result of too high work demands, low control, and low support. There were a few close calls. In Japan, because so many employees were dying as a result of chronic job stress, they devised a term called *karoshi* to depict the sudden death of employees who were overworked, working sixty to eighty hours a week.

Another dramatic impact on families, stemming in part from an unhealthy workplace environment, is an employee resignation or placement in a leave-without-pay status for months pending removal. I have personally witnessed the effects of these occurrences on employees' spouses and children. Some of the negative outcomes I have witnessed include emotional upheaval, divorce, teen drug abuse and school problems, serious financial problems, and severe stress and anxiety in day-to-day living.

Work-related employee health problems, both psychological and physical, also have a dramatic impact on families. A less dramatic but still significant impact on families occurs when employees tend to become unavailable or highly reactive because of working in an unhealthy environment for a long period of time. In my role as an EAP representative and as an internal consultant with the USPS, I became aware of many family members who were prescribed medication for depression, anxiety, and inability to sleep in order to cope with the negative fallout of the postal culture.

Impact of Postal Culture on Organizational Outcomes

1. Retention

A company's retention rate is frequently mentioned as an important organizational outcome in academic research, including in the field of OHP. The USPS has a very favorable retention rate for most career positions. Among the most important reasons for this favorable outcome are the relatively generous health and retirement benefits and long-term job security. Even with these reasons, I have witnessed talented and good performing employees resign because of an unhealthy workplace environment; one such example is discussed below.

As a result of the toxic workplace environment for field management in my district,[xxxii] a management intern, hereafter known as Ken, resigned from the USPS shortly after completing a two-year training program. Ken was hired from outside the USPS into this position, a position designed to "fast-track" employees who were identified as having a graduate degree and the requisite talent to quickly learn and manage postal operations.

Successful applicants were screened and interviewed on two separate occasions at postal headquarters. An estimated $100,000 in training and development costs were spent on Ken's training, not including the total company time spent by other managers on his training and development.

I spoke to Ken several months after he resigned from the USPS, and the reasons provided for his resignation included: lack of respect, lack of support, violations of personal dignity, unreasonable workloads, no control over resources, and expectations to work six days a week and long hours for a forty-hour paycheck. Ken indicated he felt badly about how his colleagues in postal operations were treated, but felt fortu-

---

xxxii Discussed in chapter eight and the foregoing.

nate to have found employment with a company that treated him fairly, respectfully, and had reasonable workload expectations.

2. Absenteeism and Loss Productivity

A company's absenteeism rate is another important organizational outcome highlighted in academic research, including in the field of OHP. When employees are absent from work, it negatively impacts productivity and, in many instances, more monies are spent on replacement hours.

The profile of employees' reported health concerns as presented in the chart above sheds light on the impact of an unhealthy workplace environment and its relationship to absenteeism and replacement costs. As a result of this workplace environment, two employees reported taking off work more than three months because of stress-related concerns and three employees reported taking off more than two months. It is important to note that there were a significant number of employees interviewed who were absent from their positions less than two months because of the workplace environment. In the context of assessing the impact of the workplace environment for a population of approximately three hundred management field employees, the impact of absenteeism and replacement costs are significant.

3. Management Turnover and Loss Productivity

Although a very important organizational issue, there has been little research regarding turnover in the management ranks and its relationship to a toxic workplace environment. When employees are operating in a toxic workplace environment, turnover is likely to become a very serious issue that not only impacts the management ranks, but also a company's productivity.

As a result of the subject climate workplace assessment and in the context of management turnover, it was documented that two employees voluntarily reassigned to different but same level positions, four employees voluntarily downgraded to lower level jobs, three employees voluntarily went back to postal clerk or letter carrier positions, and as mentioned previously, one employee resigned. Of those employees who went to different positions, all but one reported doing so because of the enormous job strain/stress they were experiencing in the previous nine to ten months. In the context of assessing the impact of the workplace environment for a population of approximately three hundred management field employees, the impact of management turnover and loss productivity are significant.

4. Violence and Reputation

The prevalence of violence in an organization has a clear relationship with the organization's reputation. The frequency and extent of violence in the USPS over the past three decades supports the notion that a harsh postal culture has engendered serious consequences to its reputation. Historically, the media and public have thought that there is something terribly wrong with the USPS. Not only has the USPS spent countless millions of dollars because of violence in its postal facilities, it also has spent millions of dollars attempting to change perceptions of the media and public through its public relations campaign, funding of studies, and hiring of private consultants.

Summary and Concluding Remarks

In the foregoing, I revealed the negative impact of postal culture (i.e., "toxic mix" of increased job demands, low job control, and low social support) on employees, their families, and the USPS organization. More specifically, I chronicled the impact of job strain on the health and well-being of postal employees. I provided excerpts from some of my interviews from a climate assessment conducted in late 2006 and a profile listing specific health concerns and consequences of these health concerns. Additionally, I examined the impact of the postal culture on employees' families and the organization, which was based on my personal and professional experiences from 1986 to 2007 with the USPS as an EAP representative and as an internal consultant.

It is important to note in closing this chapter that the costs associated with a harsh postal culture extend beyond employees, their family members, and the organization. There are also significant costs to our society, giving the public a sense of less safety and cohesiveness as well as putting a burden on our social services and medical resources.

For all these reasons, it is imperative that radical and comprehensive change of the postal culture becomes a national priority. Accordingly, I address *how* the USPS can shift **from** workplace tragedies and toxic work environments **to** a safe and healthy organization in the last two chapters.

CHAPTER TEN
Creating and Maintaining a Healthy Organization

In this chapter, I explore the process of how the USPS can create and maintain a healthy organization. First, however, I provide a brief overview of the job characteristics model and its relationship to unhealthy and unsafe organizations. As a result of this examination, I define the term *healthy organization* and make a moral argument for its development.

In the final section of the chapter, I discuss the means by which the USPS can shift from its current state as an unhealthy organization to a healthy and safe organization in the context of key components of organizational dynamics, including: 1) leadership, 2) organizational design and job redesign, 3) reward and performance evaluation systems, 4) selection and development, 5) change management 6) employee involvement, and 7) safety. I provide requirements and recommendations to the USPS on achieving optimal functioning for each of these key components.

Before I begin this examination, it is important to point out that healthy organizations are in general fundamentally safe. For that reason, in the subsequent discussion, when a *healthy* organization is referenced, it is also considered a *safe* one. Similarly, when an *unhealthy* organization is referenced, it is considered to be *unsafe* in terms of its impact on employees' health and well-being and potential for workplace violence.

Work Characteristics and Unhealthy Organizations

In the academic literature, a significant number of research studies have been conducted to evaluate the relationship between stressors in the workplace and their negative impact on organizations. In contrast, there have been few research studies conducted to evaluate factors that promote optimal health for organizations. The job stress model conceptualizes that chronic, negative conditions in the workplace create hazards that are detrimental to the health and well-being of the employees.

In Part 4 of this book, I assessed negative conditions in the USPS related to the larger postal culture, its organizational practices, methods, and management style. The impact of a harsh and authoritarian postal culture was shown to create negative conditions where chronic and toxic stress permeated the entire organization.

In chapter nine, I discussed the DCS theory, a work characteristics model that includes the factors job demands, control, and support. The DCS theory claims that chronic job strain or high stress levels have a significant relationship to *high job demands, low job control*, and *low job support*.

If a *toxic mix* of these three factors is prevalent throughout an organization, it then can be concluded that they are reflective of an unhealthy organization. In chapter nine, this point was supported by examining the relationship between this toxic mix and its impact on postal employees, their families, and the USPS.

Evaluating an organization's work characteristics (DCS)[161]—as part of an organizational risk assessment to identify stressors and the creation of baseline data—is very useful. By identifying a baseline for workplace stressors, interventions can be developed and their effectiveness can then be assessed.

Although the DCS theory may be useful and instructive regarding risk assessment and targeted interventions, it does not shed sufficient light on what organizational components or factors are required to create and sustain a healthy organization. Before discussing factors that I identified for the USPS to become a healthy organization, it is important first to define a healthy organization and elucidate why it is a moral obligation for corporate and public leaders to create and sustain them.

Designing Healthy Organizations: A Moral Obligation

As indicated previously, one of the initial steps in assessing the health of an organization is to conduct a risk assessment to determine dysfunctions and negative outcomes, but such an assessment does not provide sufficient information on how to design a healthy organization. In order to design a healthy organization, it is useful to have a definitional framework that sheds light on the emphases and strategic focal points of a healthy organization.

Taking in account two definitions of what constitutes a healthy organization, I offer the following definition: *A healthy organization is one which has successfully, as reflected in its organizational culture and organizational practices and methods, aligned and integrated the goals of fostering respectful relationships, validation of employee dignity, and fairness in the workplace with the goals of achieving company profitability, efficiency, and productivity.* Simply stated, a healthy organization is one that has achieved optimal systemic health by strategic focus on positive outcomes for both its employees and the organization.

These company goals provide the framework where an organization can promote employee well-being and positive employee attitudes in the context of achieving its overall mission. When these goals are maximized, healthy workplace environments become the norm and, conversely, toxic workplace environments become unsustainable. By making them unsustainable, the horrific consequences of toxic environments become a moot issue.

A wealth of quantitative and qualitative findings from the professional literature supports a clear link between work stressors and serious consequences to employees' well-being and health. It is, therefore, an unequivocal moral obligation for company leaders to design and implement measures that lead to healthy workplace environments for its employees. In the next section, I provide a pathway to how the USPS can shift from an unhealthy organization with harsh and toxic workplace environments to a healthy organization.

Creating and Sustaining a Healthy Organization within the USPS

The following programs have been implemented without significantly changing the level of turmoil and unrest in the workplaces of the USPS: training programs, stress management initiatives, emphasis on assisting employees through the Employee Assistance Program (EAP), employee opinion surveys, and dispute resolution processes. Without significant and far-reaching cultural and structural changes, these types of initiatives will only have a minimal impact regarding any hope of creating and sustaining a healthy postal organization.

In his testimony to congressional members in 1993, Postmaster Marvin Runyon[162] acknowledged that the USPS was autocratic in its management approaches and that deep structural changes were necessary. Sadly, these changes did not happen under his stewardship or under the stewardship of his successors; in fact, it worsened.

In the subsequent discussion, I discuss the means by which the USPS can shift from its current state as an unhealthy organization to a healthy one in the context of key components of organizational dynamics. Stated differently, I consider key cultural and structural changes needed in the USPS in the context of: 1) leadership, 2) organizational design and job redesign, 3) reward and performance evaluation systems, 4) selection and development, 5) change management 6) employee involvement, and 7) safety. I provide requirements and recommendations to the USPS on achieving optimal functioning for each of these key components.

Leadership

The most important or overriding factor in creating and sustaining a healthy organization is the engaged stewardship or leadership at the highest level of the organization, a leadership committed to creating and setting the tone for a culture of respect and fairness. In Appendix C, top postal management's emphases and focus were revealed by examining their strategic plans. These plans reflected a goal-driven perspective where budget and service took supra-precedence over commitment to improving the postal culture. In fact, these strategic plans contributed to making the postal culture harsher and more problematic.

Looking through the lens of a goal-driven perspective and the emphases of top-down controls of top postal management,[xxxiii] the darker side or shadow of the organization was revealed. It revealed a culture that can be characterized as supporting the end justifies the means, a lack of consideration for employee welfare, respect, or dignity, and an outcome driven bottom-line approach: do whatever is necessary to reach organizational goals.

In sum, this examination clearly revealed what top postal management paid attention to, which employees got rewarded or punished, how they reacted to key events, and who got promoted or received special privileges. Its core values and assumptions set the tone for the postal culture. The repercussions of this tone catapulted the paramilitary style of postal management at all levels of the organization, repercussions that include widespread anger, stress, and turmoil. In effect, top management's core values and assumptions created and sustained an unhealthy organization.

---

xxxiii   As previously detailed in Part 4 of this book.

So the question is: How can top postal management successfully change from an organization that focuses chiefly on the bottom line (as reflected in postal culture and its organizational practices and methods) to one that aligns and integrates the goals of a respectful workplace with the goals of achieving profitability, efficiency, and productivity?

The first step and a critical requirement is for Congress to enact legislation and the President to sign into law the abolishment of the Board of Governors. In Appendix D, I examine the statutory authority and impact of the BOG on the postal culture. Based on this examination, I am convinced that the postal culture has little or no chance of significant change unless this action is taken. Reasons for this conclusion are noted below.

The Board of Governors, in tandem with senior postal management, major mailers and advertisers, and neoconservatives, both within and outside the Bush administration, have tried but have been unsuccessful in scaling back union bargaining rights, expansion of contracting of postal positions to private enterprise, and in its attempts to virtually eliminate oversight and accountability by the United States Congress. The USPS strategic plans from 1998-2013, as approved by the BOG, have focused on top-down controls with scant attention to goals of fostering an organizational culture characterized by respectful relationships, fairness, and the validation of the dignity of its employees.

The next step and a requirement for creating and sustaining a healthy postal organization is a mandate for the Postmaster General to lead a team in the implementation of significant cultural and structural changes to the postal organization. Both of the requirements noted herein require congressional legislation and are discussed further in chapter eleven.

In order for the Postmaster General to successfully implement desired cultural and structural changes, it is also a requirement that the USPS enter a *long-term contract* with a team of organizational and occupational health psychologists to assist in design, development, implementation, and follow-up of these changes. These team members will need the requisite expertise in all of the cultural and structural components discussed herein.

Without the professional expertise in the critical areas for creating and sustaining a healthy organization, well-intentioned motives will fail. There is no easier path. Such an effort will take expertise, patience, collaboration, and an ongoing commitment for the postal organization to shift from an unhealthy one to a healthy one. It will take a fully engaged leadership.

Organizational Design and Job Redesign

Organizational Design

Organizational design has historically been a significant strategic challenge and continues to be even more so for the USPS. For this reason, it is a requirement that the USPS collaborate with major union organizations when developing far-reaching plans such as the Network Design initiative, which envisions reducing the current facility types from nine to five.

This does not mean that the USPS has to agree with their proposals or input, but it will provide an opportunity for transparency and collaboration, including better labor management cooperation. More importantly, it will improve the chances of successful development and implementation of the design initiative. For example, the 1993 RBCS agreement, an agreement between the APWU and USPS discussed in Appendix D, was highly beneficial to the Postal Service and its employees.

The RBCS agreement proved to be the highest degree of cooperation between the USPS and any postal union in its history. There were no less than ten joint union-management committees working out the details of the implementation process. These joint committees addressed all aspects of work standards and methods, including staffing, scheduling, ergonomics, training, productivity, employee performance, safety, data management, career opportunities, and minimizing administrative costs. Also, at the remote bar encoding centers, there were "crew chiefs" (i.e., higher level craft employees) that played an integral role in accomplishing its overall mission.

Even when the remote bar encoding centers were phased out, the APWU and the USPS worked diligently together to transition employees in new positions at other facilities. As an insider, it is important to point out that employee morale at the REC in my postal district was far higher than any other postal facility within the district. It also had high productivity and low absenteeism and industrial accident rates. In hindsight, the initiative was bold, innovative, and a breathtaking testament of what can be achieved when top management shares its control with key stakeholders.

Another important organizational design initiative that is considered a requirement is the development and implementation of an organizational effectiveness

<u>department</u>, including a departmental head who reports directly to the Postmaster General. This new organizational effectiveness department needs to include an office of workplace environment improvement (WEI), an office of training, an office of Employee Assistance Program, and an office of diversity under its umbrella. This new department is envisioned to work collaboratively with the above-mentioned contract team and other high-ranking postal officials in creating and sustaining a healthy postal organization.

Currently, the WEI group reports to an executive staff manager under the umbrella of the labor relations department. This is unacceptable because postal labor relations officials historically have been reactive rather than proactive in terms of workplace environment improvements. Because of WEI's distance from top postal leadership in the current organizational reporting structure, its capacity to proactively address systemic issues of workplace violence and toxic workplace environments is seriously compromised. One key example in support of this conclusion was highlighted in chapter eight in which one of my counterparts was directed to re-write her climate assessment findings from systemic in origin to individual in origin.

In late 2007, workplace environment analysts' reporting structure was changed. Instead of reporting to the district's manager of humans resources, they began reporting to an area office manager who was a direct report to the area office manager of human resources. This structural change has not and will not radically change how WEIs conduct their job duties or responsibilities, nor will there be a likelihood of improving the postal culture. As indicated previously, the seventy-five or more WEIs domiciled at the area offices and postal districts need to be direct reports to postal headquarters under the umbrella of the above-mentioned "Organizational Effectiveness Department." They need to be given broader authority to address workplace and cultural change issues in postal districts and area offices throughout the country.

Job Redesign

As discussed previously, chronic job strain or high stress levels were identified as having a significant relationship to high job demands, low job control, and low job support. It was underscored that all three of these factors were problematic in many of the workplaces throughout the USPS. When employees are repeatedly subjugated to organizational practices and methods that condone and facilitate unreasonable workload requirements, lack of resources to do the job effectively, continual monitoring and tracking of performance, and expectation to work long work hours, systemic bullying becomes commonplace within the organization.

It is critical, therefore, that job redesign be a requirement for cultural and structural change and a top priority for the above-cited team of organizational and occupational health psychologists. The priority for this team would be to assist the USPS in developing and implementing plans to reduce high workload requirements (especially for management personnel), increase employee decision-making authority, and increase support (i.e., validation of employee dignity, respect, and fairness) from employees' supervisors.

Reward and Performance Evaluation Systems

The reward and performance evaluation systems used by the USPS currently supports and fosters systemic bullying of its employees. When postal supervisors and managers are rewarded with bonuses, praise, and special privileges for achieving results by behaving unethically toward their employees (i.e., emotional abuse or bullying), the reward system is in need of dramatic change.

Likewise, when the performance evaluation system emphasizes a goal-driven perspective at the cost of employee morale and their physical and mental health, the performance evaluation system is in need of dramatic change. Accordingly, it is a requirement that the contracted team of occupational health and organizational psychologists collaborate with senior postal management to ensure that new reward and performance evaluation systems reflect what is necessary to transition from an unhealthy organization to a healthy one.

The Voice of the Employee (VOE) survey is utilized as a form of compensation in the current performance evaluation system. It is a recommendation that if a survey is used for compensation it needs to be modified and compensation needs to be significantly increased for established targets. First, however, it is a requirement that the postal unions and management organizations have input in a newly revised survey to ensure buy-in from all levels of the organizations. This buy-in will have the effect of creating employee confidence in the administering of the survey and use of the results to improve the workplace environment.

Selection and Development

In light of massive retirements of the "baby boomers" in the last ten years, the USPS has planned extensively for the recruitment and development of new postal managers. Its succession plan has provided a blueprint for successfully selecting and developing employees to carry out its mission. Sadly, these employees, especially at the higher levels of the organization, were selected essentially based upon their allegiance to the goal-driven, top-down control perspective reflective of the postal culture. Many of these selections have been employees with marginal or poor human relations skills, including a history of treating employees under their purview disrespectfully and unfairly.

Similarly, in the last ten years the development and training of postal management, especially those employees at the higher levels of the organization, have been extensive and intensive, but little emphasis has been placed on human relations, nor is fostering a healthy environment reinforced or rewarded in the workplace. Accordingly, it is a requirement that the contracted team of occupational health and organizational psychologists collaborate with senior postal management to ensure that new *selection* and *development* initiatives reflect what is necessary to transition from an unhealthy organization to a healthy one.

It is further viewed as a requirement that only employees who embrace the new postal culture be considered for promotion and those that do not live up to its ethical standards (e.g., treat employees with respect, dignity, and fairness) be removed from positions where they supervise or manage other employees. In addition to this requirement, it is recommended that organizational ethics be an ongoing component of the training and development of all postal managers, especially ethics that emphasize that respect for employees and their rights are as important as meeting corporate targets of productivity, customer service, budget, and revenue generation.

Change Management

How well a company manages significant organizational changes, both planned and unplanned, are of critical importance to employees' morale, health, and well-being. With pressures stemming from sweeping and fast-driven technological advances in methods of production coupled with privatizing agendas, the USPS has over the past twenty to thirty years seen several significant restructurings and downsizings.

As indicated previously, the USPS network plan creates new challenges regarding change management efforts. How effectively this ambitious network plan is developed and implemented will have a significant impact on the postal culture and the lives of its employees.

For these reasons, it is a requirement that the contracted team of occupational health and organizational psychologists collaborate with senior postal management to ensure any significant organizational change is developed and implemented with full consideration for employee morale, health, and general well-being.

Postal employees understand that their work methods and processes will continue to radically change overtime; they understand these change will continually impact them. What they don't accept, however, is the lack of timely, quality, and periodic communications on organizational changes. Nor should they accept the lack of sensitivity in implementing necessary changes. They don't understand why some methods and processes are implemented without their input or buy-in, especially when some of these methods and processes are ineffective and are not ready for implementation.

The USPS contends in its June 2008 Postal Accountability and Enhancement Network Plan[163] to Congress that it "approaches the task of workforce reductions with a high degree of sensitivity to employees." In my experience, generally this has not been the case. In some cases, for example, employees were excessed from their positions because of top-down pressures to reduce employee complement levels, even when it was not practicable or feasible to do so.

Because of the USPS's dismal history in managing organizational change, it is considered a requirement that change impact teams (CIT) be created at headquarters, area offices, postal districts, and all facilities designated as part of the USPS network. Team involvement by union and management organizations is highly recommended.

By maximizing participation of stakeholders on these teams there is a better opportunity for timely and quality communications, improved decision-making, and improved morale of the affected employees. It is again instructive to remind the reader of the successful change management efforts as a result of the RBCS agreement in 1993 between the USPS and the APWU. Nobody likes changes, especially changes that are disruptive to one's life, but it does make a significant difference when the changes are indeed necessary and are handled sensitively and collaboratively by postal management.

Employee Involvement

Employee involvement is an environment where employees at all levels of the organization have input and an impact on decisions and actions that affect their jobs. It is a value extolled by high-ranking postal officials as critically important to the success of the postal organization. But instead of supporting it in action, it has since 1996 continually constrained its influence with postal unions, management associations, and rank and file employees.

For example, in 1993, the USPS unilaterally eliminated the Employee Involvement Program with the NALC, a program that was implemented in 1982. The postal unions and management organizations, instead of being involved in critical developments and plans, were frequently kept in the dark, especially in the last several years as a result of the concerted efforts to privatize core postal functions.

For these reasons, it is a requirement that the contracted team of occupational health and organizational psychologists collaborate with senior postal management to ensure that broad and bold employee involvement initiatives are developed and implemented for the purpose of dramatically improving labor/management relations, including employee morale, health, and well-being.

It is also a requirement that the process of designing employee involvement initiatives include the participation of union and management organizations with the subject contract team and high-ranking postal officials. It is further recommended that consideration be given to create a headquarters team for this purpose. It is understood, however, that the charter and mission of this team would have to take in full account the APWU's historical stance on the issue of employee involvement.

One is reminded of the apparent success of "crew chief" positions created as a result of a 1993 memorandum of understanding between the two parties.[xxxiv] In short, flexibility in designing of employee involvement initiatives needs to take in account unique positions of the different union and management organizations.

Safety

Organizational safety, especially workplace violence, is integrally related to the postal culture. Based on this information and the examination of the postal culture in

---

xxxiv   As noted in Appendix D.

subsequent chapters and appendices, it became clear that, because of its ingrained paramilitary posture, the USPS is a violence-prone organization. It was shown that its stressful and toxic workplace environments were contributing factors to workplace homicide and suicides by current and former postal employees. Additionally, it was shown these environments negatively impacted the physical and mental health of employees.

For this reason, it is a requirement that the subject contract team of occupational health and organizational psychologists collaborate with senior postal management to ensure that special attention is given to current violence prevention efforts and initiatives, including improving upon them and creating new ones.

The USPS, in the 1990s, created a violence prevention program[xxxv] that in many respects served as a model for private and public organizations. Several key strategies of this program were, however, never fully implemented or satisfactorily utilized. For example, the Peaceful Parting initiative touted by the USPS to deal proactively with employees who are terminated never went beyond the pilot stages.

Even the Califano Report[164] emphasized the importance of this initiative to prevention of workplace incidences. International experts in the field of violence prevention have also emphasized the importance of having a plan to deal with employee termination as a means to prevent workplace tragedies.

Accordingly, it is a requirement that this initiative be instituted nationwide and continually monitored to ensure that appropriate management personnel are trained on how to use the methods and strategies of a Peaceful Parting initiative and routinely use them when an employee is terminated.

Another example of an excellent initiative to prevent workplace violence that has not been utilized to its potential is the identification and follow-up of hot spots in facilities throughout the USPS. As discussed in chapter eight, specific "hot spots" were identified by a headquarters staff, primarily from complaints to congressional members, complaints to the OIG, and petitions to headquarters and the national postal unions and management associations. Once identified as a hot spot, this information was forwarded to the appropriate area office and then to the appropriate postal district for action. In fact, the OIG conducted an audit[165] on August 28, 1998, on this initiative, but it is restricted information.

---

xxxv As noted in chapter five.

Again, the hot list initiative was another very good initiative, but it had no teeth or consequences for those who did not take appropriate action to address workplace issues for those facilities placed on the list. As discussed in chapter eight, its integrity and efficacy was comprised by the actions of postal executives. Accordingly, it is a requirement that the "hot list" initiative be fully implemented and monitored. There should be enforced consequences for not addressing serious workplace climate issues at all levels of the organization.

A third example of an excellent initiative, which was not fully implemented as intended, is the "Guidelines for Threats Assessment Teams." The OIG and representatives from postal headquarters periodically conducted audits on TAT compliance and found that some postal districts were not having meetings as required or were not following other required guidelines. This is unfortunate because experts in the field of violence prevention are in universal agreement that a fully functioning threat management team is a critical aspect of violence prevention. It is, therefore, a requirement that this initiative is fully implemented, monitored, and that consequences are enforced for not following the threat assessment team guidelines.

In March 2007, the USPS revised its TAT guidelines. A significant revision is that each postal district must quarterly report electronically their compliance with the TAT guidelines. This is helpful but there still needs to be consequences for those who are not following the guidelines.

Finally, it is a critical requirement that the USPS honor the 1992 "Joint Statement on Violence and Behavior"[xxxvi] agreement it signed, along with most of the major postal unions and management associations. It is a moral imperative that all postal employees, regardless of their rank, be held fully accountable for bullying and abusive behavior in the workplace, especially its occurrence by workplace bosses.

When workplace supervisors and managers continue to bully or emotionally abuse employees under their purview, despite training and other corrective actions, they need to be removed from positions of authority. Additionally, it is recommended that a "Respect, Dignity, and Fairness" policy be developed, implemented, and emphasized at all ethics training, strategic planning sessions, route adjustments activities, and postal operations audits.

---

xxxvi   As noted in Appendix D.

Summary and Concluding Comment

In the foregoing, I presented the process on how the USPS can create and maintain a healthy organization. I then provided a brief overview of the job characteristics model and its relationship to unhealthy and unsafe organizations. As a result of this examination, I defined the term *healthy organization* and made a moral argument for its development.

Finally, I delineated the means by which the USPS can shift from its current state as an unhealthy organization to a healthy and safe organization in the context of key components of organizational dynamics, including: 1) leadership, 2) organizational design and job redesign, 3) reward and performance evaluation systems, 4) selection and development, 5) change management 6) employee involvement, and 7) safety. In doing so, I provided requirements and recommendations to the USPS on achieving optimal functioning for each of these key components.

It will take diligence, patience, and a fully engaged leadership to create and sustain a healthy postal organization, but the fruits of this labor in terms of employee morale, health, well-being, and commitment to the organization are the just rewards for delivering on this moral obligation and ethical endeavor.

CHAPTER ELEVEN
Oversight and Accountability: Open Letter to Congress

January 31, 2009

Congress of the United States

SUBJECT: Oversight and Accountability of the USPS

This letter is written with a fervent hope that renewed congressional oversight and accountability of the postal culture and its violence prevention efforts will enable the Postal Service to shift from an unhealthy organization to a healthy one. The chain of events as provided below explains my motivation for writing this book.

I could not in good conscience turn a blind eye to high-ranking postal management's egregious display of arrogance and its lack of accountability for highly unethical organizational practices and behaviors and not bring it to the attention of the American public, the press, and, most importantly, to Congress. There has to be stringent oversight and accountability, otherwise the degrading, dehumanizing organizational practices and behaviors far too common in the Postal Service will continue unabated.

Since this open letter is rather lengthy, it is divided in four sections . In the first section, I discuss *my motivation* for writing this open letter and its inclusion in this book. I provide a brief overview of my book in the second section. In the third section, I present what I am convinced is required for the Postal Service to shift from an unhealthy organization to a healthy one. In the final section, I discuss some of the current, critical challenges impacting the Postal Service.

My Motivation for Writing this Letter and Book

On January 3, 2007, I retired from the USPS after nearly thirty-four years of service. Prior to my departure, my postal district became a highly toxic work environment for a very high percentage of employees in postal management. As a result of this development, under my role as the workplace improvement analyst for my postal district, I conducted a workplace climate assessment. In the climate assessment report,[166] the conditions leading to this toxic work environment and the horrific physical and psychological impact it had on at least fifty employees were thoroughly documented.

After completing this report in October 2006, it was sent to the area manager of human resources. Since there was not a timely response to the report, a copy of the report was sent to the Area Vice-President and a courtesy copy was sent to the Assistant Postmaster General. In the cover letter, it was requested that the report be brought to the attention of the Postmaster General on my behalf.

Because no response was received from these officials and the results from my meeting with the area manager of human resources were unsatisfactory, a cover letter and copies of my report were sent to the OIG director, human capital, and OIG auditor-in-charge, human capital team, with courtesy copies sent to a U.S senator, the President, NAPS, and the President of NAPUS. Sadly, to the best of my knowledge, there was no further inquiry or investigation conducted after I retired.

Now that I have addressed my initial motivation for writing this book, it is important to briefly explain how and why this book became more than just a commentary on how a specific category of employees were egregiously treated in one postal district. First, how they were treated was not unique to my district, nor was the category of employees unique to the USPS in general. In order to demonstrate this, I needed to set the foundation for this discussion by looking at the nature of violence in the workplace, both physical and psychological. Accordingly, in Part 1 of this book, I provide a comprehensive definition of workplace violence and examine its prevalence, sources, and impact in the United States in general and the USPS in particular.

Over two years have passed since the submission of my climate assessment report, and postal managers from my former postal district complain that their workplace environment remains highly stressful. Suffice to say, at this point, when top management or an organization condones or tolerates toxic work environments for its employees, it has no moral compass. Accordingly, there is a critical need for your oversight and legislative action to ensure accountability for how postal employees are treated in their workplace in postal facilities throughout the country.

Brief Summary of My Book

Parts 1-5

In Part 1, I examine the nature and prevalence of workplace violence in the United States and the U.S. Postal Service. Because it has been an important debate for experts in the area of workplace violence, and for Congress, in Part 2 I examine the notion of "going postal" to determine if there is any credence to the assignment of this controversial term to the USPS. In taking a closer look at the record, as presented in chapter four, it became very clear that the arguments by the USPS,[167] CDC,[168] Califano Report,[169] and invested consultants to frame the notion of "going postal" as a myth is not supported by the overwhelming evidence to the contrary.

Based on my review of the record, the conclusion by the Califano Report was that postal employees are no more likely to verbally abuse or physically assault their coworkers than employees in the national workforce is flawed and erroneous. Contrary to the Califano Report, the record instead supports the conclusion that the USPS work environments have been a trigger for some of its employee-directed homicides and that these incidents are far more frequent in the Postal Service when compared to other organizations. The overwhelming empirical evidence supports that this notion is both accurate and fair.

In Part 3 I review the USPS's violence prevention efforts to determine how well they were addressing this critical priority. To the USPS's credit, it developed an excellent violence prevention plan to deal with violence in the workplace, for both psychological aggression and physical workplace aggression. The main problem with the plan is that its six core strategies were not fully implemented or fully executed, especially the Peaceful Parting initiative. It is also particularly troubling that the Postal Service does not routinely enforce the "Joint Statement on Violence and Behavior" for its management personnel. These examples demonstrate a lack of commitment to follow through and are intricately linked to the USPS's emphasis on top-down controls and paramilitary approaches to solving organizational issues, which permeate and are reflective of the postal culture.

In Part 4 I assess the building blocks of postal culture and the *impact* of USPS strategic plans, congressional actions[170] and oversight, internal stakeholders, and postal law enforcement on the workplace environment and its employees. In chapter six, I briefly review the history of the USPS, including significant events and changes from the 1950s to 1992. Special attention is given to the 1970 Postal Reorganization Act[171] and the subsequent realignments, restructurings, and downsizings that transpired after its passage. In Part 4, I also discuss the impact of the postal culture on postal employees, their families, and the organization. In the following, I summarize observations, findings, and conclusions, from Appendices C-E and chapters seven to nine. I wrote these components of Part 4 in significant part with you being the intended audience.

Appendix C

In Appendix C, I provide observations and comments regarding the *USPS's seven strategic plans* (1998-2013) and I critically examine the *Presidential Commission Report of 2003*[172] and the *2006 Postal Accountability and Enhancement Act*[173] as they relate to the building blocks of the postal culture. In this examination, it became clear that the USPS had not planned or strategically focused on the creation of an empowered, participative work culture for its employees.

Further, I concluded that the main focuses of the USPS's strategic plans dealt with operations' efficiency, improved service, reduction of costs, revenue generation, and succession planning for postal management. In all these areas, the overarching focus was on top-down controls, with diminutive attention provided to create and maintain a healthy organization.

In review of the Presidential Postal Commission Report, I found its recommendations very telling. Their recommendations would have eliminated your oversight, provided massive increases in salaries for postal executives, and weakened postal unions' collective bargaining rights.

While the Bush commissioners focused on recommendations so that the USPS could become more efficient, productive, and flexible in carrying out its mission to provide universal service, they did so in order that the <u>chief beneficiaries would be the large mailers</u>. The clear losers, if their recommendations were implemented, would have been at the expense of postal employees' benefits and rights, along with the rights of residential customers. The report was simply nothing more than a blueprint for gradual USPS privatization.

Three years after the report was published, you enacted the 2006 Postal Accountability Act,[174] reluctantly signed into law by President Bush. Fortunately, you rejected virtually all the regressive measures recommended by Bush's commission. This rejection bode well for the postal and union management organizations and the employees they represent.

It is noted, however, that after the passage of the Act, the USPS Board of Governors, in collusion with high-profile business leaders in the mailing industry, continue their concerted efforts to privatize core operations of the USPS. The top-down control focus of the USPS, coupled with continual attempts to slowly and deliberately privatize its core operations, have had a very negative impact on a preexisting harsh postal culture. Postal employees are generally content with their wages and benefits, but their postal culture continues to deteriorate because employees' empowerment and participation is practically non-existent. Their trust in the intentions of top postal officials, from craft employees to senior plant and district managers, is very low. Both union and management organization leaders alike are becoming more and more allied to openly confront the USPS's arguably *uncaring* and reckless path.

Appendix D

In Appendix D, concerns of postal management are highlighted, concerns that parallel some of the findings of the workplace climate assessment previously discussed at the beginning of this letter. For example, it was noted that on March 7, 2007, the three management associations' presidents[175] (i.e., NAPUS, NAPS, and the League) wrote an historical letter to John Potter, Postmaster General, requesting a meeting to discuss their mutual concerns about the deteriorating work climate for their members in the field. In this letter, the three signatories stated:

> Postmasters, managers, and supervisors are under tremendous pressure, with more requirements, reports, and unrealistic expectations. We are concerned these conditions, if not reviewed at our level, could result in serious consequences [emphasis added].… [W]e believe that these are issues that should be a concern for both the USPS and the management associations.[176]

In response to this request, Charles Mapa, President of the League, reported on the League's website that the association presidents met with Mr. Potter, and he agreed that the numerous telecoms that postmasters and supervisors were forced to attend daily were of little value. He reported that Mr. Potter agreed to a ***task force***, including the three management association presidents and two high-ranking officials at postal headquarters. However, as noted in Appendix D, these concerns were still voiced in testimony at congressional meetings[177] on August 17, 2007, and on May 8, 2008. Sadly, I was recently informed that the subject task force was never implemented. These types of "broken promises" by the USPS regarding critical issues are far too commonplace.

In Appendix D, I also assess the role of the USPS Board of Governors, the four postal unions, and the three management associations in the context of how they have impacted the postal culture, especially in the last fifteen to twenty years. One of my central observations includes that the USPS has had a long history of using the scientific management approach, or *management unilateralism*, regarding its planning and implementation of work methods and standards. This deliberate and intentional approach discounts employee participation and input in workplace decision-making. It has generated volatile anger, high stress, low morale, and violations of employee dignity and self-esteem—not just of craft employees, but also management personnel in the field.

As further noted in Appendix D, the USPS's attempt, under the direction of the BOG, to outsource its core operations and its secret work in network realignment of facilities has exacerbated employee turmoil and anger. Together these organizational factors have accelerated the deterioration of the postal culture in the past ten years, especially the last two years. From postal employees' perspective, it would not be difficult to conclude that the USPS cares little about their input, job security, or well-being.

Postal unions and management associations have inadvertently added to the high tensions created by the approaches and decisions of the USPS. They have strongly lobbied Congress and have had numerous information pickets. They released dozens of articles critical of the USPS approach to contracting and flawed performance measurement systems. Many of these bulletins were posted on union bulletin boards at all major postal facilities and on their respective websites. As a result of its disagreements and "fighting back" with the USPS on these critical issues, it may have affected some members to take even a dimmer view of the organization and become more demoralized and angry.

The noted tensions, anger, and damaged self-esteem of postal employees do not bode well for the USPS's workplace environments or for the prevention of workplace violence. The top-down control approaches espoused and modeled by USPS top management cascades through all layers of field management, and its negative spillover effects can be seen frequently and daily on the workroom floor.

Appendix E

In Appendix E, I examine the role of both the United States Postal Inspection Service and the United States USPS Inspector General Office (OIG) in the context of how they have impacted the postal culture, especially since 2003. Postal law enforcement has had a long, reputable history of dealing effectively with issues of mail fraud, embezzlement of postal funds, and mail theft.

As a third appendage of postal management, however, they have not served postal employees well. They have not effectively or willingly investigated misconduct by high-ranking postal officials, and in its recent history, they have ostensibly aligned themselves with postal management's intent to privatize core postal operations. An exception to this history is the period from 1997 to 2003 when Karla Corcoran was the Inspector General.

In my examination of the recent history of the OIG (i.e., since 1993), the review of the record supports that the office has shown little respect for employee and union rights. It supports that they have shown little or no respect for the right to privacy on information maintained by medical providers, nor have they advised workers of their right to remain silent and have a union representative present to advise them during an investigation. In trampling on these rights, the OIG has violated the National Labor Relations Act,[178] the 2006 Postal Accountability and Enhancement Act,[179] and the National Collective Bargaining Agreements, as well as other statutory laws and rights afforded under the United States Constitution.

It became unequivocally clear that OIG's mission statement and its actual practices are aligned with the bottom line of the USPS. In practice, this means that OIG not only audits the methods and practices of the USPS as it relates to its core operations, but it also assists the Board of Governors and high-ranking postal officials in the oversight of these methods and practices. It further became clear in my review of the record that the OIG under the leadership of Mr. Williams has provided tacit approval and support for USPS privatization measures.

Some may ask the question: Why has the OIG become so aligned with the USPS's bottom line and the USPS's push to weaken the notion of universal service, thereby opening the door for major contracting out of core postal operations? The answer is, in great part, political.

All federal agencies and the USPS have experienced unprecedented pressure from the Bush administration to contract as many core functions as possible. Under the helm of the BOG, this translates in attempts to open the door for major mailers to become contractors for transportation, maintenance, mail processing, and delivery positions. The mailing apparatus in the United States is a $900 billion industry. If the universal service requirement can be relaxed by congressional legislation or by-passed, this means *huge profits* for many of these contractors involved in the mailing industry.

Chapter 7

In chapter seven, important hearings and inquiries regarding the postal culture, including reports by Kappel,[180] GAO,[181] congressional committees,[182] and the Califano commission,[183] were reviewed. As a result of this review, coupled with findings and observations from chapter six and Appendices C-E, the organizational culture of the USPS as it relates to its primary core values were discussed. The pertinent conclusions from this review as they relate to the postal culture are provided below.

The core values embedded in the USPS's organizational culture and its alignment to its organizational structure has engendered a paramilitary, authoritarian postal culture. It is a culture that promotes unilateral, top-down approaches to manage its employees and their workload. This bottom-line mentality is highly visible in postal facilities where autocratic management styles are too often reflected by use of fear, harassment, bullying, or intimidation to achieve service, financial, and productivity goals. These management styles are frequently rewarded by promotions, annual merit raises, or cash awards for achievement of corporate goals.

Consequences of the unilateral, top-down approaches employed by the USPS include widespread fear, anger, stress, and turmoil for both craft and management employees alike. Because of the concerted effort by the USPS's Board of Governors to contract out core postal operations, these fears, tensions, stress, and turmoil have escalated in the last several years. Also, since these management approaches are systemic in the USPS, many postal facilities have toxic work environments and they can be a catalyst or trigger for serious acts of workplace violence, including homi-cide and suicide.

Based on my review of a myriad of reports, studies, and investigations regarding the USPS culture, coupled with my experience as an insider, the USPS is clearly a highly paramilitary, authoritarian organization.

Chapter 8

In chapter eight, I noted my relevant experiences in the USPS from 1973 to 2007 as a career employee. In presenting critical concerns in my tenure with the USPS, I discussed those experiences that revealed the impact of unilateral, top-down man-agement styles, policies, and standards and methods and their relationship to the fostering of toxic workplace environments and workplace tragedies.

The reporting of these lived experiences served to validate the conclusion that, in agreement with the ample evidence examined and provided throughout many of the chapters of this book and its appendices, the postal culture fosters a manage-ment style at all levels of the organization that is oppressive, autocratic, and un-caring. Stated differently, these findings are in agreement with the documentary, quantitative, qualitative, and anecdotal evidence reviewed from congressional hear-ings and investigations, GAO reports, postal commission reports, and from the litera-ture in the workplace violence field.

Chapter 9

In chapter nine, I discussed the negative fallout of postal culture on employees, their families, and the organization, focusing primarily on the negative impact of the postal culture on employees' physical and psychological health. I highlighted this impact from my personal experience as an EAP representative and a WIA for the USPS from 1986 to 2007.

In Part 5, I provided a blueprint for the USPS to become a safe and healthy organiza-tion. In the following, I summarize requirements and recommendations to the USPS from chapter ten. Like Part 4, I wrote chapter ten in significant part with you being the intended audience.

Chapter 10

In chapter ten, requirements and recommendations were provided to enable the USPS to shift from an unhealthy organization to a healthy one. In order to enable this shift, these requirements and recommendations were linked to: 1) leadership, 2) organizational design and job redesign, 3) reward and performance evaluation systems, 4) selection and development, 5) change management 6) employee involvement, and 7) safety. As a means to support the Postal Service's shift from an unhealthy organization to a healthy organization, a key requirement was that the USPS enter a long-term contract with a team of organizational and occupational health psychologists to assist in the design, development, and implementation in the above-noted areas for change and improvement.

Requirements and Recommendations

I close this book with an open letter to you. It is highly unlikely that any meaningful or substantive change in the postal culture will occur unless you provide renewed oversight and accountability. Without renewed oversight and accountability, the USPS will continue to be a violent-prone organization with a culture that engenders toxic workplace environments. The blueprint provided for the Postal Service to shift from an unhealthy organization to a healthy one, as noted in chapter ten, will not be acted upon if simply left to the USPS.

Accordingly, in the following, requirements and recommendations are made on how you can ensure that the necessary changes are implemented. If acted upon, I believe these requirements and recommendations will provide the framework and direction for ensuring the necessary changes and improvements to the organizational culture of the USPS and its organizational structure.

The first legislative requirement that is necessary is the abolishment of the BOG. This would require that either the 1970 Postal Reorganization Act be amended or that the PAEA be amended. The BOG, under heavy-handed influence of the executive branch and business leaders from the mailing industry, has historically attempted and continually strives to contract-out core postal operations.

Because the BOG are appointed for long-term appointments and are essentially part-time administrators who meet infrequently, they are *tone deaf* to the issue of the postal culture and how it contributes to workplace violence and toxic workplace environments. The focus and agenda of the BOG has been almost exclusively on business and customer objectives. This limited and unbalanced focus has contributed immensely to the acceleration of the USPS becoming an unsafe and unhealthy organization. Accordingly, in order for the USPS to have any real chance of changing its postal culture, the BOG has to be abolished.

In place of the BOG, it is a corollary requirement that the Postmaster General be held responsible and accountable to improve the postal culture. As for future selections and the removal of the Postmaster General for cause, it is recommended that the General Accounting Office's (GAO) comptroller general of the United States be vested with this authority. The GAO is, as you are aware, very familiar with the postal culture and its challenges. If you consider vesting another agency with this authority, it is recommended that you rule out the Postal Regulatory Commission (PRC).

As noted in Appendix D, through the influence of the executive branch and the mailing industry, the PRC has arguably become politicized and partisan regarding the business interests of the large mailers. As a result of the current make-up of the PRC members and in view of their long-term appointments, this stance is unlikely to change in the foreseeable future.

The second legislative requirement is that you amend the 2006 Postal Accountability Enhancement Act by placing restrictions on the PRC's oversight and accountability responsibilities regarding the USPS. The amendment will need to include specific language that prevents the PRC from colluding with the postal mailers to privatize the USPS, including quarterly audits of the PRC by the GAO to ensure compliance.

The third legislative requirement is that you further amend the 1996 legislation known as the Inspector General Office Act of 1978, as amended.[184] This legislation, as you are aware, authorized for some of the auditing and investigative functions to be transferred from the USPIS to a newly created OIG within the USPS, and for the Inspector General to be appointed by and under the general supervision of the BOG.

Specifically, it is recommended that you amend this legislation to stipulate that the Inspector General will report to the comptroller general of the United States. This recommendation is consistent with my earlier recommendation that the comptroller select future postmaster generals.

The fourth legislative requirement is that you amend the 2006 Postal Accountability Enhancement Act by requiring a long-term contract team of professionals to assist the USPS in creating and sustaining a safe and healthy organization. Global recommendations in the amendment include the following: 1) the contract team to be hired and financed through monies authorized and provided to the GAO, 2) a long-term contract for five years with provisions for extensions, and 3) progress reports provided by the contract team quarterly to the comptroller of the United States, Congress, USPS, and all the union and management organizations.

The fifth legislative requirement is to enact national legislation for the prevention of bullying in the workplace. Dr. Gary Namie and his wife, Dr. Ruth Namie, founders of the Bullying Institute,[185] along with their colleague Dr. David Yamada,[186] have for years pushed for such legislation at the state and federal level. In order for national legislation for the prevention of workplace bullying to have the intended impact, it would require sanctions to employers or their representatives who are in violation of a new workplace statute that defines workplace bullying as a harmful and illegal activity.

Specifically, sanctions would need to include monetary fines and legal recourse, similar to the EEO process for the targets of bullying. Additionally, it is recommended that the legislation empower the U.S. Department of Occupational Safety and Health Administration (OSHA) with oversight and shared enforcement authority for this new statute with the National Institute for Occupational Safety (NIOSH).

In crafting the fifth legislative requirement, it is critical that language in the legislation include a provision to designate additional monies to NIOSH to research the impact of stress in the workplace in general and the effects of bullying within the government agencies (including the USPS) and private organizations. In March 2008, NIOSH, in collaboration with the American Psychological Association and Society for Occupational Health Psychology, sponsored the Seventh International Conference on Occupational Health & Stress. A significant part of the conference focused on workplace bullying and its prevention. It is further recommended that language in the legislation include a provision to empower and provide monies to NIOSH to conduct specific studies comparing workplace homicides and suicides in other federal agencies with the USPS.

The fifth legislative requirement will need specific language to address sanctions for the violations of the Federal Labor Standards Act (FLSA). As noted in Appendix D, this has been a special and ongoing concern for postal management associations and the employees they represent. In previous testimony to congressional committees, management association presidents have testified about this widespread problem for several decades.

However, the USPS continues to use organizational bullying tactics as a means to compel many field management employees to work numerous hours, way beyond the traditional forty-hour work week, and without additional compensation. In the climate assessment report regarding my former district, this organizational bullying practice was noted as a chief cause of widespread and harmful psychological and physical symptoms. It is critical that Congress address and ensure that this injurious and unsafe practice is no longer the norm within the USPS for its field management employees.

The sixth legislative requirement is to enact legislation that prevents the USPS from significant contracting out of its core Postal Services. Two bills that currently support this legislative requirement are the Mail Delivery Protection Act[187] and the Mail Network Protection Act.[188] Until these bills or similar bills are passed, Congress will be caught in the middle of the maneuvers by profiteers in the mailing industry to privatize more and more core postal operations and the union and management organizations battling to prevent it from happening.

One additional and critical requirement for dramatic improvement of the harsh, paramilitary postal culture is for Congress to ensure that, by virtue of its oversight and accountability responsibilities, the specific requirements noted in chapter 10 are fully implemented by the USPS, including that the USPS create a new "Department of Organizational Effectiveness."

If the USPS is able to make these changes, in the context of the seven structural and cultural factors delineated in chapter 10, it can successfully shift from an unsafe and unhealthy organization to a safe and healthy one. This will not happen, however, unless you maintain stringent oversight and hold the USPS fully accountable for this transition.

A Clarion Call for Post-PAEA Reform

During the last several years, there have been several unprecedented actions and events impacting the future of the USPS. For example:

1. The last two to three years in the USPS have been marked by employees' pickets regarding outsourcing of postal operations and employee treatment, the egregious tactics used by the OIG, and three separate incidences of homicide committed by current and former employees in 2006.

2. In light of a 7.6 billion dollar deficit from fiscal year 2007 to fiscal year 2008, the USPS is considering the lay-off of employees for the first time in its history and wage concessions from its management associations.

3. In 2006, the PAEA was signed into law, several post-PAEA congressional hearings[189] were held, and bills were sponsored to prevent the USPS from contracting out postal operations.

4. The PRC recently selected a contractor[190] to conduct a study on the universal service obligation, despite writings from two key members of the contractor who have expressed anti-union sentiments and the favoring of contracting of core postal operations.

5. In June 2008, the USPS submitted to you its "Network Plan."[191] On this same date, the USPS also submitted a seventy-page draft statement of work for contractors,[192] regarding proposals on contracting services involving distribution, infrastructure, and transportation for bulk mailing centers. Subsequent to these submissions, the USPS had requested authorization for early retirements for up to forty thousand career employees, which was approved by the OPM. Additionally, the USPS is reviewing the options of layoffs, four-day work weeks (ten hours a day), and two tours of duty instead of three at mail processing plants.

6. On July 24, 2008, the Congressional Subcommittee on Federal Workforce held a meeting to discuss the USPS's network plan and its potential impact on its stakeholders. As expected, the major representatives for the mailing industry and the Postal Service enthusiastically supported the plan, while the union organizations were adamantly against it.

7. In GAO testimony[193] at the July 24, 2008 subject meeting and in its previous study[194] submitted to Congress in July 2008, it was noted that the USPS had not been transparent in dealing with stakeholders, that the USPS did not have a system in place to determine savings from the plan, and that it did not provide an accounting for all of its contracting services.

Indeed, the stakes are high; addressing and dealing with issues regarding the paramilitary, authoritarian postal culture and the systematic attempts of large scale privatization of postal core services will be an arduous task. Your full attention and commitment to addressing and dealing with these issues are absolutely necessary. Safeguarding the integrity, safety, health, and rights of postal employees and their union and management organizations over the interests of profiteers in the mailing industry is the only honorable path to take. The requirements and recommendations noted herein, I believe, provide a blueprint to achieve these objectives.

The record shows that you have traveled this honorable path. Now is the time for you to meet these partisan and profiteering interests head-on, and to say enough is enough, by expeditiously enacting the required legislative changes and forwarding them to the President of the United States. Postal employees and their family members are counting on it.

Best regards,

Stephen D. Musacco, Ph.D.

APPENDIX A

Psychological and Physical Aggression in the Workplace: Its Prevalence, Source, and Impact

Psychological Aggression in the Workplace: Its Prevalence, Sources, and Impact

The Northwestern Study

The Northwestern Study[195] was conducted because of concern about the overall safety and health of employees in the workplace. It was claimed to be the first study conducted in the United States to assess the scope of fear and workplace violence and its effects in the workplace. A chief conclusion was that violence and harassment in U.S. workplaces were pervasive. Significant limitations of the study were its sample size (six hundred) and low response rate (29 percent).

Two key findings of the subject study, when extrapolating the number of employees in the sample (from the period of July 1992 to July 1993) to the national workforce, indicated that sixteen million employees were harassed and six million were threatened. This projection was based on the fact that 19 percent of the respondents stated they experienced harassment in the previous twelve months and 7 percent reported they experienced a threat of physical harm. Combined percentages indicated that in the previous twelve months of the study, **26 percent** of the participants reported experiencing abusive workplace behavior.

Other key findings of the subject study were: a) violence and harassment dramatically affected the health and productivity of victims and other workers, b) a strong relationship exists between job stress and workplace harassment, c) the majority of employees did not report their harassment (58 percent), d) non-victims were also affected as a result of witnessing the acts of harassment, e) most workplace threats were from coworkers rather than the boss (32 percent compared to 5 percent), and f) most workplace harassment was from coworkers rather than the boss (47 percent compared to 39 percent)

As indicated previously, one of the chief findings in the subject study was that there was a strong relationship between job stress and workplace harassment. Participants identified as experiencing stress as a result of the harassment reported two times the rate of stress-related conditions (e.g., depression, anger, insomnia, headaches, and ulcers) compared to those who reported no harassment. They were reported to be twenty times more likely to have reduced productivity and ten times more likely to leave their jobs, compared to those who did not report experiencing workplace harassment.

United States Hostile Workplace Study 2000

The U.S. Hostile Workplace Study[196] was a web-based survey where 1,335 respondents self-identified as directly experiencing harassment or bullying in the workplace. At the time, this was claimed to be the largest group of self-identified targets of bullying in the world. The study's chief purpose was to look at the impact of workplace bullying from the viewpoint of the health and careers of employees who were bullied.

The definition of bullying provided by the Workplace Bullying Institute is as follows: "Repeated illegitimate mistreatment of a targeted employee by one or more persons characterized by acts of commission and omission which impair the target's psychological and physical health and economic security."[197]

The Hostile Workplace Study has several limitations, one of which was the study was not random. Since the study was web-based, there was no foolproof way to prevent someone from taking the survey more than once. In reporting the findings, Gary Namie, founder and research director, indicated that targets of bullying were exposed to bullying behaviors on the average of 16.5 months with 42 percent of the targets reporting the bullying behaviors lasting eighteen months or longer.

Key findings of the Hostile Workplace Study include categories of bullying behaviors experienced by targets in the workplace. For example, targets experiencing screaming/yelling comprised 14 percent of the bullying behaviors, while 30 percent experienced controls of resources (time, budget, support, and training). Targets experiencing constant personal verbal assaults on character comprised 30 percent of the total bullying behaviors, while 36 percent reported that the bully had attempted to manipulate the impression others had of them.

Other key findings of the subject study was that 46 percent of the targets reported being humiliated by their bullies publicly, while 34 percent of the hostile behaviors were reported as completely private, and the remaining 20 percent reported that it was behind closed doors but was meant to be overheard. Gary Namie pointed out that bullying is no secret in the workplace. He reported that 96 percent of the workforce was aware of the occurrence of bullying, either by being a witness to it or by hearing about it directly from the target.

The subject study also looked at why people were targeted in the workplace. Based on a checklist used in the study, the top reasons self-identified targets reported for bullying behaviors were: a) they resisted control of the bully (58 percent), b) the bully envied their competence in the work to be done (56 percent), c) bully envied their social skills, their being liked (49 percent), d) ethical behavior, whistleblower (46 percent), and e) cruel personality of the bully (42 percent). The total percentage does not equal 100 percent because the target could report more than one reason for the hostile behaviors of the bully. Importantly, the survey for the subject study was designed to compare the frequency of bullying compared to illegal discrimination. The findings showed that 77 percent of cases involving bullying did not qualify under the law as illegal discrimination. Consequently, bullying of employees was considered to be two to three times more prevalent than illegal discriminatory behaviors such as sexual harassment, race harassment, and gender harassment combined.

The subject study focused in great detail on the effects of bullying on the targeted individuals. For example, the study focused on health impairments, which were identified in the survey by employing a thirty-five-item health impairment checklist. The top three health impairments reported were severe anxiety (94 percent), sleep disruption (84 percent), and loss of concentration (82 percent). Other significant findings reported by the targets were stress headaches (64 percent), racing heart rate (48 percent), diagnosed depression (41 percent), significant weight loss or gain (40 percent), panic attacks (33 percent), migraines (23 percent), and chest pains (21 percent).

The health impairment checklist in the study looked at the notion of work trauma or three factors related to post-traumatic stress disorder. Specifically, the three items on the checklist for the identification of work trauma were: 1) hyper-vigilance (easily startled, on guard, feeling edgy, paranoia), 2) thought intrusions (nightmares, flashbacks, recurrent memories) and 3) avoidance-dissociation (numbing of thoughts, feelings, need to avoid traumatizing location). Remarkably, of the 1,335 participants who self-identified as having been bullied, 31 percent of the women and 21 percent of the men reported having experienced all three factors.

The American Workplace Survey – 2006

The American Workplace Survey was conducted in 2006 and was reported in a journal article titled "Burned by Bullying in the American Workplace: Prevalence, Perception, Degree and Impact."[198] The survey was conducted via the Internet and the total number of participants was 469. Similar to the Hostile Workplace Study, a chief limitation of this study was that it was conducted online, and, like the Northwestern Study, the sample size was relatively small.

A significant strength of the study was that, in order to keep potential participants from inferring, the study was focused on bullying. The questionnaire not only included items from a well-established "bullying" measure, but it also included an equal amount of items that were not related to bullying behaviors. In addition to the forty-four survey items provided in the survey, using an accepted definition of bullying in the research field, the participants were asked if they had ever been bullied in the workplace by responding yes or no. Based on these data, the researchers were able to determine if there was a difference between self-identified targets of bullying and the findings from the measure (i.e., forty-four survey items) used for bullying in the questionnaire. If participants answered yes to being bullied in the workplace, they were requested to provide the duration of the bullying.

A key finding of the study was that subjects, on the average, experienced the negative behaviors associated with bullying for a duration of 18.6 months. This finding was similar to the finding of the Hostile Workplace Study, which showed the average duration of 16.5 months. These are significant findings because the longer employees are experiencing the effects of the abusive behaviors or bullying, the greater harm that can occur in terms of their health, job, family, and community. The longer the abuse lasted over time the greater the opportunity for the occurrence of harmful effects.

Another key finding of the subject study was that 28 percent of the employees surveyed were found to be bullied for a period of six months or longer where they were a target of at least two negative acts weekly or more often. Of these 28 percent, only 9.4 percent self-identified as being bullied. Such a large difference found between judging oneself as being bullied compared to what was measured by the survey on bullying is remarkable. This under-reporting of self-identified bullying may be related to concerns of self-stigmatization or being viewed as weak by others.

The subject study reported a link between the degree of bullying, stress, and job satisfaction: The more frequent the bullying was experienced, the greater the reporting of stress and lower the job satisfaction. Those who were not bullied but witnessed bullying reported higher workplace negativity, especially when the degree of bullying was more intense.

U.S. Workplace Bullying Survey September 2007

This survey[199] was conducted by Zogby International and the analysis, findings, and report presentation was provided by Gary Namie, research director of the Workplace Bullying Institute. The survey used a representative sample of the United States worker and was conducted via online interviews with 7,740 adult employees. It was the largest survey to date regarding workplace bullying and had a very low estimated margin of error ranging from +1 to -1.

Gary Namie accurately indicates in his report that workplace bullying in the United States is epidemic. Two key findings reported from the study in support of this observation was that 37 percent of the participants reported they were bullied at some point in their employment career while another 12 percent reported to have been a witness to bullying in the workplace. Based on these findings and projecting how many of the 146 million workers were impacted by bullying, the study estimated that 54 million workers had been bullied and another 17.5 million had witnessed this occurrence. It was therefore estimated that 71.5 million workers had been negatively impacted by bullying at some point in their career.

The subject study did not present a finding regarding how many employees in the last twelve months had experienced bullying in the workplace. However, using the most conservative figure of a 13 percent rate, coupled with taking in account that 37 percent of the population had at some point in their career experienced bullying, it was estimated that nineteen million workers were at risk each year. Consistent with the findings from the U.S. Hostile Workplace Study, the present study found that bullying was four times more prevalent than other forms of harassment combined; that is, sexual, gender, race, ethnicity, religion, disability, or age harassment combined.

The subject study also found that 62 percent of those who reported the bullying to their employer indicated that the problem either became worse or the employer did nothing. Based on these findings, the report concluded that an estimated 21 to 28 million employees left their jobs. Taking in account the report finding that 73 percent of the bullied targets reported having had endured bullying for more than six months, with 44 percent for more than one year, resigning from the job is understandable.

Consistent with the Northwestern Study and the Hostile Workplace Study in 2000, the subject study concluded that bullying was an urgent public health hazard. For example, findings revealed that 45 percent of bullied targets reported stress levels that affected their health (i.e., psychological or physical complications) and 33 percent of them suffered from these complications for more than one year. Other key findings reported were as follows: 1) 54 percent of those bullied reported that the mistreatment occurred in front of others, 2) 32 percent behind closed doors, in silence, and 3) 10 percent behind doors kept open so others could hear. The study showed that 72 percent of bullies were bosses and the bully's boss had the support of one or more higher level manager for the harassment.

Unlike the Hostile Workplace Survey, the participants in the subject study included five broad categories of mistreatment to choose from regarding the bullying behavior they experienced. These categories of mistreatment and the associated percentage of occurrence were reported as follows: 1) verbal abuse (53 percent) including shouting, swearing, name calling, malicious sarcasm, threats to safety, etc. 2) behavior/actions (52.5 percent)—public or private that were threatening, intimidating, hostile, offensive, inappropriately cruel conduct, etc. 3) abuse of authority (46.9 percent) including undeserved evaluations, denial of advancement, stealing credit, tarnished reputation, arbitrary instructions, unsafe assignments, etc. 4) interference with work performance (45.4 percent) including sabotage, undermining, ensuring failure, etc., and 5) destruction of workplace relationships (30.2 percent) among coworkers, bosses, or customers.

Physical Aggression in the Workplace: Its Prevalence, Sources, and Impact

Non-Fatal Acts of Physical Aggression in the Workplace

The Northwestern Study

As mentioned previously, the 1993 Northwestern Study[200] stated rationale for this study was concern about the overall safety and health of employees in the workplace and that the study had a small sample size and low response rate.

The notion of non-fatal acts of physical aggression in the study was framed as physical attack. The definition provided for "physical attack" was as follows: "Aggression resulting in a physical assault with or without the use of a weapon." The primary finding was that **3 percent** of the participants reported being physically attacked in the previous twelve months. Based on this frequency of 3 percent, it was projected that approximately **2.2 million employees** in the workforce were physically attacked in the workplace over the same twelve-month period.

The study also reported that 15 percent of the participants reported physical attack during their lifetime of employment. In terms of the perpetrator or the source of the physical attack, 44 percent reported customer or client, 24 percent stranger, 20 percent coworker other than boss, 7 percent boss, 3 percent former employees, and 3 percent someone else.

Although the subject study does not address the impact or negative effects of physical attacks perpetrated on targets, it is universally recognized by professionals in the field of workplace violence that physical assault has negative physical and psychological consequences for targets of physical aggression. This observation is more relevant considering the finding that 18 percent of the non-fatal acts of physical violence involved a lethal weapon.

National Survey of Workplace Health and Safety

The National Survey of Workplace Healthy and Safety[201] was conducted from 2002 to 2003 and was based on a nationally representative sample of 2,829 workers. The initial sample for this ambitious study was based on 34,000 telephone numbers, which later were reduced using sophisticated statistical procedures in order to safeguard the reliability and validity of the results. Of those participants selected for interviews, 57 percent actually participated in the study. Interviews of the participants lasted approximately forty-five minutes and the interviews were conducted by highly trained interviewers. Unlike in the Northwestern Study, the participants in this study were "weighted" according to standard procedures in order to make reasonable projections about the total workforce.

The overall prevalence of physical violence reported at work for the previous twelve months in the subject study was **6 percent**. Projecting the number of employees affected in this study (i.e., 6 percent), in the context of the number of employees in the national workforce, as estimated by the Bureau of Census for the same year, the total number of employees potentially impacted by physical violence was **approximately seven million.**

In the study, there were four basic questions to make a determination of physical violence. These questions and reported frequency rates for each over a twelve-month period were: a) pushed you, grabbed you, or slapped you in anger (3.9 percent), b) kicked you, bit you, or hit you with a fist 3.0 percent, c) hit you with an object, tried to hit you with an object, or threw an object at you in anger (4.2 percent), and d) attacked you with a knife, gun, or another weapon (0.7 percent). In this study findings regarding the perpetrators or sources of physical violence were compatible with findings in Northwestern Study. Like the Northwestern Study, this study did not examine the impact of physical violence on the physical and psychological well-being of the targets.

Physical Aggression in the Workplace: The Specter of Workplace Homicide

An excellent framework to classify sources or types of perpetrators of workplace violence in general and workplace homicide in particular was presented in a study conducted by the U.S. Department of Labor's Bureau of Labor Statistics (BLS) in 2006.[202] The four types classified by the BLS were:

1. **Criminal** explains when the perpetrator has no legitimate relationship to the business or its employees and is usually committing a crime in conjunction with the violence (e.g., robbery, shoplifting, or trespassing).

2. **Customer or Client** describes when the perpetrator has a legitimate relationship with the business and becomes violent while being served by the

business (e.g., customers, clients, patients, students, inmates, or any other group to which the business provides services).

3. **Coworker** describes the situation where the perpetrator is an employee, past employee of the business, or contractor who works as a temporary employee of the business and who attacks or threatens another employee.

4. **Domestic Violence** explains when the perpetrator, who has no legitimate relationship to the business but has a personal relationship with the intended victim, threatens or assaults the intended victim at the workplace (e.g., family member, boyfriend, or girlfriend).

Although the BLS classification of four types provides a useful framework for both non-fatal injuries and fatalities in its application, the primary focus in this section is workplace homicides. It is useful, however, to view the prevalence rate of workplace homicides in the context of all workplace fatalities.

Accordingly, the discussion below first focuses on the most frequent occurring work-related fatal events and then is limited to workplace homicide in general and workplace homicide committed by current or former employees (i.e., employee-directed) in particular.

In 1993, the National Traumatic Occupational Fatalities (NTOF) Surveillance System report[203] showed that from 1980 to 1989 workplace homicide was the third leading cause of death in the workplace. During the span of these ten years, 7,600 or 12 percent of all fatalities in the workplace were deemed a result of occupational homicides. The study did not show, however, what percentage of the occupational homicides was related to the BLS category of coworker, or what I termed *employee-directed homicide* in chapter two.

According to the Census of Fatal Occupational Injuries (CFOI) and data collected by the Bureau of Labor Statistics,[204] workplace homicides for the previous two years had become the fourth leading cause of death in the workplace, behind fatalities caused on the highways, falls, and struck by objects. It reported that workplace homicide had an annual decline since 2003, declining 9 percent from 2005 to 2006 or from 567 to 516.

The majority of workplace homicides in the workplace are related to robbery. According to BLS and CFO statistics over the past two decades, robberies, on an annual basis, account for around two-thirds to three-quarters of all workplace homicides.

Estimates for the annual average of workplace homicide where a coworker or former employee is the identified perpetrator are estimated to be in the range of 6 percent to 15 percent.

Although the Bureau of Labor Statistics has taken careful attention in mapping out broad categories for fatalities in the workplace (e.g., highway events, falls, struck by objects, workplace homicides), it has not identified percentages or the number of employee-directed (i.e., current or former employee) homicides on an annual basis. This explains why researchers in the field of workplace violence have reported an annual range of 6 percent to 15 percent for employee-directed homicide.

All deaths in the workplace are potentially traumatic to the physical and psychological health of their employees, including costs to the organization in terms of loss productivity, retention, absenteeism, and loss or reputation. This observation is more relevant when workplace homicide involves a current employee or former employee. The United States Postal Service knows first-hand the impact of these events. Their negative impacts underscore the need to design a healthy organization to prevent these violent tragedies.

APPENDIX B
Profile of Workplace Tragedies in the U.S. Postal Service

In presenting the history of workplace tragedies from 1983 to 2006, my sources[205] include materials from the USPS violence prevention program, textbooks and research articles, congressional reports, and Internet sites related to workplace violence.

From 1983 to 2006, there were seventeen workplace tragedies in the USPS. These workplace tragedies focused on employee-directed homicides by current and former employees. I define employee-directed homicide as *an act of murder of others or self by a current employee or former employee that has a clear nexus to the workplace and is perpetrated against another employee(s) or self in response to political, social, economic, organizational, individual, media, or the availability of guns factors.*

From 1985 to 1998, there were nine other incidences of postal workplace tragedies in the USPS. Some of these tragedies received notoriety and press while others did not. Unlike the previously mentioned seventeen workplace tragedies, there were no noteworthy links to organizational factors. There is, however, one suicide discussed that strongly appeared to involve organizational factors, but its occurrence was off postal premises.

In discussing these twenty-six postal tragedies, a brief narrative of each event is provided. The account is graphic and disturbing, especially for the seventeen workplace tragedies listed from 1983 to 2006.

Workplace Tragedies within the U.S. Postal Service from 1983 to 2006

Perry Smith – 1983

Perry Smith, *former employee*, entered into the Johnston, South Carolina, post office with a **12-gauge shotgun** and <u>killed the local postmaster and shot and injured two former coworkers</u>. Upon seeing Smith, the postmaster initially fled the post office and hid in a storage room at a convenience store across the street. Perry Smith followed him, kicked the storage room door open, and reportedly shot the postmaster twice, once in the stomach and once in the chest.

Brief Narrative

Perry Smith reportedly resigned three months prior to this workplace tragedy. He reportedly had twenty-five years of service as a postal worker. Prior to his resignation, it was reported that he was depressed as a result of his son committing suicide and this affected his work performance. It was further reported that his boss began reprimanding him for performance issues, such as exceeding his lunch break or delivering mail to the wrong addresses. He reportedly killed the postmaster on his last day of work and stated, "I told you I would get even with you, you son-of-a-bitch." Perry Smith was found incompetent to stand trial. A court-appointed attorney reportedly claimed Mr. Smith thought he was "Moses" and was on a mission.

James Howard Brooks – 1983

James Brooks, *current employee* (age fifty-three) entered into the Johnston, Alabama, post office with a **.38 caliber handgun** and <u>killed the local postmaster and shot and injured his immediate supervisor</u>. Subsequent to killing the postmaster by gunshots to the head, James Brooks ran up the stairs of the building after his immediate supervisor and shot him twice, once in the stomach and once in the arm.

Brief Narrative

Prior to this workplace tragedy, James Brooks reportedly was frustrated and angry because of issues related to forced overtime and under-compensation; that is, not getting paid for work while on duty. It was reported that he took these issues to his local union and the National Labor Relations Board but was not successful in obtaining a remedy in his favor.

Steven W. Brownlee – 1985

Steven Brownlee, *current employee* with twelve years of service, opened fire on the night shift in the Atlanta, Georgia, main post office with a **.22 caliber pistol** and killed a supervisor and a coworker, including wounding a third coworker in a mail sorting area.

Brief Narrative

Prior to this workplace tragedy, Steven Brownlee reportedly had been forced to work seventy- to eighty-hour workweeks to keep up with the supervisor's demands and heavy workloads, suggesting that organizational factors may have been involved. Steven Brownlee reportedly heard voices periodically.

Patrick Henry Sherrill – 1986

Patrick Sherrill, *current employee*, eighteen years of service, employed at the Edmond, Oklahoma, post office, armed with **two .45 Colt government-issue semi-automatics, a .22 caliber pistol, and ammunition** in his mailbag, drove to work as usual at 6:45 am. Upon entering the building, he began his systematic rampage by fatally shooting his supervisor and thirteen of his coworkers, including wounding fourteen coworkers and firing nearly fifty bullets in less than ten minutes. Most employees, like Patrick Sherrill's supervisor, were shot at close range in the chest. Later, he reportedly was seen sobbing and then fired one fatal bullet to his head, dying less than two feet from his supervisor. The Oklahoma shooting was the deadliest act of employee-directed homicide in U.S. history.

Brief Narrative

Patrick Sherrill reportedly demonstrated violent tendencies while in the Marine Corps and at his previous employment. While in the military, he reportedly pointed a loaded gun at his superior. Prior to the shooting, local postal management reportedly was highly focused on his performance. He told friends and coworkers that he was unhappy with the treatment by his supervisors. Some employees stated he was a problem employee, including that he had a poor work performance and was a complainer. However, some union officials claimed the shooting was the result of a tyrannical management style, reflective throughout the USPS.

Warren Murphy – 1988

Warren Murphy, *current employee*, entered into the New Orleans, Louisiana, postal facility with a **12-gauge shotgun** hidden under his pants and under his work apron. Later during his work shift, after an incident with a supervisor, he reportedly went to the men's room and came out brandishing the shotgun. He then fatally shot his supervisor in the face. The fired shot reportedly wounded two other postal employees. After the shooting, he held his ex-girlfriend hostage. Later two FBI SWAT agents reportedly were wounded upon finding Warren Murphy in a supervisor's office. He eventually surrendered to the agents.

Brief Narrative

Most accounts of the shooting rampage committed by Warren Murphy indicated there were no fatalities. However, the USPS in one of their reports indicated that a postal supervisor died as a result of this workplace tragedy. The report indicated that three employees were wounded in the shooting, one reportedly blinded in one eye.

Warren Murphy reportedly told coworkers he was suspicious that his supervisors were having an affair with his ex-girlfriend. He complained about family problems and his frustration with postal management. He reportedly told his ex-girlfriend that the New Orleans post office did not care about the mail or people and, on several occasions, said someday he would kill his supervisors with a shotgun while she watched.

Dan Mace – 1989

Dan Mace, *current employee,* age forty-four, walked into the Poway post office in San Diego County and, using a **.38 caliber**, fatally shot himself in the temple.

Brief Narrative

Dan Mace reportedly was frustrated with petty harassment and bullying by his supervisors and wrote a letter to the media detailing his grievances. In this statement, he reportedly stated, "By the time you receive this, I should be dead." The supervisors' harassment methods reportedly included the monitoring of his bathroom breaks and watching and "clocking" him while he took his lunch breaks at home, which ostensibly was on his route and a designated break area. A spokesman for the USPS reportedly stated that Mr. Mace had disciplinary problems. During the year Dan Mace committed suicide, there were three other postal employees working in the San Diego area who reportedly committed suicide.

John Taylor – 1989

John Taylor was a *current employee* with twenty-seven years of service. After killing his wife at home, he went to the Escondido post office in San Diego County armed with a **.22 caliber semi-automatic pistol and** fired twenty rounds, killing two co-workers at a picnic table on the loading dock outside the postal facility. He later reportedly went inside the postal facility and shot and wounded a coworker and then fatally shot himself in the temple.

Brief Narrative

John Taylor reportedly was considered a model employee, receiving numerous awards and bonuses and was well liked by most everyone. He reportedly was upset with the changes in the culture of the Postal Service, which he attributed to increased stress levels and loss of camaraderie. During his rampage, he appeared to single out certain employees.

Employees interviewed reported that John Taylor thought that Postal Inspectors were "targeting" him by planting cash along his route. It was also reported that he had a drinking problem, which he kept well hidden. He reportedly suffered from injuries to his feet, back, and shoulder as a result of carrying mail over the years.

Joseph M. Harris – 1991)

Joseph Harris, *former employee* with twelve years of previous employment with the USPS, killed his former supervisor in her apartment with a **samurai sword**. He then reportedly went to a postal facility in Ridgewood, New Jersey, armed with a **9mm Uzi handgun, a .22 caliber machine gun with silencer, three hand grenades, and some homemade ether bombs**. Upon arriving at the facility, he shot and killed two mailhandlers and injured several others before being apprehended by law enforcement.

Brief Narrative

Joseph Harris reportedly hunted down his former supervisor and killed her two years after he was fired. Prior to his murderous rampage, in a two-page letter he reportedly made references to what he considered unfair treatment by postal management. He also referenced the Edmond, Oklahoma, postal tragedy.

Thomas McIlvane – 1991

Thomas McIlvane was a *former employee* and letter carrier. The day after receiving notice that an arbitrator upheld his firing, armed with a **sawed-off .22 caliber Ruger Rimfire rifle**, he entered the Royal Oak, Michigan, postal mail processing facility. He then climbed stairs to the second floor of the facility in search of the supervisors and managers who were involved in his discipline and eventual termination. Reaching his destination, Thomas McIlvane reportedly fired one hundred rounds of ammunition, killing four people, one of which was his immediate supervisor and a labor relations representative, an advocate for postal management.

Thomas McIlvane reportedly was seeking to kill the postmaster of the facility, but was unable to find him. During the shooting spree, six employees and three civilians were reportedly shot. After the shooting spree, he fatally shot himself in the head. One report indicated that the shooting lasted less than six minutes.

Brief Narrative

Thomas McIlvane reportedly had a long history of conflict with postal management, including with superiors while in the Marine Corps. He was reportedly court-martialed for insubordination and other charges (e.g., deliberately driving a tank over a car) while in the Marine Corps. As a result of these charges, he was incarcerated for three months and later "less than honorably discharged" from the military.

Thomas McIlvane was reportedly disciplined for numerous charges while employed with the USPS, including threatening supervisors and coworkers, infractions while driving a postal vehicle, deviating from his assigned route, unauthorized lunch breaks, and time reporting discrepancies. The record further indicated that he may have assaulted a postal customer. Prior to the decision upholding his removal from the USPS, he reportedly told a union official, "If I lose the arbitration, it will make Edmond, Oklahoma, look like a tea party."

As a result of an investigation conducted by a congressional House Committee on the Royal Oak, Michigan, shooting, the committee's findings included that labor and management relations at the facility were very poor. Some of the prior discipline of Mr. McIlvane was not handled correctly, and many employees felt that discipline was used at times to harass and coerce them. In reference to supervisor harassment in the report, it stated: "[I]t is reported that Chris Carlisle would stand behind an employee and berate him, hoping to provoke a response from the employee. If the employee accosted Carlisle, he would discipline the employee." (United States House of Representatives Committee, 1992, p. 55) Chris Carlisle was one of Mr. McIlvane's supervisors.

Roy Barnes – 1992

Roy Barnes, a sixty-year-old *current employee*, went to the workroom floor at the Citrus Heights, California, post office, armed with a **.22 caliber pistol, and then fatally shot himself in the heart** in front of his coworkers.

Brief Narrative

Roy Barnes reportedly was reacting to pressure and harassment from his postmaster. Because of the alleged harassment, he reportedly tried to obtain a restraining order on the postmaster with the help of the local union, but was unsuccessful. After the suicide, the postmaster reportedly was suspended and later transferred to another facility.

Lawrence Jaison – 1993

Lawrence Jaison, *current employee*, a postal mechanic with twenty-four years of service, went into the garage area at a Dearborn, Michigan, post office and began his deadly rampage. In carrying out his mission, he was armed with a **.38 caliber revolver and a shotgun**. He reportedly killed two coworkers, wounded two other employees (including a supervisor), and then committed suicide.

Brief Narrative

Lawrence Jaison reportedly was upset over being bypassed for a promotion, which a coworker received. Prior to the killing rampage, he reportedly made threats to coworkers and had received several letters of warning and a suspension. The record showed that employees told reporters they hoped the tragedy would lead to a change of management style in the USPS.

Note: The same day of this tragedy, Mark Hilburn, a former letter carrier, went to the Dana Point, California, post office to kill a female coworker, but was unable to locate her. In the process, he killed a male letter carrier. The rampage began with Mark Hilburn killing his mother. The motive for the killing at the worksite was reportedly related to a "love interest" he had with a female coworker.

Bruce Clark – 1995

Bruce Clark, *current employee* and a postal clerk with twenty-five years employment with the USPS, subsequent to an argument, punched his supervisor in the back of the head at the City of Industry, California, mail processing center and left the work area. About ten minutes later, he returned to the work area with a brown paper bag in his hand. Upon being asked by his supervisor what was in the bag, he reportedly pulled out a **.38 revolver and at close range fatally shot the supervisor twice, once in the upper body and once in the face.** Two employees reportedly took the gun away from Bruce Clark and held him down until the police came. Seventy-five postal employees reportedly witnessed the shooting.

Brief Narrative

Bruce Clark reportedly told a coworker shortly before the tragedy that he thought his supervisor was picking on him and driving him crazy. He reportedly told others at the scene of the tragedy and later to the police that he only intended to kill his supervisor.

A few days before the tragedy, he reportedly contacted a private investigator and told the investigator that he feared his supervisor and wanted to find out if his supervisor had a criminal history. According to the private investigator's statement, Bruce Clark claimed to have information that showed that his supervisor was stealing from the USPS and that he planned to share it with his supervisor's superiors. Based on the record, Mr. Clark allegedly told police that some employees thought he was a Postal Inspector and that one employee had followed him on at least two occasions.

Charles Edward Jennings – 1996

Charles Jennning, *former employee*, went to the parking lot at the Las Vegas, Nevada, postal facility and shot and killed a labor relations specialist. Mr. Jennings reportedly indicated in his statement to investigators that the labor relations specialist struggled to take the **gun** away from him and was shot in the process.

Brief Narrative

Charles Jennings reportedly was recognized for excellent performance in his carrier duties, but also had a number of letters of warnings and suspensions. He was removed from the USPS on the charge of falsification of records and fraud. He reportedly went to the Las Vegas postal facility with the intent to kill the plant manager and several other officials who were involved in his termination. However, after killing the labor relations specialist in the parking lot of the facility, he fled the scene and was later apprehended. In his statement to investigators, he reportedly stated that he had no intention of killing the labor relations representative.

Anthony James Deculit – 1997

Anthony Deculit, *current employee*, at a Milwaukee, Wisconsin, mail processing facility, armed with **a 9mm pistol**, shot and killed a coworker and wounded two others, one of which was his supervisor. Afterwards, he reportedly put the gun in his mouth and fatally shot himself.

Brief Narrative

Anthony Deculit reportedly had difficulty adjusting to the work demands and management style of the Postal Service, especially after the birth of his first child. Prior to the shooting, he reportedly had been admonished by his supervisor for sleeping on the job. His numerous attempts to transfer to the day shift had been denied. Anthony Deculit reportedly told his therapist sixteen months prior to the shooting that he was under a lot of stress and, if it continued, he would kill his supervisor and his manager. Although the therapist reported this information to the USPS threat assessment team, she did not consider him an imminent threat. He was later sent for a fitness-for-duty examination. Based on the examination, the physician reportedly did not view him as posing an acute danger and found him fit for duty.

Jennifer San Marco – 2006

Jennifer San Marco, *former employee*, after fatally shooting a former neighbor, drove to the mail processing facility in Goleta, California. Once she reached her destination, she drove through the gate of the secured facility by using an employee's identification badge she took at gunpoint. While inside the facility, **using a 9mm Smith & Wesson pistol and reloading at least once, she killed six postal workers and then herself**. Approximately eighty people were reportedly at the postal facility at the time of the shooting, many of whom fled to a fire station across the street as the event unfolded. The shooting was the "bloodiest postal tragedy in twenty years, the deadliest ever by a woman, and the deadliest in the United States, since 2003.

Brief Narrative

Jennifer San Marco, prior to her employment with the USPS, reportedly had worked as a Santa Barbara police dispatcher in the mid-1990s. As a requirement for that employment, she passed an extensive background check and a psychological exam. While employed with the USPS, she was observed talking to herself and making offensive, racially-motivated comments. On February 5, 2001, she reportedly was extremely irrational and subsequently was removed from the mail processing facility with handcuffs and placed in a county mental health facility on a seventy-two-hour involuntary hold. Because of Jennifer San Marco's ongoing mental health concerns, she reportedly was granted a medical retirement from the USPS.

After retiring from the USPS, Jennifer San Marco reportedly moved to New Mexico and displayed bizarre behaviors and created disturbances where the police were called. On several occasions, she allegedly harassed an office worker and reportedly appeared naked at a local gas station. While in New Mexico, she reportedly tried to obtain a business license for a newspaper called the *Racist Times*.

Jennifer Marco reportedly had written over a hundred-page journal detailing disputes and conflicts with others. The details of this journal reportedly provided a context for the motive of the killings and her suicide. Investigators reported that they were not looking at racial animus as a motive for the killings.

Grant Gallaher – 2006

Grant Gallaher, *current employee* and letter carrier of thirteen years, while on duty as a letter carrier in Baker City, Oregon, reportedly went home and got his **.357 Magnum revolver** and drove to the city post office with the intention of killing his postmaster. Arriving at the parking lot, he reportedly ran over his supervisor several times. Subsequently he went into the post office looking for his postmaster. Not finding the postmaster, he went back out to the parking lot and shot his supervisor several times at close range, ostensibly to make sure she was dead. He reportedly then fired three bullets in the windshield of her car and three more in the hood.

Brief Narrative

Grant Gallaher reportedly was on a new route for three weeks and had felt pressured by a week-long work-time study and an extra twenty minutes added to his new route. On the day of his rampage, he reportedly was ahead of schedule on his route and his supervisor brought him more mail to deliver. He allegedly decided to take the matter up with his postmaster on his cell phone and then went home to get his .357 Magnum revolver to exact his revenge. The work climate had reportedly improved from what it was in 1998, the year a union steward, age fifty-three, at the Baker City post office committed suicide.

Julius Kevin Tartt – 2006

Kevin Tartt, *current employee*, with eighteen years of service, employed at the Napoleon Street Carrier Annex in San Francisco, went to his supervisor's residence armed with a **revolver** and shot her in the back of the head outside of her house. He then reportedly left the scene and fatally shot himself in the head with the same gun.

Brief Narrative

Early in the investigation, homicide investigators were reportedly looking at links between disputes between Julius Tartt and his supervisor, including what one police official referred to as a discipline issue. One of the homicide officials stated that there were indications that Julius Tartt was dissatisfied with work and with the supervisor. During the timeframe of the tragedy, he was absent from work and had called in sick the previous day. Some employees reportedly stated in a blog on Postalreporter.com, an insider website for postal employees, there were some issues between Kevin Tartt and his supervisor.

Additional Postal Tragedies Worth Citing (1985-1998)

New York, New York, May 31, 1985

David Perez, a forty-five-year-old letter carrier, entered a New York City post office, pulled a rifle from a mailbag, and aimed it a supervisor. A postal clerk who came to the supervisor's aid was shot and wounded. Perez, who had been suspended several times, held the supervisor hostage for two hours before surrendering.

Chelsea, Massachusetts, June 29, 1988

Dominic LuPoli killed a coworker in the postal parking lot. After fleeing, LuPoli committed suicide.

Dana Point, California, May 6, 1993

Just four hours after the postal shooting in Dearborn, Michigan, **Mark Hilbun**, a former employee, killed his mother and her dog. He then went into a Dana Point, California, post office looking for a former female coworker in whom he reportedly had a love interest. Unable to locate her, he fatally shot a letter carrier and wounded a postal clerk. He left the post office and continued his shooting spree, wounding three civilians before his capture a day and a half later. Mark Hilbun reportedly had been diagnosed as having a substance abuse problem and bipolar disorder. Prior to his discharge from the USPS, he was sent for a fitness-for-duty examination and had received disciplinary actions from postal management.

Montclair, New Jersey, March 21, 1995

Christopher Green, former employee, robbed a post office armed with a 9mm handgun, killing two postal clerks whom he reportedly knew well and liked. He killed two customers and wounded another. He fled with $5,000.

Portland, Maine, August 17, 1995

Judith Coffin a forty-six-year-old project engineer, worked twelve years with the USPS. After receiving a promotion in 1993 where she was responsible for overseeing workers who installed and maintained mail-processing machines in the city's largest post office, her work life reportedly became very stressful. From the beginning of her new position, she reportedly was relentlessly sexually harassed and verbally abused by male subordinates and male supervisors under her purview.

Ms. Coffin complained to postal officials, who reportedly did nothing to alleviate the situation. On August 17, 1995, after almost two years of the harassment and postal officials not dealing with the problem, Judith Coffin reportedly met with a superior to discuss her job status. That same day, Ms. Coffin reportedly left a suicide note blaming the USPS for her decision to end her life. She then reportedly took an overdose of insulin and died six days later.

Palatine, Illinois, August 29, 1995

Dorsey Thomas, a fifty-three-year-old postal clerk, walked within a few feet of a fellow postal clerk and, without a word, drew a .380 caliber semi-automatic pistol and fired five rounds, wounding him. Thomas then calmly went down to the lobby of the facility and, seeing another coworker, stopped, withdrew the gun, and fired the remaining two bullets at his coworker. In the confusion, Thomas calmly went to his car and went home. Police arrested him shortly after his arrival.

Paterson, New Jersey, August 15, 1996

Thirty-eight-year-old **Danny Isku**, who had nine years of service, called in sick on August 15, 1996, but reportedly changed his mind and showed up at work that morning. He went to the office where supervisor Jerry Peterson and a USPS labor representative, Richard Anastasi, were meeting. As the two stood up, Isku reportedly pulled a .22 semiautomatic pistol from a **brown paper bag** and ordered Peterson to step into the hallway. Peterson lunged at Isku and reached for the weapon. At the same time, Anastasi reportedly leaped into the fray and tried to subdue Isku. The gun went off and a bullet pierced Peterson's hand. Anastasi sustained a fractured hand resulting from his attempt to subdue Isku.

Denver, Colorado, December 24, 1997

David Jackson, former employee, entered the Denver general mail facility brandishing a weapon and took seven postal employees hostage. After approximately ten hours, Jackson surrendered.

Dallas, Texas, April, 17, 1998

Maceo Yarbough, a twenty-seven-year-old non-career letter carrier, shot and killed a coworker after they reportedly argued in the break room of the Northaven post office. Yarbough then fled the scene. He was apprehended shortly after the shooting. He reportedly was found mentally incompetent (i.e., paranoid schizophrenic) to stand trial. Yarbough reportedly feared that his victim was planning to kill his family and that she had her boyfriend and Postal Inspectors follow him.

APPENDIX C

Impact of Strategic Plans and Congressional Oversight on Postal Culture

In this appendix, I review significant events over the last ten years as they relate to the building blocks of the postal culture. I provide observations and comments about seven strategic USPS plans (1998-2013),[206] the Presidential Commission Report of 2003,[207] the 2006 Postal Accountability and Enhancement Act (PAEA),[208] and post PAEA congressional oversight hearings[209].

It is important to note that the Government Performance Results Act of 1993[210] mandated the USPS and other government agencies to develop five-year strategic plans. The Act requires that these plans be *updated* annually and that the five-year strategic plan be *revised* at least every three years. The strategic plans of the USPS prior to 1998 were not listed on their official website. Accordingly, the first plan I discuss is the 1998-2002 Strategic Plan.[211]

Strategic Plans of the USPS 1998-2006

1998-2002 Strategic Plan (aka Customer Perfect!)

The efficiency and timeliness of postal mailings were greatly improved during the tenure of Marvin Runyon, Postmaster General, 1992-1998. Before he took the helm, service was deplorable in many parts of the country. The improvement of customer service under Runyon was achieved, however, in a top-down manner, with very little or no involvement of the postal unions and management associations, and the costs to employee morale were very high. Mr. Runyon indicated that the efficiency of the USPS was accomplished by implementing a culture of *performance management*. In describing this culture, he stated: "Four years ago, we decided we needed a better way of running the USPS. So we installed the Baldridge Concepts. We called it *Customer Perfect!* Because that's what we really aimed at—the customer."[212]

The performance management system utilized by the USPS in the context of this strategic plan incorporated a mission statement, goals, and strategies. Within this framework, a process was developed to evaluate not only the outcome of the strategies employed to achieve goals but also the progress made toward reaching goals. The primary emphases throughout the USPS were on improving customer service, reducing costs, and generating new business. Improvement of the workplace environment received minimal attention compared to the other voices, like the Voice of the Customer and the Voice of the Business.

One of the key performance goals under the Voice of the Employee in this strategic plan was framed as enhancement of workplace environment to improve relationships. Interestingly, instead of having targets and indicators for this performance goal, the plan merely indicated that the USPS, over the next five years, would "develop indicators and targets for enhancing the workplace environment to improve relationships with employees while developing the capability to survey employee attitudes."[213]

In my role as workplace improvement analyst during the timeframe of this strategic plan, there were no formal targets and indicators developed by the USPS to improve its relationship with employees. Also, during this period of time, postal executives in the USPS received the vast amount of their end of year merit pay based upon on how well service improved, costs were reduced, and improvement achieved in total productivity.

2001-2005 Strategic Plan

Similar to the 1998-2002 strategic plan, this new plan's[214] strategic goals focused heavily on generation of revenue, reducing costs, and improving productivity and service. A sub-goal of the plan to address the workplace environment was: "[I]mprove understanding of employee issues and concerns."[215] Differing from the previous strategic plan, rather than having no formal targets and indictors to address the workplace environment, there were two formal targets and one indicator.

For example, under the heading of this sub-goal, it stated: "The VOE survey, along with other 'listening' methods, will be adapted, improved, and integrated into the management process."[216] Although I can validate that VOE survey results were formally used as a target with indicators in my role as a workplace improvement analyst, I am not aware of any other "listening methods" adapted, improved, and integrated into the management process during this timeframe.

2002-2006 Strategic Transformation Plan

This particular plan[217] was delivered to the Senate and House in April 2002, with a tone marked by a sense of urgency. Because of the critical challenges facing the USPS regarding the organization's short- and long-term financial and commercial viability, congressional action was considered paramount. There was enormous concern over significant declines in the nation's first-class mailings, related to the impact of the Internet and e-mail. Compounding these concerns, letter carriers' delivery points across the nation were increasing at the same time. This was especially troubling from a financial perspective.

Arguably, the unfair requirement to fund 20-plus billion dollars of annuity benefits to employees that were attributable to their prior military service was another significant concern. This was particularly alarming because of the high percentage of "baby boomers" planning to retire over the next twenty years.

Although in the executive summary of this plan it is stated that the Postal Reorganization Act of 1970[218] was successful, the USPS recommended congressional legislation to assure future success. For example, in the concluding remarks of the executive summary it stated:

> The USPS does not have the flexibility essential for successful management of a modern business. Postal laws create a tension between a public policy mission and structure and the businesslike necessity to deliver what customers want and will pay for in the marketplace. Until transformation is accomplished, the ability of the USPS to finance a continually growing universal service obligation without a government subsidy will be in serious doubt.[219]

For these reasons, recommendations for future success included more flexibility in purchasing and regulation of pricing. It also called for the weakening of the bargaining rights of the postal unions through binding arbitration by switching to a compulsory mediation process when there were impasses.

The plan in its entirety places substantial emphasis on preparing for the challenges of technology and business requirements in a global age, but offers little on improving employee treatment in the workplace, with the exception of holding managers accountable for the results of the Voice of the Employee (VOE) survey, for dealing with "troubled work sites," threat assessment teams, and several other issues. Suffice to say at this point, management accountability for these issues generally was not realized.

Strategic Plans of the USPS 2004-2013

2004-2008 Strategic Plan

This five-year strategic plan,[220] as mandated by the Government Performance and Results Act, was released shortly after the Presidential Commission Report of 2003. The plan's focus, similar to the ones that went before it, focused on four strategic goals, including improve service, manage costs, enhance performance-based culture, and grow revenue. Unlike the previous plans, it added one additional strategic goal, which was to adjust civil service retirement contributions by pursuing legislative reform.

In the plan, the means to improve the workplace environment was framed within the context of the USPS *goal to enhance performance-based culture*. For example, the plan stated: "The overall objective, which cannot be measured precisely, is to maintain an accountable, motivated, and diverse workforce empowered to maximize performance in a safe and secure work environment."[221] It is interesting and telling that the first adjective in this statement to describe the desired work environment is **accountable**. It is also interesting and disingenuous that the adjective **empowered** was used to describe what kind of workforce was desired, especially when viewed in the context of the unilateral dismantling of programs that had provided increased opportunities for employee input in the 1990s.

Two specific sub-goals, strategized from the goal to enhance performance-based culture, were the VOE survey and safety as it relates to employee illness and injury rates. The compensation program for management employees regarding these two factors accounted for 10 percent of the potential compensation with regard to annual merits. The targets for these two sub-goals were set in terms of reduction of the illness and injury rates and increases in the VOE survey index, which is based on the average of six items in the survey. The six items of the VOE survey include statements about recognition, accountability, exclusion, sexual harassment, being treated with dignity and respect by the supervisor, and workplace communications by the supervisor.

What is most troubling about the discussion of workplace improvement and safety in this plan, in light of the level of workplace tragedies and violence in the USPS, is the following statement:

> When the previous strategic plan was under development, there was considerable concern that the postal work environment was hostile and unsafe. An independent commission was established to examine the issue in detail, and found that the postal work environment was much better than expected and was indeed safe and secure.[222]

This statement ostensibly is nothing more than a disguised public relations ploy rather than an accurate characterization of the true state of affairs. In several chapters of this book, I make the case that this independent commission (i.e., the Califano Report) skewed and misrepresented its own data to place the USPS in a more favorable light.

2006-2010 Strategic Transformation Plan

In a message from Chairman of the Board James Miller III and Postmaster General John Potter they stated, as a prelude to the USPS's 2006-2010 Transformation Plan, it is "focused on our core business and the strategies we know produce operational and business processes … *The Strategic Transformation Plan* will be updated annually."[223]

In this sixty-five-page plan, the USPS cites four strategic goals, including: 1) generate revenue, 2) reduce costs, 3) achieve performance-based culture, and 4) improve service. As in previous plans, the USPS listed numerous performance objectives and strategies as the criteria to reach these goals. However, regarding the ***sub-goal of engaging employees***, under the goal to achieve performance-based culture, metrics to suggest that workplace environment was improving include improvement in the VOE survey score and reduction of disputes (e.g., union grievances and EEO formal complaints). In discussing the VOE survey score, it stated:

> Under the 2002 Transformation Plan the U.S. Postal Service began to build a highly effective and motivated workforce. The Voice of the Employee (VOE) survey is an employee opinion survey designed to assess the workplace environment ... The VOE survey reveals that the workplace environment has improved substantially and continues to improve. Current efforts, initiatives, and systems have all contributed to an increase in the USPS's VOE survey index. The index is comprised of six questions about key workplace factors that can impact employee performance and thus affect business outcomes. The index rating is composed of favorable responses to these six questions. Nationally, the VOE index rating has improved steadily, from 58.1 in 2001, to the current 2005 rating of 63.3.[224]

This conclusion that the VOE survey supports the notion that the workplace environment has improved belies what is presented in chapters six through eight and Appendices D-E. Based on my experience with the VOE survey, the scores essentially improved because management compensation was tied to their improvement. A significant amount of monies were spent to "recognize employees." Recognition efforts across the country included giving employees shirts, hats, lunches, gift certificates, and a host of other prizes. These efforts did help employee morale, but not significantly.

With all this intense and focused attention on management compensation and monies spent for employee recognition, the VOE survey score only improved 5.2 percent over a four-year period. In my professional opinion, this is not significant. Even with compensation incentives for postal management to make improvements in the workplaces across the country, the VOE survey score in recent years still declined. The index scores for 2006 and 2007 were lower than 2005, and for 2008 it was the same as 2005.

2006-2010 Strategic Transformation Plan Update

In 2007, the USPS submitted an update[225] to their 2006-2010 transformation plan. Regarding the issue of employee treatment, under the heading "The Voice of the Employee," it was indicated that the USPS would "continue to rely on the Voice of the Employee survey to identify and address areas of concern."[226] Again, here we have another plan without substantive initiatives, strategies, or targets to improve the postal culture.

2009-2013 Strategic Plan

The USPS titled this particular five-year strategic plan "Vision 2013."[227] It is by the far the briefest account of all the previously discussed plans. The document is only sixteen pages. Compared to previous strategic plans, it provides no meaningful discussion on improving the workplace environment. As far as metrics to measure success in key areas, none are provided. Instead, in the conclusion portion of the document, it is stated: "We will expand our current performance metrics with measurements that are more relevant to customers and profitable results."[228] Based on this statement and review of the document, it does not appear that the USPS has complied with the criteria set forth in the Government Performance Results Act of 1993.

Under the heading "Partner to Create New Customer Value," it is stated that the Postal Service "will pursue innovative outsourcing and insourcing approaches where they provide … customers with greater benefits."[229] This statement is consistent with the major thrust by the USPS in recent years to contract out core postal operations.

Presidential Commission Report of 2003

At this point, it is relevant to discuss significant recommendations in the President's Commission on the United States Postal Service, submitted on July 31, 2003. In the executive order on December 11, 2002, President George W. Bush outlined the broad goal for the commission as follows:

> The mission of the commission shall be to examine the state of the United States Postal Service, and to prepare and submit to the President a report articulating a proposed vision for the future of the

United States Postal Service and recommending the legislative and administrative reforms needed to ensure the viability of the Postal Service.[230]

The commission's report title, "Embracing the Future: Making the Tough Choices to Preserve the Universal Mail System," was not only foretelling, it also provided some bold and highly controversial recommendations, one that primarily represented the broad business interests of the mailing industry. While focusing on ways the USPS could become more efficient, productive, and flexible in carrying out its mission to provide universal service, it did so in a manner where the chief beneficiaries would be the mailers, at the expense of postal employees' benefits and rights.

Some of the commission's key recommendations, if adopted, would have shifted the authority and historical oversight of the USPS from Congress to solely in the hands of the executive branch. One key recommendation, for example, was that three members of the USPS's Board of Governors (BOG) be selected by the President, with the concurrence of the Secretary of the Treasury, instead of being selected by the President with the consent of Congress.

It was further recommended that these three appointed members select the remaining eight members of the BOG. Shifting accountability and public policy oversight of the USPS from Congress to a new Postal Regulatory Commission (PRC) was another key recommendation. This new PRC, as recommended by the commission, would have the authority to clarify and periodically review the scope of the mail monopoly. Both of the measures, if adopted by Congress, would have placed the USPS in great jeopardy of being privatized. It could reasonably be argued that these two key recommendations were developed with that end in mind.

In addition to the above recommendations, the commission made three recommendations from the Private Sector Partnership Subcommittee. These recommendations were premised on the notion that the USPS should focus on ways to outsource some of its functions to the private sector. The commission also made several recommendations that employees' benefits, such as health benefits and retirement benefits, be subject solely to bargaining agreements between the USPS and the postal unions. This recommendation, if adopted, would have weakened the fringe benefits and other protections of the rank and file postal employees. Historically, USPS employees have shared the same benefits (i.e., health and retirement benefits) of other federal employees under congressional mandates.

As a final note, it is interesting and telling that *the commission recommended that the Board of Governors be authorized to establish pay rates for top USPS officers and executive employees that are competitive with the private sector.* Like private enterprise, the rewards for those at the top would be dramatically increased, while at the same time increasing ways in which to decrease the wages and benefits of the rank and file employees.

2006 Postal Accountability and Enhancement Act

More than three years after the presidential commission examined the state of the USPS and made far-reaching recommendations to overhaul it, the Postal Accountability and Enhancement Act (PAEA) of 2006 was passed by Congress and reluctantly signed by President Bush on December 20, 2006.

The Act was the most comprehensive reform of the USPS since the Postal Reorganization Act of 1970. One key provision, after a very protracted battle with the executive branch, was that the Act relieved the USPS of the 27 billion dollars unfunded liability of military pension benefits, which was rightly returned to the Treasury Department. The Act would have passed sooner, perhaps several years sooner, if it was not for President Bush's persistent opposition to this transfer.

The PAEA was not as sweeping as the Act of 1970, but it did profoundly affect the way the USPS set rate increases and how it was to be governed and regulated. The Act authorized the USPS to adjust prices each May and limited postage increases to the rate of inflation, as measured by the Consumer Price Index. This was a great benefit to the public and private sector, especially business mailers (i.e., advertisers and publishers) in terms of forecasting costs. However, under special circumstances and with the approval of the Postal Regulatory Commission (PRC), the USPS could raise postage rates higher than the rate of inflation. Aside from this provision, in an e-newsletter by the Magazine Publishers of America,[231] it was estimated that publishers would save billions of dollars in coming years. The newsletter also underscored that the Mail Publishers Association would participate at the PRC in review of the 2008 postal increase, as mandated by the PAEA.

It is interesting to note that the USPS did not exercise their right to raise postal rates one last time under the old, pre-reform law; that is, under the PAEA requirement to have rate increases no higher than the rate of inflation. The rate increase went into effect on May 12, 2008. This is particularly troubling because the USPS had a 5.1 billion dollar deficit in 2007 and a 2.8 billion dollar deficit for 2008. Accordingly, it is likely that the USPS will attempt to use this provision of law to justify layoffs, privatization measures, and restricted cooperation with union and management organizations.

In many ways, however, the Act was an enormous victory to the postal unions and the postal employees they represent. Congress rejected nearly all the regressive and anti-union recommendations of the 2003 presidential commission. One single exception was that postal employees injured on the job would not be entitled to workers' compensation pay for loss of time during the first three days. Congress sent a very clear message in the Act that the postal unions would continue to be major stakeholders in the bargaining of wages and benefits for its employees. For example, it stated:

> [N]othing in this Act shall restrict, expand or otherwise affect any
>
> of the rights or privileges of either employees, or of labor organiza-
>
> tions representing employees, under existing law, including Title 39
>
> of the USC, and the National Labor Relations Act, any labor contract,
>
> or any USPS handbook or manual.[232]

Despite this provision in the PAEA, upon examination of the postal record after the passage of the Act, it becomes clear that the USPS's Board of Governors, its law enforcement apparatus, and its collusion with the high-profile mailers serve to undermine these rights and privileges.

Post-Postal Enhancement and Accountability Act

The Congressional Subcommittee on Federal Workforce conducted three hearings[233] since the passage of the Act, which were held on April 17, 2007, May 8, 2008, and July 24, 2008. The first two of these hearings were conducted to explore issues and concerns of the USPS's operation and business practices, mail growth, delivery, and how it has taken advantage of provisions provided in the Act to enhance its overall economic situation going forward. The third meeting was conducted to discuss the USPS's network plan[234] and its potential impact on all stakeholders.

Although Congress' intent was to legislate an act that provided long-term viability and relative stability for the USPS to operate like a business, and which would inspire the support and blessings from the union and management organizations, serious concerns emerged shortly after it was signed into law. The context for these concerns is provided in the following examples.

On April 17, 2007, Oscar (Dale) Goff, Jr., President, National Association of Postmasters of the United States, testified[235] at a congressional subcommittee hearing regarding the PAEA. In this testimony, he indicated that the jury was still out on the PAEA because a conference report did not accompany the legislation, which was necessary to clarify many of the provisions in the Act. In his testimony, Mr. Goff pointed out that service was declining because postmasters on a daily basis faced inadequate staffing for window service, mail processing, and mail delivery. He indicated that these problems would give voice to the corporate mailers who were poised to complain about service problems, and perhaps residential customers as well, to the Postal Regulatory Commission.

In light of recent contracting of letter carrier positions to private contractors, as discussed below and in Appendix D, Mr. Goff suggested that corporate mailers have forged an alliance with the USPS to dig deeper into the pockets of the highly lucrative 900 billion dollar postal industry. For example, in his testimony he stated:

> [T]he agency must resist the temptation to subordinate the expertise of its homegrown dedicated postal employees – the professionals who actually provide Postal Service – to green eye shaded gurus who declare the bottom line is the only line. [I]t appears that postal privateers have allied themselves with a cadre of postal operational personnel in a quest to squeeze the lifeblood out of postal facilities – large and small – and to private postal functions that are, in fact, inherently governmental in nature.[236]

In support of this observation, in no less than nine National Letter Carrier Association (NALC) union bulletins from November 1, 2006 to July 6, 2007, the NALC informed their members of their epic battle with the USPS on contracting and its lobbying efforts with congressional members to stop the contracting out of letter carrier jobs to private contractors. When it became clear that Congress was poised to take legislative action, the USPS began to roll back its contracting out of letter carriers jobs to private contractors.

Supportive of Mr. Goff's observations and comments are the recent concerns and actions expressed by the American Postal Workers Union (APWU). For example, an APWU article[237] posted April 2, 2008 discussed the recent decision of a federal court to dismiss a suit where the APWU and the Consumer Alliance for Postal Service (CAPS) sought the records and minutes from the Mailers Technical Advisory Committee (MTAC) meetings. The MTCA committee members are comprised of high-ranking USPS officials and representatives of large corporate mailers.

The APWU and CAPS argued that the MTCA records should be available for public scrutiny under the Federal Advisory Committee Act. In response to the judge's decision in overturning the suit, APWU President William Burris, in contrast to Mr. Goff's previous comments, described the alliance between the large corporate mailers representatives and the USPS as more fact than a mere appearance. In commenting on the alliance between the two parties, Burris unequivocally stated:

> The APWU is deeply concerned that the USPS has relinquished its strategic policy-making to the largest mailers, and that it has done so in secret. Using MTAC, and similar forums, big mailers have set the USPS agenda. This may explain why the USPS has repeatedly proposed postal rates and policies that favor large mailers at the expense of individuals and small businesses.[238]

Sadly, this is reminiscent of Vice-President Dick Cheney meeting in private with energy industry executives (e.g., Enron, Shell Oil, BP, etc.), and the records of these meetings have been ruled by the U.S. Supreme Court as privileged and as such not open to public inspection. It is an example of a pattern of secrecy that has permeated President Bush's administration, and the USPS has also fallen under that wide umbrella of secrecy. This type of secrecy poisons labor-management cooperation because of the lack of transparency. It leads to mistrust and places concerns back in the lap of Congress.

On March 25, 2008, in an APWU update[239] and in support of Mr. Burris' concluding sentence in the above excerpt, the Postal Regulation Commission (PRC) issued a strong warning to the USPS in what was deemed "excessive rate discounts" to large corporate mailers in its proposed rate adjustments scheduled for May 12, 2008. Ironically, despite this finding by the PRC, the USPS was afforded a reprieve for this particular case. The PRC did warn, however, that such discounts in the future would not be permitted without sufficient justification. In short, this case clearly demonstrates that the USPS and large corporate mailers have a formidable alliance. It is not accidental that this APWU update was titled *PRC Ruling Exposes Unhealthy Relationship Between USPS and Influential Mailers*.

Another example to illustrate unresolved issues regarding the PAEA: In an *APWU News* article dated April 14, 2008,[240] Mr. Burris informed his membership that he had written the Postmaster General and later President George Bush to apprise them that, under the Postal Reorganization Act and the PAEA, the Postmaster General was required to appoint eleven members to a <u>USPS Advisory Council</u>, including four members nominated by postal labor unions, four representatives of major mail users, and three representing the public at large. Other members of the council were to include the Postmaster General as chairperson and the Deputy Postmaster General as co-chair. Specifically, in Mr. Burris' letter to President Bush, he stated:

> At this critical juncture in the history of the USPS, the APWU insists that an Advisory Council be established and consulted in accordance with statute. Matters of critical importance to the USPS and its employees, including realignment of the postal mail processing network, implementation of a major new flat sorting program, establishment of service standards, and implementation of the new rate-setting provisions enacted by the PAEA, make consultation with the Advisory Council more important now than at any time since the passage of the Postal Reorganization Act.[241]

Subsequent to the subject letters to the Postmaster General and President Bush regarding the issue of the USPS Advisory Council, the APWU filed suit[242] against both in District Court on July 17, 2008 because of their failure to implement the council as authorized by the Postal Reorganization Act and PAEA. To further complicate unresolved issues since the enactment of the PAEA, the PRC selected a contractor,[243] whose members are on record as anti-union and favoring of contracting postal operations, to conduct a study on the universal service obligation (USO), a study required to be submitted to Congress and the executive branch by January 8, 2009. I discuss this disturbing and egregious issue in Appendix D.

It is important to note that in October 2008, the USPS submitted its report[244] to Congress on the USO. Although the Postal Service shows support for the USO as it pertains to private express statutes (PES) and the mailbox rule, the report emphasizes flexibility on how the USPS meets its universal service obligation. It does not address, however, its plans to privatize core postal operations.

As I mentioned previously, the third meeting by the Congressional Subcommittee on Federal Workforce,[245] on July 24, 2008, was held to discuss the USPS's network plan and its potential impact on all stakeholders. As expected, the major representatives for the mailing industry and the Postal Service favorably supported the plan, while the union organizations were adamantly against it. In Appendix D, the unions concerns with the subject plan are discussed.

The battle to contract out postal core functions has escalated over the last several decades, particularly the last five years and after the passage of the PAEA. Until the new Congress starts its business in 2009, it is unlikely that the Board of Governors, President Bush and the neo-conservatives, and corporate mailers will substantially back away from this battle.[xxxvii]

Summary and Concluding Remarks

Summary

In this appendix, I examined important events over the last ten years as they relate to the building blocks of the postal culture. I provided observations and comments about seven strategic USPS plans from 1998-2013. In this examination, it became clear that the USPS has not planned or strategically focused to create an empowered, participative work culture for its employees. The only area where there was any significant strategic focus was related to the VOE survey and linking it to incentive-based compensation for postal management. The main focuses of the USPS's strategic plans dealt with operations' efficiency, improving customer service, reducing costs, revenue generation, and succession planning for postal management. In all these areas, the overarching focus was on top-down controls.

In 2003,the Bush commission released its report titled the "Presidential Postal Commission Report." Its recommendations would have eliminated congressional oversight, provided massive increases in salaries for postal executives, and weakened postal union collective bargaining rights. While the commissioners focused on recommendations where the USPS could become more efficient, productive, and flexible in carrying out its mission to provide universal service, they did so in order that the chief beneficiaries would be the large mailers. The clear losers, if their

---

xxxvii   The ubiquitous influence of the board of governors in this battle is examined in Appendix D. Required legislation to address post-PAEA issues is presented in the last chapter to this book—an open letter to the Congress of the United States.

recommendations were implemented, would have been at the expense of postal employees' benefits and rights, along with the rights of residential customers. Read closely, the report was simply nothing more than a blueprint for gradual USPS privatization.

Three years after the report was published, Congress enacted the 2006 Postal Accountability Act, reluctantly signed by President Bush. Virtually all the regressive measures recommended by Bush's commission were rejected by Congress. Despite the victory of the postal unions and the management associations in persuading Congress to reject these measures, upon examination of the postal record after the passage of the Act, it becomes clear that the USPS's Board of Governors, its law enforcement apparatus, and its collusion with the high-profile mailers continue their concerted efforts to undermine postal employees' and their representatives' benefits and rights and to privatize core operations of the USPS.

Concluding Remark

The top-down control and goal-driven focuses of the USPS, as provided in its strategic plans from 1998-2013, coupled with continual attempts to slowly and deliberately privatize its core operations, have had a very negative impact on a preexisting harsh postal culture. Postal employees are generally content with their wages and benefits, but their postal culture continues to deteriorate because employees' empowerment and participation is practically non-existent.

Employees' trust in the intentions of top postal officials, from craft employees to senior plant and district managers, is very low. Both union and management organization leaders alike are becoming more and more allied to openly confront an arguably uncaring and reckless path the USPS is pursuing.

APPENDIX D
Impact of Internal Stakeholders on Postal Culture

In this Appendix, I assess the impact of internal stakeholders on postal culture. Top management of the USPS has the largest overall role in impacting organizational culture, especially the less conspicuous but very powerful Board of Governors (BOG). The BOG is empowered to hire and fire the Postmaster General. Accordingly, the examination of top management primarily focuses on the role of the BOG.

In contrast to top management, other critical internal stakeholders play a lesser, but important, role regarding impact on the postal culture. These stakeholders include the four postal unions and the three management associations. Like top management, they are assessed in light of their impact on the postal culture.

Top Management

As noted in chapter six, the Postal Reorganization Act of 1970[246] was a comprehensive postal reform measure that created the context for the newly formed USPS. It transformed the post office department into a semi-independent federal agency. The Act allowed for the creation of a postal corporation under the direction of a nine-member Board of Governors (BOG). These nine members are nominated by the President and then selected with the advice and consent of the Congress. The BOG selects the Postmaster General and the Assistant Postmaster General and both become members of the board. Since the Act has been implemented, there have been eleven postmaster generals at the helm of USPS.

The USPS's Board of Governors' duties and oversight responsibilities are similar to the board of directors in a private corporation, and its members generally have a

strong business background, enabling them to evaluate the efficiency and productivity of the USPS in light of economic criteria and theoretically manage it more like
a private business. Their goal, as required by the Act, as decision-makers for the USPS,
is to ensure that the USPS is self-sufficient; in other words, that it functions without
budget deficits and federal subsides.

The BOG was the final authority in approving reorganizations, restructurings, and
realignments efforts, with the most comprehensive occurring under Marvin Runyon
in 1992. Likewise, since required by Congress in 1994, the BOG was the final authority in approving the USPS's strategic plans.[247] The BOG was a major ally with George
W. Bush's presidential commission[248] regarding attempts to weaken the bargaining
rights of the postal unions by switching to a compulsory mediation from the binding
arbitration process and aligning itself with several other regressive recommendations. The 2003 report issued by this commission on the United States Postal Service
would have given greater power to the executive branch and the BOG, and thereby
nullify most of Congress' oversight and accountability. This battle was waged by the
advocates of the Bush commission and the key players of the BOG, especially James
C. Miller III, its chairman.

Mr. Miller was appointed by President Bush to the BOG through a recess appointment on April 22, 2003. He served as the BOG chairman from January 2005 to January 2008. Mr. Miller is recognized as a very conservative economist who has been
affiliated with conservative organizations such as the Hoover Institution and the
American Enterprise for Public Policy Research. The Hoover Institution, led by Milton
Friedman, drafted Ronald Reagan's supply-side economics policies in the 1980s. Mr.
Miller did not vacate his position on the BOG until the postal unions defeated the
regressive measures proposed by Bush's postal commission and the BOG's failure to
expand contracting of letter carrier positions to private contractors in several major
cities.[249] Later in my discussion about the role of the National Association of Letter
Carriers (NALC), I assess the Postal Service's persistent attempts to the contracting of
letter carrier positions.

Interestingly, on April 2, 2008, the BOG honored Mr. Miller for his three years as chairman and he was given the honorary title of chairman pro tempore.[250] "Pro tempore"
has been defined as a designation for an individual to act as consul. These formal
actions by the BOG are **telling** because it suggests that the current composition of
the BOG will continue down the path of Mr. Miller, weakening the postal unions and
providing major advantages to the major mailers, including advertisers and publishers. As outlined previously, this battle wages on and will continue to do so for the

foreseeable future, unless Congress explicitly resolves the issue by further legislation.

The neo-conservatives in the Bush administration, Congress, and the Board of Governors under Chairman Miller were unsuccessful in their attempts to scale back union bargaining rights, expansion of contracting postal positions to private enterprise, and to virtually eliminate oversight and accountability by Congress. This battle, however, still rages on behind closed doors and, less often, right out in the open. In the next section, I discuss the postal unions' response to these issues and other critical issues.

Postal Unions

The USPS has four major unions, all of which I assess in the context of their impact on the postal culture and their legitimate rebuke to the top-down control and goal-driven emphases of the Postal Service and its attempts to scale back their bargaining rights and to privatize core postal operations. The four major unions include the National Association of Letter Carriers (NALC), American Postal Workers Union (APWU), National Postal Mail Handler Union (NPMHU), and the National Rural Letter Carriers Association (NRLCA).

In reading this examination on postal unions, some readers may infer that I am biased toward unions in general, or postal unions in particular, or both. I do not consider such an inference a valid observation. Instead, I have concluded that, throughout history, unions have played legitimate and honorable roles in representing the rights and personal dignity of employees. I readily acknowledge that sometimes unions have not represented the best interests of all stakeholders, including the postal unions. Postal unions have no doubt been rightly cited for excesses in their history, but their excesses pale in comparison to some of the egregious tactics and command and control measures employed by the postal management and its third appendage, postal law enforcement.

Labor unions in the United States historically came into power to remedy widespread and unchecked exploitation by employers. Prior to their emergence, wages, benefits, and safety and health conditions were deplorable. In this context, many employers embraced the principles of scientific management, principles that devalued employees' participation and their inherent integrity. These principles provided the impetus to autocratic management styles where employees were disempowered in the decision process regarding everyday work life.

Beginning in the 1950s and extending to the early 1980s, scores of companies began to look at alternatives to scientific management or top-down control approaches. Some embraced and implemented philosophical approaches affiliated with the human relations movement where employees were viewed as vitally important in the decision-making process. Not only were they viewed as important in the day-to-day decision process, but their input into company work standards and methods were also deemed very important.

With the accelerated expansion of a global economy in the 1980s, however, employers once again began to view employees as dispensable and unworthy of livable wages and benefits. As this became the dark reality for many of the blue collar workers in the 1980s, it also became the reality of white collar workers beginning in the 1990s. The maximization of profits by corporate interests, at enormous costs to American workers and workers globally, had become the staple of the 1980s and continued full stride into the twenty-first century. Accordingly, today there is a greater need for labor unions, including postal unions—not less.

National Association of Letter Carriers

Currently, there are approximately 225,000 city letter carriers in the USPS. The NALC is the representative union for all these employees. The NALC was the first craft in the old Post Office Department to organize and lobby Congress. The GAO report of 1994 outlined its early history as follows:

> At a time of unsatisfactory working conditions, low pay, and arbitrary management, postal workers were the first federal employees to join a union. In 1889, city letter carriers were the first craft in the old Post Office Department to organize. From the beginning, the city letter carriers, along with other crafts and management associations, developed relationships with Congressional efforts to improve their poor working conditions and poor pay.[251]

Although some of the more contentious issues between the USPS and the NALC have been longstanding, the examination of these issues is limited to the years after the implementation of the Postal Reorganization Act of 1970. Accordingly, the major contentious issues discussed in this section include: 1) the dispute resolution process regarding the resolving of grievances and contractual issues, 2) employee involvement, 3) top-down work standards and methods, 4) joint statement of violence and behavior, and 5) contracting of letter carrier positions to private enterprise.

1. Dispute Resolution Process

In the GAO report of 1994, the NALC indicated that a joint, cooperative process, called Union Management Pairs, had been put in effect with excellent results at various pilot sites for ten years, but the USPS had refused to expand the program nationally. At the nineteen pilot sites that utilized this joint process, grievances were reportedly reduced by 59 percent. After years of contentious disagreements, in 2002 the USPS and the NALC finally agreed to an initiative called the dispute resolution process to address an unsustainable backlog of grievances. The initiative gave broad authority to full-time representatives from the NALC and postal management at postal districts to settle grievances. It created the context for these representatives to reduce third-party interventions by settling grievances at their level.

In many of the postal districts the dispute resolution process is working well. In some other postal districts, however, district managers through their subordinates or directly are interfering with the process. Grievances sent to arbitration have been reduced markedly in the past three years because a merit compensation initiative rewards management officials for these reductions.

Despite the significant reductions of grievances, the USPS-NALC dispute resolution process does not solve the root causes of adversarial labor-management difficulties, nor does it address concerns and behaviors regarding the postal culture and how employees are treated in the workplace. In a December 2006 union bulletin, William Young, the current president of NALC, stated it this way: "[T]he traditional paradigm of adversarial confrontation at the workroom floor remains."[252]

2. Employee Involvement (EI)

In announcing the USPS's employee involvement initiative in October 1981, Postmaster General William Bolger said, "I have taken a first step in a redirection of postal philosophy, away from the **traditional, authoritarian style of management** [emphasis added] and toward an increasing worker involvement in finding solutions of the workplace."[253] The EI initiative was initially established between the NALC and the USPS. Over the next several years, hybrid employee involvement initiatives were established between the USPS and the other postal unions and management organizations with the exception of the APWU.

In the 1994 GAO report, it was indicated that the real *hope* of the EI initiative between the USPS and the NALC was to redirect the traditional style of postal management, providing employees the opportunity for involvement in the day-to-day work tasks and processes and thereby enhancing their dignity and self-worth. In spite of this hope, EI was unilaterally discontinued by the USPS in 1996 to the dismay and outrage of the NALC. For example, in the 1997 GAO report, Vincent Sombrotto, former president of the NALC, stridently stated in a letter to a high-ranking postal official:

> When the NALC and USPS jointly initiated this program in 1982, it was hailed as a remarkable achievement. We were early—and eager—for joint ventures in the new labor-management era of "jointness"—and we were jointly proud of our innovative effort … What was once the largest program of employee involvement in the nation (involving hundreds of thousands of employees) is soon to be history—by the mere stroke of your pen … [P]ostal management appears to be determined to attempt to reassert its long discredited effort to dominate its workforce through an authoritarian, unilateral system of top-down controls.[254]

Based on my work experience and first-hand witnessing of the unilateral, top-down controls applied in the USPS, I wholeheartedly agree with this assessment. It is consistent with the long history of the USPS adherence to the scientific management principle that any advantages of employee participation or input in workplace decision-making are far outweighed by its inherent disadvantages.

One high-ranking postal official was credited with stating that the initiative was discontinued because it no longer significantly contributed to the goals of the Postal Service and it did not address the roots causes of workplace conflict. It was also advanced that a new initiative called "Customer Perfect" (see Appendix C) was being emphasized in place of EI. This was a new initiative that was implemented without any prior input from the postal unions.

Another high-ranking postal official indicated that discontinuance of EI occurred because EI facilitators were full-time positions and thereby restricted employees from their core duties of mail processing and delivery. According to Mr. Sombrotto, a critical reason for the discontinuance of EI was the lack of progress in delivery redesign, which is discussed below under the heading of Top-Down Work Standards and Methods.

Many reasons were provided to explain why the USPS unilaterally terminated the NALC-USPS EI initiative. The over-arching reason, however, was the USPS's desire to implement top-down controls without the participation of the NALC and its employees. The introduction of *Customer Perfect*, contrary to what the USPS proffered to the GAO in 1994, did not provide any substantive or meaningful input from the postal unions and management organizations on work standards and methods utilized in the USPS.

3. Top-Down Work Standards and Methods

The issue of top-down work standards and methods has been a burning issue for the NALC for over a hundred years. Concerted efforts to monitor letter carriers' work performance on their routes by "spotters" go back to the late nineteenth century. The work standards and methods I discuss under this heading focus on the facets of office management and street management of city letter carriers, primarily emphasizing the latter. Accordingly, I highlight important commentaries, initiatives, and events in the past twenty-one years.

In chapter seven I briefly noted that delivery redesign was a huge opportunity for the NALC and the USPS to jointly devise work standards and methods for both office and street management on behalf of the city letter carrier force. In this context, it was also a critical opportunity to jointly address root causes of employee conflict, violence, stress, and turmoil in the workplace.

Beginning in 1987, the USPS and the NALC established a joint task force to address work standards and methods for city letter carriers. Although there were numerous discussions about establishing evaluated routes similar to the rural carrier craft, no agreement was realized. In 1996, the year that EI was discontinued, the USPS unilaterally pursued delivery redesign pilot sites without input from the NALC. According to Mr. Sombrotto, prior to this unilateral action, the USPS rejected repeated invitations to join the NALC in efforts for meaningful dialogue. In a blistering rebuke to this unilateral action, in a letter to a high-ranking postal official, Mr. Sombrotto stated:

> I would have hoped and expected that management's bunker mentality would not apply to so central a matter of our common concern as performance standards for letter carriers. In view of all that has been said about the deplorable state of the labor-management culture of the USPS, the need for cooperation and the desirability of joint action, the intention of the USPS to change its historical autocratic, top-down managerial mind-set, I would have expected even the hard-liners at L'Enfant Plaza to perceive the wisdom of proceeding cooperatively.[255]

Again, this type of unilateral top-down control is consistent with the long history of the USPS's adherence to the scientific management principle that union and employee involvement in work standards and practices has far more disadvantages than advantages. This type of unilateral action is consistent with the prevailing business philosophy in the United States. When viewed in this historical context, it is understandable why the USPS's Board of Governors did and would seek to manage the USPS along a path of *management unilateralism*. Below, I present the negative impact of this stance in greater detail.

Many of the delivery redesign pilot sites that the USPS unilaterally implemented in 1996 were later disbanded because of their requirement to abide by national contract agreement issues. Consequently, in 1997, postal management heightened their micromanagement and monitoring techniques and practices regarding the office and street management of city letter carriers. In 1992, one of the chief by-products of these efforts was a sophisticated information system called <u>Delivery Operations Information System (DOIS)</u>.

During subsequent years, the end result of DOIS was a dramatic increase in city letter carriers' tensions and turmoil in the workplace, having the overall effect of creating more stressful and toxic work environments within postal installations throughout the USPS. The immediate focus of this examination, however, is how DOIS has been utilized at many postal facilities throughout the country and its current status.

Before the implementation of DOIS, the USPS had several less sophisticated information systems to track individual letter carriers' performances. These previous information systems like DOIS frequently "pitted" the first-line supervisor in conflict with the city letter carriers. Both GAO reports of 1994 and 1997 indicated how close monitoring of the letter carriers by postal supervisors exacerbated problematic union-management relations and tensions on the workplace floor. Many of the tensions in the workplace chronicled in these reports were the result of performance management tools that tightly limited dialogue and compromise between letter carriers and their supervisors regarding workload issues.

Over the past twenty years, postal supervisors have relied on various information systems to determine the workload requirements for city letter carriers in the office and on the route. City carriers were expected by their supervisors to adhere to these determinations. When letter carriers failed to meet these determinations, they frequently faced increased negative attention from the supervisor. As indicated previously, DOIS is a more sophisticated information system compared to earlier ones. What they share in common is the emphasis on accounting for, and monitoring of, the office and street time of letter carriers and the implicit promise of reducing their work hours.

In August 2004, the NALC and the USPS entered into a memorandum of understanding (MOU) allowing for a freeze on all route adjustments, using the traditional route inspection process, and for a national task force, comprised of representatives from the USPS and NALC, to devise a new inspection and adjustment method. Shortly after reaching this agreement, the USPS rescinded the agreement and unilaterally implemented DOIS. There was a provision in the MOU permitting either side to terminate the agreement within fourteen days of advance notice, and the USPS exercised this option. In response to this action, Mr. Young, NALC President, stated that "management chose to throw away the opportunity and gave managers a go-ahead to resume daily bickering on the workroom floor."[256]

Although the NALC had contested the use and misuse of DOIS from the very outset, heightened concerns and outrage became more evident in several 2006 NALC publications. Below are relevant excerpts taken from these publications:

> The NALC is actively pursuing grievances over the uses—and abuses—of the DOIS computer system, but top USPS managers are still dragging their feet on it … More than a year ago we gave man-

agement a list of DOIS violations—chapter and verse, right out their own manuals and handbooks and our National Agreement ... One of the union's major concerns is how the corrupt data is used by supervisors to project letter carriers' work load on a daily basis.[257]

DOIS isn't broken—it never worked right in the first place ... What was supposed to be a data management tool has become an electronic mismanagement device. It's a perfect example of 'garbage in-garbage out' technology. The scary part is, they are using the corrupt DOIS numbers as a basis for all their planning, budgets, staffing levels, the works ... Too many carriers on the workroom floor are struggling with supervisors who believe they can use DOIS as a tool of intimidation to squeeze carriers more and more.[258]

[T]he system was deliberately misprogrammed to ignore elements needed to calculate a carrier's standard office time ... [A]n example of mismanagement linked to DOIS—is overtime. It starts when supervisors using DOIS projections to push carriers to speed up, a few minutes one day, a few more the next. If the letter carrier wants to avoid conflict, or "help out" the Service or the supervisor, or simply do the job and go home, he or she may absorb these minutes cutting corners, skipping a break—whatever it takes to make up the stolen time.[259]

For years, NALC has complained, and rightly so, about postal management abuses in their inflexible reliance on various information systems to monitor, control, and manage letter carriers' office and street time. The NALC has frequently filed formal grievances, arguing that postal facilities were using inaccurate data to determine letter carriers' office and delivery time expectations. They have argued, for example, that daily projections for letter carriers' workload and time expectations were based on inaccurate route adjustments or partial route adjustments or just unethical use of the data.

I personally had supervisors tell me that they were instructed not to use fair judgment in management of the letter carriers' duties, but instead were told to hold them accountable to whatever DOIS projected. I was told by some higher-level managers that DOIS estimates for carriers' productivity in their offices were based on flawed data. They were disturbed by the expectation from their "superiors" to discipline letter carriers based on this flawed data.

In the postal district that I had worked at, there were several facilities where city letter carriers were excessed (i.e., transferred) out of their offices based on flawed DOIS projections. In one station, letter carriers were excessed over three hundred miles, only to return as a result of grievances that supported that their positions were still needed, in accordance with the national contract and based on total employee hours worked at the station. Overtime, in many of these offices, soared to over 20 percent in the interim, creating hardships for the remaining employees.

In addition to the monitoring of city letter carriers' workload expectations through DOIS, city letter carriers were also electronically monitored before they left the office, while on the routes, and upon their return to the office. These electronically monitored points are called managed service points (MSP). In practice, letter carriers use mobile data collection devices (DCD) to scan barcodes placed at seven basic scan points. The scan points for the city letter carriers include: 1) hot case (i.e., resorted mail usually amounting to less than twenty letters, 2) depart to route, 3) first delivery, 4) last delivery before lunch, 5) first delivery after lunch, 6) last delivery, and 7) return to office.

In chapter two, I examined factors associated with workplace violence, including organizational factors. Two specific organizational factors that can lead to violence are high control and pressure. Dupree[260], for example, found employees were more likely to act out aggressively toward supervisors who tended to over control and pressure them to work at a specified standard or in a particular way. In the spring of 2008, the USPS entered a contract[261] for implementation of a Global Positioning System (GPS)/ Global Information System (GIS) to track letter carriers' whereabouts on the street.

At a delivery operations presentation in a September 2008 meeting for top postal management,[262] it was noted that the USPS had implemented a GPS/GIS program in five hundred vehicles in Chicago. It was further noted that the "global tracking system" recorded the following information from each vehicle: miles traveled, deviations from the route, idle time (with engine on and with engine off), number of stops and park points, and a "breadcrumb trail" of vehicle activity. The annual estimated cost for the GPS/GIS system for five hundred vehicles was 138 thousand dollars. The break even on the costs per route per day with the tracking system was noted as 1.4 minutes.[263]

Sadly, the USPS is not satisfied with DOIS and MSP; it wants more control in the form of surveillance. In order to meet its goals, postal management ostensibly believes that city letter carriers have to be monitored minute by minute while on their postal routes. In chapter eight, I provided examples of over control and pressure exerted and its impact on employees by postal management.

Fortunately, as a result of NALC pressure through the grievance procedure and the collective and bargaining processes, the USPS and the NALC reached agreement on DOIS in their most recent contract.[264] In this 2007 agreement, three major points were agreed upon, including: 1) DOIS is a management tool for estimating a carrier's workload, 2) DOIS projections are not the sole determinant of a carrier's leaving or return time, or daily workload, and 3) management is responsible for accurately recording volume and other data in DOIS. In addition to the above agreement on DOIS, the NALC and USPS also agreed to establish a national task force to jointly explore alternative methods of evaluating, adjusting, and maintaining routes.

On October 22, 2008, the USPS and APWU signed a breakthrough agreement for an interim alternate route adjustment process.[265] The agreement allows for a NALC/USPS route evaluation team at each postal district. The team responsibilities include "data analysis, route evaluation, and oversight of jointly conducted carrier consultations and adjustments."

It is too early to know if these agreements will have a significant effect on how letter carriers are managed in their daily operations by postal management. Sadly, based on the history of the postal culture, there is little reason to believe that this initiative will provide significant change regarding how employees are treated in the workplace, or that the level of stress or turmoil experienced by employees will be abated. Furthermore, the October 22, 2008, agreement has several contingencies, which are noted in a subsequent discussion on contracting.

Why not be more hopeful? Too many times, as described throughout this book, including this appendix, the USPS has not followed through on joint initiatives, one of which I discuss below, the "Joint Statement on Violence and Behavior".

4. Joint Statement on Violence and Behavior

In February 1992, shortly after the Royal Oak postal tragedy, the USPS and the union organizations and management associations signed a "Joint Statement on Violence and Behavior". All major union organizations entered into the agreement with the exception of the American Postal Workers Union.

After several drafts, Mr. Sombrotto was credited with authoring the entire statement. Two key phrases in this document, which were later ruled by a national arbitrator as a contractually enforceable agreement, include: 1) There is no excuse for and will be no tolerance of violence by anyone, at any level of the USPS. There is no excuse for and will be no toleration of harassment, intimidation, threats, or bullying by anyone, and 2) Those who do not treat others with dignity and respect will not be rewarded or promoted. Those whose unacceptable behavior continues will be removed from their positions.

Although a national arbitrator ruled that the joint statement was enforceable, and a few arbitrators "enforced" the agreement by "removing" management officials from their positions, subsequent decisions by the Merit System Protection Board (MSPB) and higher courts found such action infringed on the due process rights of these management officials. Aside from the contention that the joint statement was an enforceable agreement, an important question is: Has the "pledge" been honored by the USPS? It is the contention of the NALC, and from this insider's perspective, that the answer to this question is an unequivocal "no."

Since the joint statement agreement and my subsequent years as a postal employee, I became aware of a high number of management personnel who routinely harassed, intimidated, threatened, and bullied employees and later were rewarded or promoted to higher-level positions within the organization. For many of these individuals, treating employees with respect and dignity was not a priority and was rarely practiced. Specific examples of these observations were chronicled in chapter eight.

5. Contracting of Letter Carrier Positions to Private Enterprise

In chapter six and Appendix C, the burning issue of union bargaining rights was addressed. It was noted that Bush's presidential 2003 commission on the USPS recommended highly regressive reforms, including weakening of the postal unions' collective bargaining rights. The U.S. Congress, however, did not include any of these reforms in the December 2006 Postal Accountability and Enhancement Act (PAEA).

The postal unions have historically been concerned about the mailing industry's plans and attempts to privatize the USPS. More recently, the NALC has vociferously opposed the USPS's unilateral decision to contract out letter carrier positions at urban and suburban areas of the country, including cities in New York, New Jersey, and Iowa. This unilateral decision by the USPS occurred shortly after the BOG and neo-conservatives failed to have their regressive labor reforms incorporated into the 2006 PAEA. Besides highly organized picketing at contract sites, the NALC successfully lobbied congressional members[266] to support their cause to halt contracting of city letter carrier positions. While waging this battle to protect letter carriers' jobs, the NALC was concurrently involved in protracted negotiations for a new postal contract.

In no less than nine NALC union bulletins from November 1, 2006 to July 6, 2007, the NALC informed their members of their epic battle with the USPS and its lobbying efforts with congressional members to stop the contracting out of letter carrier jobs to private contractors. Before the USPS agreed to stop hiring private contractors to deliver the mail in various cities, Congress was posturing to pass legislation to prevent them from this practice. In fact, they had a bill in the Senate that had numerous co-sponsors to do just that.

The USPS and NALC agreed to restrictions on contracting out of city letter carriers positions in the new contract, which was ratified in November 2007. Shortly after a tentative agreement was reached with the USPS and the NALC on this issue, Mr. Young gave testimony in a Senate subcommittee where he eloquently stated:

> At a time of so-called prosperity, the ranks of workers without health insurance or pension protection have surged into the United States. Even as Wall Street profits have exploded, wages on Main Street have stagnated and middle class living standards have eroded. The federal government and the United States USPS should not contribute to these disgraceful trends by adopting an outsourcing strategy.[267]

I wholeheartedly agree with these sentiments as stated by Mr. Young, especially because of their relevance to our country's recession in 2008. Because of private enterprise's unparalleled pursuit of profits, regardless of the negative costs to employees and society at large, we are now witnessing a crisis in real estate, lending, banking, energy, unrealized since the Great Depression of 1929.

Fortunately, as previously mentioned, USPS and the NALC entered an agreement on a joint process to address route adjustments.[268] Additionally, this agreement extends the moratorium on contracting out of city carrier positions through November 20, 2011. This moratorium is contingent upon, however, the implementation of the agreed upon interim alternate route adjustment process. The agreement duration is also contingent upon future decreases in mail volume. If there are future decreases in mail volume and the parties cannot reach an agreement on a new process by June 30, 2009 or June 30, 2010, the original agreement will terminate.

American Postal Workers Union

The American Postal Workers Union (APWU) represents over 330,000 clerks (i.e., mail processing and customer service craft employees) and maintenance and motor vehicle service employees. It is the world's largest postal union. Like the NALC, the APWU contended with poor working conditions and poverty level salaries until the 1970 Wildcats strikes propelled the U.S. Congress to pass the Postal Reorganization Act of 1970. Major contentious issues between the APWU and the USPS can be subsumed under three categories: 1) violence in the workplace, 2) union-management partnership, and 3) contracting of postal positions.

1. Violence in the Workplace

From 1980 to 2001, Moe Biller was the president of the APWU. His tenure was marked by controversy, a no-nonsense approach to negotiating with the USPS, and a reputation for getting right to the point. Some just considered him a maverick. One quote from Mr. Biller that embodies these attributes is: "It is time that the USPS realized APWU is a stand-up union. We will not back away from our determination to achieve justice and dignity for all the Postal Workers we represent."[269]

In his testimony to Congress at the 1993 Joint Hearing to Review Violence in the U.S. Postal Service, Mr. Biller was the only voice from the postal unions and management associations who spoke with clarity and passion on the extent and nature of employee-directed homicides in postal facilities across the country. As a reminder to the reader, this congressional joint hearing was the result of numerous postal shootings in postal facilities by current or former employees.

It was noted in chapter four that the Postal Service, at this hearing and afterwards, provided meaningless statistics to detract from the "reality" of postal violence, particularly employee-directed homicide. In this light, below I provide two poignant remarks from Mr. Biller's testimony at the subject hearing.

> When the issue is faced squarely, what we see is not a meaningless industry-to-industry comparison, but a form of violence in the USPS that is reaching alarming proportions … I find it disingenuous that USPS management would rely on deceptive statistics to mislead the committee into believing the problem is not that serious.[270]

> Violence in the USPS must be addressed from an organizational and institutional perspective without pinpointing blame on an individual. USPS management must be held accountable for the safety and the health of its employees and that's what the contract reads.[271]

I unconditionally agree with both of these observations, and they are, to a certain extent, the underpinnings of this book. Organizational factors clearly play a key role in acts of workplace violence and a broader perspective is warranted. In order for the USPS to fully address workplace violence and its prevention in the workplace, honesty and transparency are prerequisites. Detractors of the APWU are eager to point out that Moe Biller was the only postal union president not to sign the 1992 "Joint Statement on Violence and Behavior".

Based on the fact that the USPS has not enforced key parts of the joint statement after its signing, many of Mr. Biller's reservations proved to be warranted. In 1997, he correctly pointed out the consequences of the lack of a viable internal procedure for addressing abusive managers in the workplace:

> Recent inquiries by the union to employees to identify abusive managers has generated hundreds of responses detailing the abuse acts of specific managers and repeated efforts by employees to have the abuses investigated. The results have been a "siege mentality" approach where abusive managers are at best assigned to other employees or, at worst, the requests are ignored. The refusal to hold managers accountable to the same standards as employees has

created a climate of distrust and lack of respect and unavoidably affects performance.[272]

Sadly, from the time of this statement and my retirement in January 2007, there remained a lack of accountability for management personnel who emotionally abused or bullied their employees, and a number of them were even promoted to higher-level positions. It would be an error in judgment to infer that this lack of accountability is not still the case today.

2. Union-Management Cooperation

Mr. Biller in his tenure routinely rejected any initiative where the APWU was not a bona-fide stakeholder in the outcome. Before rejecting the 1992 joint statement initiative, he rejected the employee involvement (EI) process adopted by all the unions with the exception of APWU in 1981. His perspective on the initiative was that these EI committees would have too much input regarding issues like safety, health, and work standards and methods. In his view, EI would create a wedge between APWU union representatives and the employees they represent, thereby serving to undermine the collective bargaining rights of the union.

In 1995, in solidarity with the other postal unions, the APWU boycotted the use of the "Employee Opinion Survey" (EOS) when its results were used by postal officials during collective bargaining deliberations. Mr. Biller noted that, as a response to the 1997 GAO report,[273] not one single question on the EOS was developed or approved by the APWU and questions that were formally objected to by the APWU remained. In support of the APWU position that they had no inherent objection to the use of, and cooperation with, surveying of employees, Mr. Biller pointed out that the USPS and APWU jointly designed a survey on dependent care[274] issues where the APWU had a role in its implementation and analysis of its results.

For several of the reasons noted above, the APWU rejected and later boycotted the new EOS implemented in 1998, which was renamed Voice of Employee (VOE) survey. It is important to note that too often complaints were lodged by branch AWPU officials in the field about misuse of the survey results to higher-ranking APWU officials.

Evidence of cooperation between the APWU and the USPS in the 1990s, besides the mentioned dependent care survey initiative, include: 1) 1990 MOU for "crew chiefs,"[275] 2) 1993 labor-management agreement,[276] 3) 1993 MOU for remote bar encoding system agreement,[277] and 4) 1994 meditation of grievances initiative.[278] The 1990 MOU for "crew chiefs" was a pilot program permitting craft employees to provide leadership and direction to rank and file workers. The view was that this initiative would *empower* these line employees to work more as a team. More importantly, the APWU viewed the crew chief position as a step removed from the autocratic management styles reflective of the postal culture. This initiative, however, was unilaterally tabled by the USPS commencing with the 1994 national agreement.

In the context of congressional oversight stemming from workplace tragedies at postal facilities,[279] the APWU and USPS entered two agreements on the same day in 1993, including the Labor-Management Cooperation Agreement and the Remote Bar Encoding System (RBCS) Agreement. Interestingly, the 1997 GAO report referred to the signing of the non-binding labor-management agreement as a quid pro quo between the USPS and the APWU, ostensibly because the USPS considered it as a prerequisite to its committal to the binding RBCS agreement. The essential points in the labor-management agreement were that the parties reaffirmed their commitment to, and support of, labor-management cooperation and that the parties pursue strategies that emphasize improving working conditions, improving service, and reducing costs.[280]

From the AWPU perspective, the critical agreement was not the labor-management agreement, it was the RBCS agreement. Before this agreement, the USPS was pursuing efforts to contract all work associated with RBCS to private contractors. The RBCS sites were set up in key geographical areas across the country and were viewed as transitional centers. They were to be used for a limited time span, with key responsibilities for coordination and processing of mail that involved change of addresses for postal customers.

The RBCS agreement proved to be the highest degree of cooperation between the USPS and any postal union in its history, the antithesis of top-down controls. There were no less than ten joint union-management committees working out the details of implementation. These joint committees addressed all aspects of work standards and methods, including staffing, scheduling, ergonomics, training, productivity, employee performance, safety, data, career opportunities, and minimizing administrative costs. All the RBCS sites included the previously discussed "crew chiefs," who played an integral role in accomplishing the overall mission of the RBCS.

Even when the remote bar encoding centers were phased out, the APWU and the USPS worked diligently together to transition employees to new positions at other facilities. As an insider, it is important to point out that employee morale at the center in my postal district was far higher than any other postal facility within the district. It had high productivity and low absenteeism and accidents rates. The initiative in hindsight was bold, innovative, and a breathtaking testament of what can be achieved when top management is willing to share "controls" with key stakeholders.

In 1994, a mediation of grievances process was established between the APWU and the USPS through the collective bargaining process. This initiative provided for the joint training of union and management officials on contractual issues and for the parties to collaborate to resolve grievances at the lowest level. However, the initiative did little to address the root causes of employee turmoil in the workplace and poor union-management relations.

In September 2008, the Postal Service unilaterally terminated a program with the APWU that fostered cooperation between employees and postal management. It was a pilot program that provided for a "team lead" for window retail services or clerks providing retail services. The "team lead," like the crew chief previously discussed, would, among other responsibilities, have been a voice to make recommendations to management regarding proper staffing for retail services. It was planned to be implemented nationwide, but APWU reports[281] that the program was terminated because bottom-line numbers did not improve.

Another example of the USPS acting unilaterally was reported in an APWU update, October 2008, regarding the elimination of Tour 2 at postal plants. For example, William Burris, APWU President, upon receiving complaints from field offices, stated:

> Postal management has failed to inform the national union of this plan, and no discussions on the subject have taken place. The union believes that this lack of consultation at the national level violates the employer/union relationship, and we will respond appropriately…The termination of Tour 2 mail processing may be intended to force senior employees to retire or accept unfavorable hours of work.[282]

Accordingly, the prevailing posture of the USPS to continue with its overall implementation of top-down controls with respect to work standards and methods remain unabated. The USPS attempts to weaken postal unions' bargaining rights by allying itself with President Bush's 2003 postal commission, and the contracting of positions to private contractors has served to further compromise the labor/management relations between the two parties.

3. Contracting of Positions

As an alternative to contracting out mail processing functions to private enterprise, the previously discussed 1993 RBCS agreement between the APWU and the USPS was the only mutually agreed upon initiative between the parties. To the chagrin of the APWU, for decades and subsequent to the 1993 RBCS agreement, the USPS has attempted to hire private contractors in mail processing, retail, maintenance, and transportation functions. In some cases, they have been successful and in many other cases arbitrators have ruled in favor of the APWU.

In 2005, or perhaps earlier, the USPS was embarking on an ambitious plan called Evolutionary Network Design (END),[283] which envisioned reducing their network of nine existing facilities types to five. This plan was requested by the Postal Rate Commission (PRC) on February 14, 2006, but was not provided to the PRC until July 25, 2006. The END plan contained a list of 139 facilities as "potential candidates" for consolidation.

Although the USPS was required by the Postal Reorganization Act to obtain an opinion from the PRC about plans that would have a "substantially nationwide" affect on mail delivery, they did not share this information with the PRC for nearly a year.[284] The USPS was also required, under its collective bargaining agreement with the APWU, to notify the union with its plan to consolidate facilities. However, the APWU did not become aware of the plan until it was disclosed in testimony to the PRC on February 14, 2006.

The APWU was so concerned about the veil of secrecy surrounding the END plan and its ramifications for its members, especially the potential of massive contracting of mail processing and transportation positions, that its national executive board raised union dues five dollars, biweekly, effective April 7, 2006, to help pay for a grassroots ad campaign and for the lobbying of congressional leaders.[285] In 2007 and 2008, two congressional bills[286] to prevent the USPS from unilaterally contracting out mail processing, transportation, or delivery positions gained widespread support in Congress.

It is important to note that the USPS never went completely ahead with its consolidation plans ostensibly because provisions in the Postal Accountability and Enhancement Act of 2006 were not finalized until December 2006. Congressional leaders later requested that the USPS submit its network redesign plan to Congress by June 20, 2008. In addition to this plan[287] and on the same date, the USPS submitted to Congress a seventy-page draft statement of work for contractors to submit proposals on contracting core postal operations[288] involving distribution, infrastructure, and transportation for bulk mailing centers. The Government Accounting Office also submitted a report, as requested by congressional leaders, on contracting of core postal operations in late July 2008.[289]

In the context of the USPS pressing for contracting of core postal operations, the PRC was tasked by Congress to conduct and complete a study on the universal obligation requirement and the postal monopoly by the end of 2008. The selection of the contractor by the PRC for this study has raised the ire and dismay of the postal unions and management associations, with the APWU the most vocal. In testimony to a congressional post-PAEA hearing on May 8, 2008, Myke Reid, APWU legislative director, stated:

> My concern is that the PRC has selected as its contractors people who are on the record as favoring privatization and as believing the postal monopoly is not needed. One of these individuals has written extensively on postal topics … In his testimony before the presidential commission, he characterized the postal monopoly as having insidious effects: stating that the postal monopoly: makes the Postal Service a victim, corrodes labor relations, intimidates customers, excuses endless political interference from members of Congress, and is the "chain the binds the Postal Service hand and foot" … The other principal contractor selected by the PRC is also on record favoring dismantling the postal monopoly.[290]

Since the BOG and the major mailers strongly appear to be unrelenting in their attempt to contract core postal operations under the auspices of the Postal Accountability and Enhancement Act of 2006, these issues will continue to be a source of high concern for the APWU. Not until they are resolved by congressional legislation, the fight over the privatization of core postal operations will wage on. Hopefully, the new Congress of 2009 will provide the leadership and subsequent legislation to stop the attempts of profiteers to "dismantle" the Postal Service. My open letter to Congress in chapter eleven provides a blueprint for these efforts.

National Postal Mail Handlers Union – NPMHU

The NPMHU represents approximately fifty-five thousand employees. The primary duties of the mailhandlers include the transporting or moving of the mail, principally within mail processing and bulk mail centers and plants. The NPMHU, like the NALC and APWU, historically have voiced concerns about the employee opinion survey (i.e., survey used between 1992 and1995), strained employee relations, and concerns about contracting postal positions to private contractors.

William Quinn, former president of the NPMHU, expressing concerns about strained employee relations and Postmaster General Runyon's responses to changing the postal culture, stated:

> One way to shake that managerial complacency is to make a dramatic change in accountability [emphasis added]. Just as not making the budget numbers can result in discipline of managers, so too should poor interpersonal relations with employees.[291]

In a recent publication to their members regarding contracting of positions, the NPMHU expressed concerns about the USPS's ongoing review of an option to contract postal positions at or near bulk mailing centers. In congressional testimony[292] on May 8, 2008, NPMHU President John Hegarty noted his concerns about network realignment, including plans for facility consolidations and contracting of postal positions. He indicated in this testimony that the union was fortunate to have the support of House Representatives for the Mail Network Act, an act that would prevent the USPS from unilateral contracting of postal positions.

National Rural Letter Carriers Association - NRLCA

Representing approximately sixty-eight thousand career rural carriers, the NRLCA, until recently, had very high morale and positive views of postal management regarding how they are treated in the workplace. A chief reason for these positive views is that full-time rural carriers' routes are evaluated, meaning that they receive a fixed salary based on route evaluations. In contrast to the city letter carriers, who are paid by the hour and receive overtime pay after eight hours, the rural carriers do not receive overtime.

Since the rural carriers routes are based on fixed salaries, they are paid the same each day, regardless if they work six hours or twelve hours. For this reason, historically the rural carriers' performance in the office and on the street was not a primary concern of postal management. Unlike the close monitoring of the performance of city letter carriers by postal management, rural carriers were generally granted more latitude in their starting time, how they cased their routes, and when they actually left the office to deliver the mail. Unlike city letter carriers, in the office they were allowed to routinely talk to each other while working.

Sadly, in the past three to four years, the way rural carriers were treated by postal management dramatically changed. Two of the last three contracts between the USPS and the NRLCA went to binding arbitration. The NRLCA twice filed national grievances, the most recent filed March 20, 2008. In the national grievances, the NRLCA argued that the previous route evaluations were improperly conducted.

I recall these types of concerns regarding route evaluations conducted in my postal district for rural carriers in 2005. In this particular evaluation, there were a significant number of rural carriers whose salaries were substantially cut as the result of the evaluations, some as much as 20 percent of their pay. From 2005 to 2007, I personally observed an increased focus on reducing rural carriers' hours by increased monitoring of their office and street duties, especially prior to their day off when they would be replaced by their substitutes.

These changes in the last several years have had an adverse affect on the morale of many rural carriers. At one time, it appeared most were exempt from a highly insensitive management style and the rigid work standards and methods embedded within the postal culture, but that has dramatically changed at many postal facilities.

The NRLCA disillusionment with the Postal Service unilateral and bottom-line approaches to solving postal issues is exemplified by its National Board decision to withdraw from the joint Quality Work Life/Employee Involvement (QWL-EI program) with the Postal Service January 1, 2009. NRLCA had participated in this program with the Postal Service for 26 years. As for the reason provided for withdrawal, the Board stated:

> We have concluded that the Postal Service's commitment to im-
> prove the workplace environment has been pushed to the bottom
> of the list of concerns. More and more, the Postal Service has insist-
> ed that the QWL/EI process work exclusively on issues that support
> its corporate goals.[293]

Like with the NALC, an employee involvement initiative of great promise comes to end because of lack of commitment by the USPS for genuine workplace improvement in the area of employee empowerment and decision-making.

Management Associations

The USPS has three management associations, including the National Association of Postal Supervisors (NAPS), National Postmasters of the United States (NAPUS), and the National League of Postmasters of the United States (League). Collectively, these three management associations give voice to approximately sixty-five thousand field management employees. Since these organizations represent postal management in the field and there are not many differences in their approach and relations with officials at postal headquarters, they are discussed both collectively and individually.

In the early 1980s, NAPS, NAPUS, the League, and the USPS agreed to an initiative titled "Management by Participation (MBP)." The purpose of this initiative was to improve communication flow and to provide more input by the management associations regarding postal policy, standards, and methods on behalf of management personnel in the field. In the 1994 GAO report, it was indicated that all three management associations' presidents and a headquarters official agreed that the MBP initiative over the years had improved relations between the parties.

However, as a result of the massive postal restructuring in 1993, the MBP initiative was discontinued. A high-ranking postal official reported to GAO investigators that the need for the initiative would be eclipsed by the management associations' eventual participation on leadership teams at each of the eighty-five postal districts. This initiative, designed for management associations to participate on leadership teams at the postal districts, never was implemented at some postal districts and, at the vast majority, the management associations presidents' participation on the teams were short lived.

Despite general agreement between the management associations and the USPS that the MPB initiative had been making a positive difference in employee relations, and similar to what was discussed with the postal unions, this termination of the MPB initiative is another sad example of the USPS unilaterally terminating an initiative with appreciable benefits. William Brennan, President of the League, in response to reading the draft of the 1997 GAO report, summed it up as follows:

> The USPS and the seven organizations' [three management associations and four postal unions] inability to jointly solve problems is not primarily caused by the leaders of this organization not being able to agree, but because not a lot of effort is being expended by the USPS to explore root causes when seeking solutions … Instead, it seems that going to the easier route of putting a Band-Aid on the effect is their solution … starting up initiatives that sound good, but never get off the ground, doing studies and then only using part of the data collected which is easiest to implement, ignoring causes of pressures in facilities, etc.[294]

Like the postal unions, the management associations have had strained relationships and concerns about the top-down controls employed by the USPS. Over the past several decades, critical and burning issues for management employees and the management associations who have represented them are increased demands with fewer resources, translating into working extra hours without additional monetary compensation.

In 1993, in testimony at a congressional hearing on postal violence, James Miller, former NAPUS president, indicated that there were many postal facilities with a shortage of staff and resources, unrealistic budgets, and excessive overtime. Mr. Miller indicated in his testimony that this state of affairs had improved in some facilities. Aside from this observation, he saw it relevant and critical to provide the committee a copy of his letter to postal headquarters officials, dated September 28, 1992, which stated:

> NAPUS surveyed our postmasters for their deepest concerns in 1990. The results of those surveys, shared with PMG Tony Frank, DPMG Mike Coughlin and other senior managers, indicated as serious problems: lack of complement, staff and budget, resulting in postmasters

working 10-12 hours a day, 6-7 days a week, taking administrative
work home to get it done, and creating unwarranted stress. CUR-
RENT [emphasis in the original] policies have compounded these
problems and escalated them to dangerous proportions [empha-
sis added]. The potential for violence has escalated accordingly and
now includes postmasters. As a result of stress, the violence would
include as dangers for postmasters—heart attacks, strokes, suicide,
and even murder. From our standpoint, this is unnecessary; it can
and should be prevented.[295]

It is important to note the above-referenced letter was titled "Consideration of Withdrawal by NAPUS from Participation In and Attendance at National Committee Meetings for Prevention of Violence in the Workplace." This committee was set up shortly after the 1993 Royal Oak tragedy with all the postal unions and management associations and representatives from postal headquarters.

The state of affairs described by Mr. Miller, in my opinion, became less of a concern from 1994 to 1996 because budget pressures were lessened under Postmaster General Marvin Runyon. After this brief period of relief, employee tensions and tur-moil began to dramatically change partly because of promotions of results-driven managers to high-ranking positions in the USPS and the budget becoming salient. Consistent with Mr. Miller's concerns, on March 7, 2007, the three management as-sociation presidents wrote an historical letter to John Potter, Postmaster General, requesting a meeting to discuss their mutual concerns about the deteriorating work climate for their members in the field. In this letter, the three signatories stated:

Postmasters, managers, and supervisors are under tremendous
pressure, with more requirements, reports, and unrealistic expectations. We are concerned these conditions, if not reviewed at our l
evel, could result in serious consequences [emphasis added] …
[W]e believe that these are issues that should be a concern for both
the USPS and the management associations.[296]

In response to this request, Charles Mapa, President of the League, reported on the League's website that the management association presidents met with Mr. Potter and he agreed that the numerous telecoms that postmasters and supervisors were forced to attend daily were of little value. He reported that Mr. Potter agreed to a "task force" to include the three management association presidents and two high-ranking officials at postal headquarters. Unfortunately, I was recently informed that this task force only met once and none of the issues were resolved. In fact, the management organizations' concerns and stress levels have exacerbated,[297] especially in light of a hiring freeze and further reduction of staff allocations in October 2008.

It is important to note, consistent with some of the previous concerns voiced by management association presidents, that Mr. Mapa in his testimony to congressional leaders on August 17, 2007 and May 8, 2008, expressed concerns on how their members were being treated in the field and concern about the privatization of core postal operations. In 2007, he testified that "[t]he Postal Service's style of managing postmasters is becoming more and more one of intense micromanagement, with an overlay of fear and intimidation."[298] In this testimony, he expressed concern about burnout of its members because of their working very long hours with fewer resources.

Similarly, in his 2008 testimony,[299] Mr. Mapa expressed concern about postmasters working long hours without sufficient resources and that higher-level management were using PAEA as an excuse to mandate postmasters to work six days a week, in violation of Public Law 89-116. In this testimony, he expressed concerns about union busting and the contracting of postal positions. In his 2008 congressional testimony, Dale Goff, President, NAPUS,[300] also expressed concerns with staffing shortages throughout post offices nationwide and attempts to weaken the USPS's universal service obligation.

Ted Keating, President, NAPS, in his testimony to Congress in 2008,[301] expressed concerns how the PRC was not providing adequate transparency and public review regarding the selection of a George Mason School of Public Policy contract to study the universal service obligation and the postal monopoly. Although the management associations were not invited to the July 24, 2008, congressional hearing on the postal network plan, Mr. Keating sent the subcommittee a letter for inclusion in the hearing record.

In this letter, he asked the following questions as they related to the postal network plan and the USPS's possible motivations:

> What is the ultimate goal? Is this the first phase of wider reliance on privatization of mail processing and distribution? Does the Service ultimately intend to contract out all processing and distribution of mail, if it believes

that service standards and customer service can be maintained at accept-

able levels?[302]

Summary and Concluding Remarks

Summary

The Board of Governors, in tandem with senior postal management, major mailers and advertisers, and neoconservatives, both within and outside the Bush administration, have tried but have been unsuccessful in scaling back union bargaining rights, contracting core postal operations to private enterprise, and in their attempts to virtually eliminate oversight and accountability by the United States Congress.

In the past fifteen to twenty years, the four postal unions, with the exception of the NRLCA, have had serious management labor relations problems with the USPS, mainly because of the USPS's implementation of top-down controls for work standards and methods. This management position is consistent with the long history of the USPS's adherence to the scientific management principle that any advantages of employee participation or input in workplace decision-making are far outweighed by its inherent disadvantages. The other main concern for the postal unions, especially in the last two years, has been the posture of the USPS to contract core postal operations, including mail processing, delivery, maintenance, transportation, and retail services.

In examining the three management associations, especially in the last several years, major, ongoing concerns regarding their members include: 1) working without appropriate staff complements and resources 2) ongoing intimidation by their managers 3) unreasonable expectations and workload requirements, and 4) burnout out due to working a six-day work week and over eight hours a day, on an ongoing basis. The management associations' presidents have all voiced concerns about the USPS attempts to contract out core postal operations.

Broken promises by the Postal Service in agreements with the postal unions and management associations have occurred too often in its recent history. Some of the broken promises discussed in this appendix included: 1) participation by management associations at district leadership meetings, 2) task force to address stressful working conditions of management personnel, 3) lack of enforcement of a zero tolerance agreement with postal unions and management associations, 4) termination with APWU on a "team lead" program for window retail services, and 5) termination of the 2004 agreement with NALC on a national task force for new inspection adjustment.

Concluding Remarks

On September 15, 2008, John Potter, Postmaster General, met with the four national unions and three management associations seeking their support to work with Congress as a result of declining revenue and a budget deficit of 7.5 billion dollars over the past two years. To the best of my knowledge, this is the first such meeting with these stakeholders with any PMG in nearly fourteen years. I find it disingenuous for Mr. Potter to meet with these officials in light of these concerns.

Why weren't these stakeholders invited to consult on issues of contracting of delivery operations, the network plan, and the overall direction of the Postal Service in the past several years? What expediency does this meeting provide for the BOG and future leveraging?

The USPS has a long history of using the scientific management approach, or <u>management unilateralism</u>, regarding the planning and implementation of work methods and standards. This approach discounts employee participation and input in workplace decision-making. Because of this deliberate and intentional stance, it has generated incredible anger, high stress, low morale, and violations of employee dignity and self-esteem—not just craft employees but also management personnel in the field.

In light of the Postal Service's history of broken promises with the management associations and union organizations, it is unlikely that they will honor the process for the duration of the USPS/NALC contract, which expires in 2011. Unless there are dramatic changes in the Postal Service, as outlined in chapters 10 and 11, the probability is that broken promises will continue to be the rule, not the exception.

The USPS's attempt to contract its core postal operations to private contractors and its secret work in network realignment of facilities has created high turmoil and anger. Together, these organizational factors have accelerated the deterioration of the postal culture in the past ten years, especially the last two years. From the postal employees' perspective, it is not difficult for them to conclude that the USPS not only does not care about employee participation or input, but it also does not care about employees' job security.

The postal unions and management associations have inadvertently added to the high tensions created by the approaches and decisions of the USPS. Postal unions have strongly lobbied Congress and have had numerous information pickets. They have released dozens of articles criticizing the USPS approach to contracting and flawed performance measurement systems, which were posted on union bulletin boards at all major postal facilities and their respective websites. Therefore, as a result of the unions' disagreements and "fighting back" with the USPS on these critical issues, they may have influenced their members to take even a dimmer view of the organization. And as a result, some may have become more demoralized and angry.

Employee tensions, anger, and damaged self-esteem described in this appendix do not bode well for the USPS's workplace environments at postal facilities throughout the country, nor does it bode well for prevention of workplace violence. The top-down control approaches, espoused and modeled by top management in the USPS, cascade through all layers of field management, and the fallout of its negative effects can be seen frequently and daily on the workroom floor. If these issues are not systematically addressed, they will worsen.

APPENDIX E
Impact of Postal Law Enforcement on Postal Culture

Since its inception, postal law enforcement has had a dubious history. In the areas of mail fraud, embezzlement of postal funds, and mail theft, it has had a remarkable and noble reputation. However, postal law enforcement has also functioned as a dark, vital third appendage of postal management, with the exception of a brief period in its history from 1997 to 2003. The old Post Office Department, from its inception, used inspectors to provide surveillance and enforcement within the confines of postal facilities and carriers on their routes.

Historically, surveillance in postal facilities included "cat walk" areas between the ceiling and the roof and "peep holes" within the circumference of the facility, and even inside locker rooms and bathrooms. Personal privacy of employees was generally not considered relevant or important. This practice of installing and utilizing "peep holes" in locker rooms and bathrooms reportedly did not stop until the 1950s. In postal law enforcement's early history, before the emergence of postal unions, surveillance on the letter carriers' routes included reporting back to postal management the smallest of infractions. Letter carriers were sometimes fired merely on the reported observations of a Postal Inspector.

Besides the issue of surveillance and privacy concerns being problematic in the history of postal law enforcement, there has been a seemingly lack of concern with employee due process and an overt inclination to "turn a blind eye" to the waste and even fraud of high-ranking postal officials. Less problematic, yet telling and very serious, has been postal law enforcement's apparent inclination to "over-protect" the image of the Postal Service. This was a notable concern conveyed in the 1992 congressional report[303] regarding the investigation of the Royal Oak massacre, where relevant records were not kept.

In this review, I assess the role of both the United States Postal Inspection Service (USPIS) and the United States Postal Service Inspector General Office (OIG) primarily in the context of their respective, recent history. The documents reviewed include several dozen OIG audits, OIG quarterly reports to Congress over the past eleven years, and postal union bulletins and legislative updates.

United States Postal Inspection Service (USPIS)

The USPIS is one of the oldest federal law enforcement agencies in the United States, initially set up by Benjamin Franklin in 1737 to protect the sanctity of the mail. Today, the USPIS employs approximately 1,770 Postal Inspectors and an additional 830 uniformed postal police officers to support them in their mission to secure the mail and to ensure the public trust in the mail. Their annual budget is 464 million dollars. Under current policy, the Chief Postal Inspector reports directly to the Postmaster General.

In a survey of nine thousand citizens, when asked by the Ponemon Institute in 2008[304] who was the most trusted agency, the USPS was named the top government agency four years in a row. What most people are unaware of, however, is that every year since 1998, "U.S postal authorities have approved more than 10,000 law enforcement requests to record names, addresses, and other information from the outside of letters and packages of *suspected* criminals."[305] Records obtained by *USA Today* under the Freedom of Information Act include years from 1998 through 2006.

Of the records obtained from 1998 to 2003, it was found that 97 percent of the information requests on "suspected criminals" were approved, and 99.5 percent were approved for 2004 to 2006. Requested records for 2007, under the Freedom of Information Act, were denied. The director of the American Civil Liberties Union described these activities as alarming. Considering that the figures do not include national security matters, it is even more alarming.

Besides the privacy concerns related to recording information from letters and packages of postal customers, President Bush added a statement to the signing of the 2006 Postal Accountability and Enhancement Act claiming the executive branch has unequivocal power to open mail without judicial review or warrant.[306] Interestingly, in response to these findings, a USPIS spokesperson indicated there was nothing new with the USPS or the executive branch having this authority.[307]

In addition to USPIS responsibilities to protect the mail and public trust, they are also charged with the responsibility to help secure a safe work environment for postal employees. Accordingly, they are active participants in many postal districts' threat assessment teams (TAT), which is discussed in chapter five. Their participation includes providing additional information to TAT members and assisting the TAT in developing risk abatement plans when a serious risk is present. In chapter eight, I discussed USPIS involvement on the TAT from an insider's perspective. The USPIS is charged with the responsibility of investigating credible threats and assaults committed by postal employees in the workplace or by customers on postal employees, while on duty.

Effective November 3, 2008, Al Lazaroff, Chief Postal Inspector, resigned under a "cloud of impropriety." Shortly before his retirement, he was under the spotlight of an ABC News investigation[308] and a congressional inquiry from Senator Chuck Grassley's office for the Inspector General Office to conduct an investigation. Allegations of impropriety from whistleblowers in the USPIS include that he wasted postal traveling funds to be near gambling casinos, spending 300,000 dollars in two years on travel while "on the road" from his duty station 70 percent of the time. Mr. Lazaroff also allegedly placed pressures on his subordinates to hire his "friends" as private contractors, and he had retaliated against the whistleblowers in his department who notified Senator Grassley of their concerns.

In response to Mr. Lazaroff's retirement announcement, John Potter, Postmaster General, stated that Mr. Lazaroff "has demonstrated a powerful focus on operational excellence and an unwavering commitment to this organization."[309] In the ABC News article,[310] it was further noted that Postal Inspectors reportedly indicated that the Postmaster General or his deputy approved all of Mr. Lazaroff's travel expenses. Senator Grassley reportedly stated in response that this raised questions about the judgment of the Postmaster General and it was "that attitude that there's nothing wrong, that's part of the culture of the agency, that we're going to protect ourselves."[311]

Office of Inspector General (OIG)

Brief History

In 1996, Congress passed the Inspector General Office Act of 1978, as amended:[312] authorizing the transfer of some of the auditing and investigative functions from USPIS to the newly created OIG and empowering the OIG with statutory oversight regarding the USPIS. The OIG currently employs more than one thousand one hundred auditors and investigators with an annual budget of more than 130 million dollars. The Inspector General is appointed by, and is under the general supervision of, the Board of Governors (BOG). It takes seven of the nine appointed members of the BOG to remove the IG for cause.

It is important to pause and to review relevant postal history at this juncture. In 1991 and 1993, two very important congressional reviews were conducted pertaining to postal culture and workplace violence within postal facilities. Also, in 1994 and 1997, the General Accounting Office (GAO) released two extensive reports[313] on the postal culture.

Accordingly, because of mounting congressional concerns and documented reports from the GAO about workplace violence and a problematic postal culture, coupled with the documented impression of some congressional members that the USPIS was not proactive in dealing with issues of workplace violence and had too close of an alliance with postal management, it is reasonable to conclude these were reasons that Congress included the USPS under the umbrella of the Inspector General Office Act of 1978, as amended.

First Inspector General (1997-2003)

Based on my observations as an insider, including documentary and anecdotal evidence, the USPIS has been too protective of postal executives over the years, especially at the officer level of the organization. With the appointment of Karla W. Corcoran by President Bill Clinton as the first Inspector General in 1997, the OIG was initially very aggressive in pursuing fraud, waste, and abuse at all levels of the organization. The first several years of Ms. Corcoran's tenure, postal officers, senior plant managers, and district managers were investigated by the OIG for allegations including sexual harassment, fraud, and waste. As a result of these investigations, several of these high-ranking officials resigned from the USPS.

Another fundamental and critical shift was that the new "OIG team" was ambitious in reviewing and making appropriate recommendations regarding the USPS's workplace violence program and was responsive to employees' allegations about abusive, intimidating, harassing, and bullying behaviors from postal management. Despite these achievements in the area of employee relations and in the accounting for fraud, waste, and abuse at all levels of the organization, Ms. Corcoran resigned as the Inspector General because of pressure from the BOG, Congress, and activist citizens groups. The President's Council on Integrity and Efficiency found a pattern of questionable expenditures and personnel practices during her tenure.[314]

In order to support the claims that under Ms. Corcoran's tenure the OIG was highly focused on employee concerns and workplace violence and actively investigated employees' concerns about abusive management practices, I have taken excerpts from seven of the OIG's semiannual reports to Congress from March 1999 to March 2003, and they are provided below.

> Excerpt 1: What are we doing to add value? To support manage-
> ment's effort the OIG participates in and monitors activities of the
> USPS Threat Assessment Team … The OIG meets regularly with
> committee representatives of the USPS Workplace Environment
> Improvement Human Resources and Labor Management to discuss
> strategies for improving labor and employee relations.[315]

> Excerpt 2: The OIG generally does not review individual employee
> complaints. However, over the past six months, we have performed
> 24 individual reviews of workplace violence and climate issues that
> resulted from Congressional requests. As a new agency, we under-
> took these reviews to develop a greater understanding of the Postal
> culture and to establish a working relationship with Postal Manage-
> ment to ensure that employees' concerns are addressed.[316]

> Excerpt 3: [T]he OIG determined that a plant manager treated em-
> ployees in an abusive manner … despite the fact that the district
> manager was aware of the plant manager's behavior, the labor cli-
> mate at the center continues to be hostile and intimidating.[317]

Sadly, despite this finding from the OIG, as noted in excerpt 3 above, the report stated that management did not accept their conclusion or their recommendations.

It is important to note that in each of the OIG's semiannual reports to Congress from September 30, 1999 to September 30, 2001, under the heading of "Workplace Climate," it stated: "The Postal Service believes that signs of workplace stress are present, and that they need to take comprehensive steps to address issues of improving workplace environment. This must be accomplished by the emphasis of **aligning human resources with business requirements** [emphasis added]."[318]

In subsequent reports from March 2001 to September 2003, the heading of "Workplace Climate" was changed to "Workplace Environment Reviews" and it stated: "The Postal Service has identified signs of workplace stress in many of its facilities and is developing comprehensive steps to improve the workplace environment, including improving relations between managers and employees and aligning human resources with business requirements."[319]

> Excerpt 4: The OIG reviewed and substantiated allegations of a hostile working environment that increased the risk for violence at a Southeast post office. The audit disclosed evidence that some managers verbally abused, harassed, and intimidated employees. There was also evidence that managers singled out employees for unwarranted discipline, resulting in monetary awards and settlements of about $70,000 to employees. The audit disclosed district officials knew of employees' concerns for about three years, but did not address employees' issues or respond to Congressional inquiries in a timely manner.[320]

> Excerpt 5: OIG audits at four postal locations, which occurred because of abusive management styles and aggressive measures used by managers to improve employee performance.[321]

> Excerpt 6: A review of allegations that a hostile work environment existed at a Virginia post office confirmed that it was potentially volatile because of harassment and intimidation by the postmaster. As a result of this review, the postmaster was reassigned to another facility and performance and conduct were monitored at the new assignment. We verified with Postal Service management, district management, and union officials [emphasis added] that the work environment improved as a result of the actions taken.[322]

Excerpt 7: A review was conducted in response to a Congressional inquiry relating to Postal Service management's treatment of
employees at a New York mail service center. [A] hostile work environment might have existed at this postal facility … Postal management developed several initiatives to resolve labor relations
problems at the facility.[323]

The excerpts and comments from the OIG semiannual reports to Congress cited
above during this timeframe (i.e., 1999-2003) illustrated the OIG's commitment to understand the postal culture, improve upon the USPS workplace violence prevention
efforts, and attempts to foster a positive workplace climate in the Postal Service.

Interestingly and telling, there were *no* OIG audits conducted *between August 1,
1997 and March 5, 2003*, regarding the implementation and utilization of methods
and practices used by postal management to control mail delivery, mail processing, and retail operations. To some observers, the absence of audits for these postal
operations by the OIG may seem irresponsible. If the auditing of these operations
also takes in account how specific management methods and practices impact the
postal culture and how their design and intent could be deleterious to productivity
or revenue generation, then the audits would be of high value.

In this next section, I discuss audits conducted by the OIG *after March 5, 2003*, that
focused on the methods and practices of postal management regarding delivery,
mail processing, and retail operations. None of these audits substantially reviewed
or took in account negative impacts resulting from inherent flaws in the methods
or practices from an operational perspective or from a management perspective.
These audits eventually served to significantly add to the stress, fear, anger, and turmoil in the workplaces of postal facilities nationwide.

It is also significant and telling that numerous audits were conducted by the OIG
between August 1, 1997 and March 5, 2003, regarding the *use of* outside contractors
by the Postal Service. In a significant number of these cases, impropriety (i.e., fraud,
waste, misconduct, etc.) of high-ranking postal executives and officers and agents
of the USPIS were noted. Many of these audits are listed on the OIG website but
are restricted and can only be obtained through Freedom of Information Act (FOIA)
requests. Aside from this obstacle, there is one audit on their website dated February 27, 2001 titled "Contracting Practices for the Procurement of Mail Transport
Equipment Services."[324] A chief finding in the report was that the USPS had obtained

three non-competitive bids where they did not follow appropriate procurement protocol. One of the chief conclusions was that the USPS could have possibly saved 53 million dollars if competitive contracts were sought and awarded.

Second Inspector General (2003-Current)

Since August 2003, David C. Williams has been the Inspector General of the USPS. He previously served as Treasury Inspector General for the Tax Administration, including with the Social Security Administration and Nuclear Regulatory Commission. His civilian government experience spans four presidents, from Ronald Reagan to George W. Bush. Before his civilian government service, Mr. Williams was an Army special agent with military intelligence in Vietnam and was honored for his service with the medal of honor and bronze star.

Beginning in 2003 with the appointment of the new Inspector General, Mr. Williams, the status quo of protecting the image of the Postal Service and its bottom-line approaches began to take precedence over responsive oversight of the postal culture, violence prevention initiatives, and the aggressive pursuing of fraudulent and wasteful practices of high-ranking postal officials. Since Mr. Williams' appointment as the Inspector General, the OIG's priority and focus increasingly became more in conformance with the strategic goals of the USPS in general, and their practices and methods in particular. In Appendix C, I examined the strategic goals of the Postal Service from 1998 to 2013.

There is ample evidence to support the conclusion that the OIG has become increasingly strident in its enforcement approaches in alignment with the USPS's strategic goals, practices, and methods. Accordingly, this conclusion is examined below in the context of: 1) OIG mission statement, 2) OIG audits of postal work methods and practices, 3) OIG privacy violations and surveillance of employees, and 4) OIG disregard for national collective bargaining agreements and the National Labor Relations Act. Before examining these four specific issues, however, I provide three relevant excerpts from the OIG's semiannual reports[xxxviii] from September 2005 to September 2007, below.

> Excerpt 1: Controlling delivery costs is critical for the Postal Service
> because mail delivery requires a significant infrastructure investment,

---

xxxviii   Reports are required submissions to the U.S. Congress.

especially as delivery points increase each year with population growth … Delivery operations are the Postal Service's largest cost center, making up 42 percent of the total labor hours in the FY 2006 Field Operating Budget. At the end of FY 2005, 100 percent of the DOIS facilities (6,198) have implemented AMSOP. DOIS provides delivery supervisors and managers with data (such as workload status reports and carrier performance information) to improve daily delivery operational performance … One of our initial Value Proposition Agreements is with the Vice President of Delivery & Retail to assess management of City Letter Carrier Operations [emphasis added]. During this reporting period, we expanded our ongoing assessment of city letter carrier operations to the Pacific and Great Lakes Areas.[325]

Excerpt 2: A management challenge facing the Postal Service is to control costs, especially given the significant infrastructure investment required to meet its universal service obligation. Delivery now extends to more than 144 million delivery points with about 290,000 city and rural letter carriers, and more than 6,000 highway route contractors with box delivery. Based on these facts and our work in related areas, we believe cost control continues to be a significant challenge for the Postal Service. The greatest opportunities to reduce costs are in the areas of optimizing the network to control delivery costs, increasing efficiencies of technology investments, and maximizing the cost effectiveness of contracts [emphasis added].[326]

Excerpt 3: In response to BOG questions about the Automation Category Management Center's (CMC) practice of awarding contracts to a limited number of suppliers, often noncompetitively [emphasis added], we reviewed the commodity sourcing activities within the Automation CMC. In general, the Postal Service effectively identified and maintained a mail automation supplier base consistent with its policies and business objectives.[327]

These excerpts highlight OIG focus and tacit support for the USPS Board of Governors' desire to maximize the contracting of postal operations, including minimizing findings with non-competitive contracts. It also illustrates the OIG's alignment with postal management in support of practices and methods utilized to monitor and control its operations and employees. These emphases in the tenure of IG Mr. Williams are in stark contrast to IG Ms. Corcoran (1997-2003).

In contrast to Ms. Corcoran's tenure as the IG, where there was a high emphasis on addressing a problematic postal culture and aggressive oversight of the USPIS and postal executives, in Mr. Williams' tenure there has been very little attention provided to the betterment of the postal culture, high tacit support of contracting of postal operations and other contracts, and reduced attention to misconduct, fraud, and waste by high-ranking postal executives or postal officers. The ensuing examination will clearly reveal that under Mr. Williams' tenure the OIG has contributed to the deterioration of the postal culture and has been delinquent in its oversight responsibilities as envisioned by statutory law.

1. OIG Mission Statement

The mission statement of the OIG is consonant with the USPS's **bottom line** and reveals their foremost intentions. For example, their mission statement is as follows:

> The USPS OIG achieves its mission of helping maintain confidence in the postal system and improving the USPS's bottom line [emphasis added] through independent audits and investigations. Audits of postal programs and operations help to determine whether the programs and operations are efficient and cost effective. Investigations help prevent and detect fraud, waste, and misconduct and have a deterrent effect on postal crimes.[328]

Interestingly, the mission statement on each of the OIG's semiannual reports to Congress differs from the one noted above, simply stating: "The mission of the U.S. Postal Service Office of Inspector General is to conduct and supervise objective and independent audits, reviews, and investigations relating to Postal Service programs and operations to:

- Prevent and detect fraud, theft, and misconduct.

- Promote economy, efficiency, and effectiveness.

- ***Promote program integrity***. [emphasis added]

- Keep the Governors, Congress, and Postal Service management informed of problems, deficiencies, and corresponding corrective actions."

The main difference between the two mission statements is the absence of the reference to ***promote program integrity*** in the subject semiannual reports and the addition of improving the Postal Service's ***bottom line*** on the website. Some may consider this distinction splitting hairs. However, after reading the subsequent examination, it is likely many will have a different perspective.

If, for example, the concept of *promoting program integrity* is viewed in the context of conducting audits for the purpose of assessing both the negative impacts and the positive impacts of methods and practices employed by postal management, then the issue of integrity is relevant. However, if the audits are conducted primarily to help the USPS with *its bottom line*, program integrity is at risk of being compromised. In other words, the negative impacts of methods and practices, ostensibly used by postal management to improve productivity, revenue generation decrease hours, and other sought-after organizational outcomes may be overlooked. With the change of "leadership" in the OIG in 2003, their audit emphasis reflects overlooking or ignoring the negative impacts of methods and practices employed by the USPS on the employees in the organization.

2. OIG Audits of Postal Work Methods and Practices

From July 26, 2003 to October 16, 2006, numerous OIG audits were conducted to evaluate the methods and practices used by postal management to control mail delivery, mail processing, and retail operations.[329] Initially, there were four audits conducted on mail processing operations, and later ten on delivery operations, five of which were conducted from August 8, 2005 through March 28, 2006. In September 2006, there were nine OIG audits conducted, assessing mail delivery, mail processing, and retail operations, within the nine postal areas of the Postal Service.

The five OIG audits of mail delivery operations from August 8, 2005 through March 28, 2006[330] were conducted under an agreement titled "Value Proposition Agreement" between the OIG and the Postal Service Vice President of Delivery and Retail. The purported objective of these audits was to assess the management of city carrier delivery operations. The common themes or findings of these audits, as they related to the management of city carrier operations by *facility supervisors and managers*, were as follows:

1. They did not always timely view the delivery operations information system (DOIS) reports to manage daily operations.

2. They did not adequately match work hours with workload when approving Postal Service Form 3996, Carrier—Auxiliary Control.

3. They did not effectively use the manage service points (MSP) base information to monitor carrier performance.

4. They did not always properly document letter carriers' unauthorized overtime occurrences and take appropriate corrective action.

What is interesting and revealing about these reports is that the OIG submitted them without indicating any concern about the reliability and validity of DOIS. The audit reports also did not take in account the enormous pressure and workload requirements on field management or how the use of the DOIS measure has negatively impacted the postal culture.

As mentioned previously, in September 2006, there were nine OIG audits conducted on mail delivery, mail processing, and retail operations within the nine postal areas of the Postal Service. These audits, like those previously discussed, were conducted under the agreement titled "Value Proposition Agreement," an agreement between the OIG and the Postal Service Vice President of Delivery and Retail. The nine subject audits assessed compliance with a myriad of standard operating procedures (SOP) required for field management, including SOPs for the management of rural carriers, city letter carriers, and retail clerks.

Some of the Postal Service's SOPs, as a plan to manage employees, are not necessarily problematic. What is problematic is how they are implemented and how they are monitored. For example, they are implemented with little or no regard for the already overburdened and understaffed supervisory personnel. They are implemented and monitored with little or no regard to how many hours supervisors or managers are required to work and without additional compensation, which is in violation of the Fair Labor Standard Act (FLSA).

Postal headquarters then cascades the SOP to the area offices, which add more reports and tracking tools to ensure compliance from the districts. The districts in turn add more reports and tracking tools to ensure compliance from large and medium-sized postal facilities throughout the district. Now, here comes the OIG to seek more compliance. This spiraling of reports, audits, reviews, telecoms, have had an extreme, deleterious effect on postal culture, especially for field postal management and the city letter carriers.

The OIG, in its consolidation report of the nine audits conducted in September 2006,[331] recommended more monitoring to ensure compliance with SOPs. Specifically, they recommended: 1) Area Vice-Presidents direct area managers of delivery program support to develop plans to address delivery SOPs, 2) Area Vice-Presidents direct district managers to follow SOPs and adhere to policies for matching work hours to workload, and 3) Area Vice-Presidents direct district managers at all units with ten or more rural routes for certification or self-review, and 4) Area Vice-Presidents to direct district managers to require unit managers to staff retail window operations using retail mart window operations surveys.

In the above-referenced OIG consolidation report, dated February 22, 2007, there is no mention of an understaffed or overworked supervisory staff or the additional burdens on supervisors, managers, and postmasters arising from nationally cascaded SOPs or the numerous violations of the FLSA. There is no mention of the serious flaws associated with the reliability and validity of DOIS. Also, there is no mention of how these top-down controls are negatively affecting the postal culture.

Clearly, what we see here is just another third arm of postal management turning a blind eye to issues and concerns that arguably are part of their official responsibilities. What we see is a radical departure from the focal points of the first OIG era, focal points that included the addressing of violence prevention, improving the postal culture, eliminating waste and fraud by high-ranking postal officials, and the wasteful and unnecessary contracting of core postal operations.

3. OIG Privacy Violations and Surveillance of Employees

As indicated previously, historically there have been numerous concerns regarding privacy violations of postal employees by postal law enforcement officials. On January 17, 2008, the APWU and NALC filed a joint lawsuit against the USPS and the OIG for violating postal employees' medical privacy.[332] The claim from the postal unions was that the OIG illegally obtained information from employees' medical providers, without their authorization. The claim stated that the OIG prepared and sent form letters to medical providers. These form letters purportedly advised the medical providers that the HIPAA privacy rule normally applies when releasing protected medical information, but "the OIG requests that you refrain from this notification."[333] In a similar form letter to medical providers in a request for medical records of employees, the OIG letter purportedly stated that "compliance with this request is mandatory."[334]

According to NALC officials, OIG agents illegally obtained protected information from medical providers regarding employees' on-the-job injuries and medical conditions related to FMLA or, in some cases, just questioning an employee's claims of being sick or not. The complaint as filed in District Court stated:

> In particular, Defendants (USPS and OIG—emphasis added) have adopted a policy and practice of interviewing employees' physicians and other health care providers and reviewing their personal medical files, with no notice to the employees.[335]

This is an egregious example of postal law enforcement acting as a dark, third arm for postal management and matching their zeal to accomplish objectives without concern for legal due process, basic fairness, or decency. Mr. William Burrus, APWU President, rightfully and passionately stated, "I am outraged that OIG would use the tactics of a police state to investigate workers' compensation or sick-leave cases. The OIG has no legitimate business investigating routine personnel matters. The use of these methods demands the strongest possible response."[336]

Surveillance of letter carriers by the OIG ostensibly took on a new low in 2006 to 2007. For example, in the NALC *Postal Record*, dated April 2007, Mr. Young noted:

> A wave of mass suspensions based on unsupported charges of mishandling mail, inappropriate interrogation techniques involving on-the-street interviews in OIG vans, and violations of the union's rights under Article 16 of the National Agreement have alarmed and angered NALC members and local officers across the country.[337]

Mr. William Young, NALC President, further outlined his concerns to the Postmaster General and Inspector General in a letter dated February 27, 2007. In this letter, he requested that these unwarranted abuses stop and stated:

> The OIG is supposed to save money not waste it. Surely, the OIG has better things to do with its $200 million budget than to harass letter carriers who are trying to do their jobs. Given the current controversy over the treatment of USPS funds allocated for the OIG's budget in the Senate appropriation process, perhaps this is a question for Congress.[338]

As an update to its members, an article in the December 2007 *Postal Record*, titled "Good Cop/Bad Cop—right here in the USPS," Mr. Young discussed some of the specific, alleged abuses of letter carriers by OIG agents.[339] He noted that OIG agents who investigated the alleged mishandling of mail by letter carriers in three cities led to more than one hundred removals. He also noted that, as a result of arbitration decisions and grievance settlements, virtually all letter carriers who were removed from their positions were allowed to return to duty, with full back pay, including lost overtime.

Mr. Young estimated the cost to the rate payers for these wrongful suspensions and removals exceeded well over one million dollars, plus several hundred thousands dollars for replacement workers. In one arbitrated removal case, a letter carrier with thirty-five years service was awarded not only full back pay, but also was awarded an additional half pay for each day he was in a non-pay status—a highly unusual award. In the decision, the arbitrator stated:

> The Postal Service's case against the Grievant was so lacking in substance that it bordered on an unconscionable act to place him on emergency suspension and then remove him … The Grievant testified that he has endured what can be described by the Arbitrator as a living nightmare. The Grievant lost his home, has alienated his family due to the mental strain he has endured, had the phone cut off, and has otherwise been dehumanized by the stripping of his career.[340]

In the article "Good Cop/Bad Cop—right here in the USPS" Mr. Young also "blasted" the OIG agents for illegally acting as a "health oversight agency" in obtaining protected medical records on employees, and "blasted" Mr. Williams' testimony in a 2007 congressional hearing, where he accused him of supporting a slow de facto privatization of letter carrier positions.[341]

This article presumably raised the ire of Mr. Williams. He wrote a memo to all OIG staff, dated January 16, 2008, "Subject: Response to National Association of Letter Carriers recent President's Message Referencing OIG," which was subsequently posted on the OIG website. In this memo, Mr. Williams attempted to address the issues and concerns expressed by Mr. Young.[342] In reading his response, I found no meaningful or cogent argument to support the egregious actions of OIG agents under his direction. I view the response as a very poor public relations attempt and arrogance reflective of eight years of rule by George W. Bush and his administration.

4. OIG Disregard for National Collective Bargaining Agreements and the National Labor Relations Act

Since the advent of the Postal Reorganization Act of 1970, postal unions have had bargaining rights on wages and benefits, including the percentage of employees' contribution to national health plans administered through the Office of Personnel Management and negotiated with the USPS in collective bargaining agreements. In spite of the relevance of collective bargaining agreements between the USPS and postal unions, the OIG conducted a "voluntary" audit where it demonstrated that the USPS would save 1.073 billion dollars annually, provided that the USPS contribution to employees' health plans was equal to other federal agencies.

William Burris, APWU President, delivered a "stinging rebuke" to the study, pointing out that it lacked relevance and completely ignored bargaining rights of the postal unions. Mr. Burris in a letter to IG Williams, with copies to the other postal unions and National Vice-President of Human Resources, dated November 16, 2007, stated:

> I am troubled that the Office of Inspector General has elected to
> insert itself into the collective bargaining arena without portfolio.
> Because the law does not confer such responsibility to the OIG, the
> audit report serves no constructive purpose ... Rather than produc-
> ing an irrelevant comparison of postal benefits to those in other

federal agencies, your office would better serve the public interest by exposing this collusion between major mailers and postal management, which circumvents the legal requirement of universal rates.[343]

Another recent concern of the APWU not only deals with the issue of the collective bargaining rights of the union, but also deals with the National Labor Relations Act and constitutional and statutory considerations. The APWU contends that OIG agents have displayed a disregard for employees' rights while they investigated them either as a suspect or a witness. For example, the APWU contended that the OIG denied employees a right to have a union steward present during an investigation and the use of intimidating and coercive tactics in attempts to obtain statements.

Initially, these contentions were placed in the November/December 2005 issue of *The American Postal Worker Magazine* in an article entitled "What's Behind Changes in Internal Investigations." The article engendered a written response from IG Williams to Greg Bell, AWPU director of industrial relations, dated January 11, 2006.[344]

In his response to Mr. Bell, IG Williams stated that the OIG was **voluntarily** complying with relevant bargaining right provisions.[345] In the letter, IG Williams did not deny or affirm any intimidating or coercive tactics used by OIG agents, but did defend the use of the new "advise of rights" form used by OIG in their investigations of suspected employee misconduct. In response to IG Williams' letter, on March 27, 2006, Mr. Bell stated:

> The Postal Service and its 'law enforcement agents' (Postal Inspection Service or OIG) obligation to adhere to the APWU collective bargaining agreement is mandatory, not optional or voluntary [emphasis added].[346]

Mr. Bell also noted in his letter that union stewards can appropriately advise the employees that they are not legally required to sign the new forms used by the OIG in their investigations and that they have the right to remain silent until they have legal counsel. It is important to note at this juncture that the Inspector General Act of 1978, as amended, sets unequivocal and clear boundaries regarding limits of OIG authority in the Postal Service. For example, it is stated:

Nothing in this Act shall restrict, eliminate, or otherwise adversely affect any of the rights, privileges, or benefits of either employees of the United States Postal Service, or labor organizations representing employees of the United States Postal Service, under chapter 12 of title 39, United States Code, the National Labor Relations Act, any handbook or manual affecting employee labor relations with the United States Postal Service, or any collective bargaining agreement.[347]

Mr. Young , as previously mentioned in the article titled "Good Cop/Bad Cop—right here in the USPS," also expressed concerns with the inappropriate use of interrogation techniques by OIG agents in their investigations of employees and their disregard for union rights afforded to them under the national collective bargaining agreement.

Summary and Concluding Remarks

Summary

Postal law enforcement has had a long, reputable history of dealing effectively with issues of mail fraud, embezzlement of postal funds, and mail theft. As a third appendage of postal management, however, it has not served postal employees well and has not effectively or willingly investigated misconduct by high-ranking postal officials. In its recent history, the OIG has ostensibly aligned itself completely to postal management's intent to privatize core postal operations. An exception to this history is the period from 1997 to 2003, when Karla Corcoran was the Inspector General.

In examining its recent history, the OIG has shown little respect for employee and union rights. It has shown little or no respect for employees' rights to medical privacy, the right to remain silent, and the right to have a union representative present to advise them during an investigation. In trampling on these rights, the OIG has violated the National Labor Relations Act, the 2006 Postal Accountability and Enhancement Act, the national collective bargaining agreements, as well as other statutory laws and rights afforded under the United States Constitution.

As a result of the examination of recent OIG history (i.e., 2003 to the present day), it becomes unmistakably clear that its mission statement, focal points, and emphases are aligned with the bottom line of the USPS. This means that the OIG not only audits the methods and practices of the Postal Service as it relates to its core operations, it also assists the Board of Governors and high-ranking postal officials in the oversight of these methods and practices. It is clear that the OIG under the "leadership" of Mr. Williams has provided tacit approval and support for privatization efforts of the postal Board of Governors.

Concluding Remarks

As I previously indicated in this book, one of the reasons why Congress may have amended the Inspector General Office Act of 1978 was concern that the Postal Inspection Service was too aligned with the image and "bottom line" of the Postal Service. However, it took "whistle blowers," a congressional inquiry, and a network investigation to bring to light the alleged impropriety of the USPS Chief Postal Inspector. It makes me wonder if the OIG was on top of this, and, if not, why.

Some may ask the question: Why has the OIG become so aligned with the USPS's bottom line and the USPS's push to weaken the notion of universal service, thereby opening the door for major contracting of core postal operations? The answer is in great part political. All federal agencies and the USPS have experienced unprecedented pressure from the Bush administration to contract as many core functions as possible.

Under the helm of the BOG, this unprecedented pressure translates into attempts to open the door for major mailers to become contractors for transportation, maintenance, mail processing, and delivery positions. Recall that the mailing apparatus in the United States is a 900 billion dollar industry. If the universal service requirement can be relaxed by congressional legislation, or the USPS is allowed to contract postal core services, this means huge profits for many of these contractors involved in the mailing industry. It also would mean the "Wal-Martinizing" of future employees who will transport, process, and deliver public and private mailings.

When looking at the political climate that existed under the Bush administration, it becomes clear why the agenda and tactics of the postal OIG were reflective of having no respect for the rights of employees, unions, national bargaining agreements, National Relations Act, or statutory and constitutional law. Not only has the Bush administration pushed hard on the issue of contracting, it has also uniformly used its influence through the courts and other federal departments to weaken and lessen the influence of all unions, including postal unions. Additionally, this administration has set up a government-wide policy through the Attorney General Office, where high-ranking law enforcement agents of the government were required to rigidly limit public access to information and authorized unprecedented authority to obtain private information on its citizens, including federal and civilian employees.

The results of the focus, mission, and tactics of the OIG has had a far-reaching, negative impact on the postal culture. Although it may have been initially envisioned by Congress as a major contributor to the oversight and improvement of postal culture and violence prevention efforts when it amended the Attorney General Act in 1996, instead it has **significantly** worsened the USPS's organizational culture.

What employee would trust to call or write the OIG to address an abusive management official? It's now back on Congress' doorstep, and it is unlikely that any of the major concerns noted herein will be fully addressed until the advent of the 2009 Congress. In the meantime, the OIG will remain as the unabated third appendage of the BOG and the postal culture will continue to worsen. The specter of more toxic work environments at postal facilities throughout the USPS and an increased potential for workplace violence are the end result.

ENDNOTES

Chapter One

1   The American Heritage Dictionary 3rd edition (1996, p. 1994). Houghton Mifflin Company, NY.
2   Medical Research Council (2001). Draft paper: The impact of crime and violence on the delivery of state health care services in the Western Cape. Presented by Sandra Marais on 10/18/2001 at Unisa Institute in Lenasia. Retrieved 5/2/08 from http://www.icn.ch/SewWorkplace/WPV_HS_SouthAfrica.pdf.
3   Hershcovis, S.M., Turner, N., Barling, J., Arnold, K.A., Dupree, K.E., & Inness, M. (2007). Predicting workplace aggression: A meta-analysis. Journal of Applied Psychology, 92 (1), 228-238.
    Schat, A.C, Frone, M., & Kelloway, K. (2006). Prevalence of workplace aggression in the U.S. workforce. In: E.K. Kelloway, J. Barling. & J.J. Hurrell (Eds.) (2006). Handbook of Workplace Violence. Thousand Oaks, CA: Sage.
    Baron, R.A., Neuman, J.H. (1996). Workplace violence and workplace aggression: Evidence on their relative frequency and potential causes. Aggressive Behavior, 22, 161-173.
    Keashley, L., & Newman, J. H. (2005). Bullying in the workplace: Its impact and management. Employee Rights and Employment Policy Journal, 8, 335-373.
4   Brodsky, C. (1976, p. 46).The harassed worker. Lexington, MA: D.C. Health and Company.
5   Ibid., 2.
6   Leymann, H. (1990). Mobbing and psychological terror at workplaces. Violence and Victims, 5, 119-126.
7   Leymann, H. (1996, p. 168). The content and development of mobbing at work. European Journal of Work and Organizational Psychology, 5 (2),165-184.
8   Einsaren, S., Raknes, B. (1997). Harassment in the workplace and the victimization of men. Violence and Victims, 12 (3), 247-263.
9   Keashley, L. (1998). Emotional abuse in the workplace: Conceptual and empirical issues. Journal of Emotional Abuse, 1 (1), 85-117.
10 Ibid.
11 Keashley, L., & Harvey, S. (2005, p. 205). Emotional abuse in the workplace. In S. Fox & P. Spector (Eds.), Counterproductive work behaviors (pp. 201-236). Washington DC: American Psychological Association.
12 Namie, G. (2003). Workplace bullying: Escalated incivility. Ivey Business Journal, Nov/Dec, 1-6.
13 Meglich-Sespico, P., Faley, R.H., & Knapp, D.E. (2007). Relief and redress for targets of workplace bullying. Employee Responsibilities and Rights Journal, 19 (1), 31-43.
14 Issacs, A. (2001, p. 6). Workplace Violence: Issues in Response. Critical Incident Response Group, National Center for Analysis of Violent Crime, FBI Academy, Quantico, VA. Retrieved from 4/2/08 from http://www.fbi.gov/publications/violence.pdf.
15 National Center on Addiction and Substance Abuse at Columbia University (2000). Report of the USPS Commission on a Safe and Secure Workplace. New York: Author.

Chapter Two

16 Northwestern National Life Insurance (1993). Fear and violence in the workplace: A survey documenting the experience of American workers. Minneapolis, MN: Author.
17 Namie, G. (2000). The WBTI report on U.S. hostile workplace survey 2000. Retrieved 9/26/07 from www.bullyinginstitute.org.
18 Lutgen-Sandvik, P., Tracy, S., & Alberts, J. (2007). Burned by bullying in the American workplace: Prevalence, perception, degree and impact. Journal of Management Studies, 44 (6), 837-862.

19   Namie, G. (2007). The WBTI 2007 U.S. Workplace Survey on bullying. Retrieved 9/26/07 from www.bullyinginstitute.org.2007.

20   Schat, A.C , Frone, M. & Kelloway, K. (2006). In: Kelloway, K., Barling, J., & Hurrel, J.J. (Eds.), 47-61. Handbook of Workplace Violence. Thousand Oaks, CA: Sage.

21   DHHS (1995). Preventing homicide in the workplace: NIOSH ALERT: May 1995. DHHS (NIOSH) Publication No. 93-109. Author. Retrieved 1/20/08 from: http://www.cdc.gov/Niosh/homicide.html.

22   Bureau of Labor Statistics (2006). National census of fatal occupational injuries in 2006. Author. Retrieved 1/20/08 from: http://www.bls.gov/iif/oshcfoi1.htm.

23   Ibid.

24   Babiak, P., & Hare, R.D. (2006). Snakes in suits: When psychopaths go to work. HarperCollins Publishers, New York.

25   Mantell, M., & Albrecht, S. (1994, p. 42). Ticking Bombs: Defusing violence in the workplace. Irwin Publishing, New York.

26   Coleman., C. (2004). The Copycat effect: How the media and popular culture trigger the mayhem in tomorrow's headlines. Pocket Books: New York.

27   Lasseter, D. (1997). Going postal. Kensington Publishing: New York.

28   National Center on Addiction and Substance Abuse at Columbia University (2000). Report of the USPS Commission on a Safe and Secure Workplace. New York: Author.

Chapter Three

29   National Center on Addiction and Substance Abuse at Columbia University (2000). Report of the USPS Commission on a Safe and Secure Workplace. New York: Author.

30   Wikipedia (2008). This term first appeared in print on December 17, 1993 in the St. Petersburg Times. Retrieved 2/10/08 from http://en.wikipedia.org/wiki/Going_postal.

31   NIOSH (1993). Fatal Injuries to workers in the United States, 1980-1989. Retrieved 3/2/08 from http://www.cdc.gov/NIOSH/93-108.html.
     Centers for Disease Control and Prevention (CDC) (1994). Occupational injury deaths of postal workers—United States, 1980-1989. MMWR 43(32):587, 593-595. Retrieved 3/2/08 from http://www.cdc.gov/mmwr/preview/mmwrhtml/00032345.htm.

32   NIOSH (1993). Fatal Injuries to workers in the United States, 1980-1989.

33   Centers for Disease Control and Prevention (CDC) (1994). Occupational injury deaths of postal workers.

34   National Center on Addiction and Substance Abuse at Columbia University (2000).

35   Ibid., 1.

36   Ibid., 1.

37   Ibid., 1.

38   United States Postal Service (1997). "Going Postal": Myth or reality. Postal Life. Retrieved 2/10/08 from http://www.usps.com/history/plife/pl011697/cover.htm.

39   United States Postal Service (1998). USPS 1998 Postal Publication 45. Retrieved 2/10/08 from www.nalc.org/depart/cau/pdf/manuals/pub45.pdf.

40   Ibid.

41   United States Postal Inspection Service (2000). Annual Report of Investigation 2000. Retrieved 2/4/08 from http//www.usps.com-postalinspectors-ar00_02.pdf.

42   United States Postal Service (2006). USPS commission on a safe and secure workforce. United States Postal Service (2006). Public Affairs and Communications Department, 1/31/06. Retrieved 3/1/08 from http://www.usps.com/communications/news/press/2006/pr06_0131commission.htm.

43   Howland Group (2008). Interview with Dennis Johnson. Retrieved 1/5/08 from http://www.howlandgroup.com/johnson.htm.

44 Rendon, J., & Dougherty, J. (2000). "Going postal": A new definition and model for employment ADR. Retrieved 3/4/08 from http://www.txmediator.org/toolkit/Going%20Postal.htm.

45 Anderson, G. (2006). Avoiding aggressive behavior at work. Retrieved 3/1/08 from http://www.andersonservices.com/blog/?p=256.

46 Ibid.

47 Temple, P. (2000). Real danger and postal mythology: Dealing with workplace violence. Workforce, 79 (10), 4.

48 VandenBos, G., & Bulatao (1996, Introduction to Part IV). Violence on the job: Identifying and developing solutions. American Psychological Association (APA): Washington D.C.

49 Kurutz, J.G., Johnson, D.L., & Sugden (1996). The United States Post Service employee assistance program: A multifaceted approach to workplace violence prevention. In Violence on The Job: Identifying and Developing Solutions, (Eds). VandenBos, G., & Bulatao. American Psychological Association (APA): Washington D.C.

50 Paludi, M., Nydegger, R. & Paludi, C. (2006, p. 3) Understanding workplace violence: A guide for managers and employees. Praeger Publishers: CT.

Chapter Four

51 Centers for Disease Control and Prevention (CDC) (1994). Occupational injury deaths of postal workers—United States, 1980-1989. MMWR 43(32):587, 593–595.

52 National Center on Addiction and Substance Abuse at Columbia University (2000). Report of the USPS Commission on a Safe and Secure Workplace. New York: Author.

53 Centers for Disease Control and Prevention (CDC) (1994, editorial note).

54 Ibid.

55 DHHS (1995). Preventing homicide in the workplace: NIOSH ALERT: May 1995. DHHS (NIOSH) Publication No. 93-109.

56 Fearn-Banks, K (2007). Crisis Communications. Lawrence Erlbaum Associates, Publishers: New Jersey.

57 Ibid., 241.

58 Ibid., 243.

59 National Center on Addiction and Substance Abuse at Columbia University (2000, p. 1).

60 Fox, J. A. (1994, p. 25). Firing back: The growing threat of workplace homicide. Annals of the American Academy of Political and Social Science, 536 (1), 16-30.

61 Baxter, V.K. (1994, p. 188). Labor and politics in the U.S. Postal Service. Plenum Press: New York.

62 Joint hearing to review violence in the U.S. Postal Service: Joint hearings before the Subcommittee on Census, Statistics, and Postal Personnel and the Subcommittee on Postal Operations and Services of the Committee on Post Office and Civil Service, House of Representatives, One Hundred Third Congress, first session, August 5; October 14 and 19, 1993 United States (1994, p. 59). Congress. House. Committee on Post Office and Civil Service. Subcommittee on Census, Statistics, and Postal Personnel: Washington.

63 National Center on Addiction and Substance Abuse at Columbia University (2000, cover letter to report & p. 1).

64 Ibid., 2.

65 Ibid., cover letter to report & 1.

66 Schat, A.C , Frone, M. & Kelloway, K. (2006, p. 56). Prevalence of workplace aggression in the U.S. workforce. In: E.K. Kelloway, J. Barling. & J.J. Hurrell (Eds.). Handbook of Workplace Violence. Thousand Oaks, CA: Sage.

67 Ibid., 28.

68 Ibid., 26, Chart 6.

69 Ibid., 29, Chart 11.

70 Northwestern National Life Insurance (1993). Fear and violence in the workplace: A survey documenting the experience of American workers. Minneapolis, MN: Author.

71 Namie, G. (2007). The WBTI 2007 U.S. Workplace Survey on Bullying. Retrieved 9/26/07 from www.bullyinginstitute.org.2007.

72 National Center on Addiction and Substance Abuse at Columbia University (2000, p. 13 & p. 28).

73 Ibid., Appendix C.1, Question 18.

74 Northwestern National Life Insurance (1993). Fear and violence in the workplace.

75 Schat, A.C , Frone, M. & Kelloway, K. (2006). In: Kelloway, K., Barling, J., & Hurrel, J.J. (Eds.), 47-61. Handbook of Workplace Violence. Thousand Oaks, CA: Sage.

76 National Center on Addiction and Substance Abuse at Columbia University (2000, appendix C.1, question 33).

77 Ibid., 26, Chart 6.

78 Ibid., 29, Chart 11.

79 Ibid., 13 & 286.

80 Ibid., Appendix C.1, question 34.

Chapter Five

81 General Accounting Office (GAO) (1986). Postal Service: Employee-Management relations at the Evansville, Indiana, post office. Report to congressional requestors.
General Accounting Office (GAO) (1988). Postal Service: Labor-management relations and customer services at the Simi Valley, California, post office. Report to Chairman, Committee on Post Office and Civil Service, House of Representatives.
General Accounting Office (GAO) (1989). Postal Service: Improved labor/management relations at the Oklahoma post office. Report to the Honorable Mickey Edwards, House of Representatives.
General Accounting Office (GAO) (1990). Postal Service: Employee-management relations at the Indianapolis post office are strained. Report to congressional requestors.

82 U.S. Congress, House of Representatives (1992). A post office tragedy: The shootings at Royal Oak (Serial 102-7): Hearings before House Post Office and Civil Service Committee. Government Printing House: Washington D.C.

83 General Accounting Office (GAO) (1994). U.S. Postal Service: Labor management problems persist on the workroom floor. Report to congressional requestors.
General Accounting Office (GAO) (1997). U.S. Postal Service: Little progress made in addressing persistent labor-management problems. Report to Chairman, Subcommittee on Government Reform and Oversight, House of Representatives.

84 Joint hearing to review violence in the U.S. Postal Service: Joint hearings before the Subcommittee on Census, Statistics, and Postal Personnel and the Subcommittee on Postal Operations and Services of the Committee on Post Office and Civil Service, House of Representatives, One Hundred Third Congress, first session, August 5; October 14 and 19, 1993 United States (1994). Congress. House. Committee on Post Office and Civil Service. Subcommittee on Census, Statistics, and Postal Personnel: Washington.

85 National Center on Addiction and Substance Abuse at Columbia University (2000, p. 43). Report of the USPS Commission on a Safe and Secure Workplace. New York: Author.

86 Joint hearing to review violence in the U.S. Postal Service: U.S. Congress (1994, p. 61).

87 National Center on Addiction and Substance Abuse at Columbia University (2000, p. 48).

88 United States Postal Service (1997). Threat Assessment Team Guide. Retrieved 4/1/08 from www.nalc.org/depart/cau/pdf/manuals/pub108.pdf.

89 Joint hearing to review violence in the U.S. Postal Service: U.S. Congress (1994, p. 97).

90 National Center on Addiction and Substance Abuse at Columbia University (2000, pp. 83-84).

91   United States Postal Service (2001). Publication 106, Guide to Professional Parting: Details on Handling Separations. No longer available.

92   National Center on Addiction and Substance Abuse at Columbia University (2000, p. 49 & p. 86).

93   Mantell, M. & Albrecht, S. (1994, p. 165). Ticking Bombs: Defusing violence in the workplace. Irwin Publishing, New York.

94   Baron, A.S., Hoffman, S.J., & Merrill, J.G. (2000). When work equals life: The next stage of workplace violence. Pathfinders Publishing, Inc.: California.

95   United States Postal Service (2000) Presentation by Suzanne Milton, former manager, Workplace Environment Improvement, in August 2000. Retrieved 2/5/08 from http://www1.va.gov/vasafety/docs/wcc072-1.ppt.

96   National Center on Addiction and Substance Abuse at Columbia University (2000, p. 49 & p. 86).

Chapter Six

97   Postal Reorganization Act of 1970 (39 U.S.C. § 206).

98   Wikipedia (2008). Origin of the word postmaster. Retrieved 4/2/08 from http://en.wikipedia.org/wiki/Mail.

99   Towards postal excellence: The report of the President's Commission on postal organization (1968, p. 3). Government Printing Office: Washington D.C. Author.

100 Postal Reorganization Act of 1970 (39 U.S.C. § 206).

101 National Association of Letter Carriers (2008). The Postal Service is self-sufficient. Retrieved 2/4/08 from http://www.nalc.org/postal/perform/selfsufficient.html#selfsufficient.

102 Baxter, V.K. (1994, p. 95). Labor and politics in the U.S. Postal Service. Plenum Press: New York.

103 General Accounting Office (GAO) (2008). U.S. Postal Service: USPS has taken steps to strengthen network realignment planning and accountability and improve communication. Testimony before subcommittee on Federal Workforce, Postal Service, and the District of Columbia, Committee on Oversight and Accountability and Government Reform, House of Representatives.

104 Towards postal excellence: The report of the President's Commission on postal organization (1968).

105 Kick, E. L., Fraser, J. C., & Davis, B.L. (2006, p. 140). Performance management, managerial citizenship and worker commitment: A study of the United States Postal Service with some global implications. Economic & Industrial Democracy, 27(1), 137-172.

106 Baxter, V., Margavio, A. (1996, p. 284). Assaultive Violence in the U.S. Post Office. Work & Occupations, 23(3).

107 Ibid., 293.

Chapter Seven

108 Towards postal excellence: The report of the President's Commission on postal organization (1968). Government Printing Office: Washington D.C. Author.

109 Ibid.

110 Ibid., 3.

111 General Accounting Office (GAO) (1986). Postal Service: Employee-Management relations at the Evansville, Indiana, post office. Report to congressional requestors.

General Accounting Office (GAO) (1988). Postal Service: Labor-management relations and customer services at the Simi Valley, California, post office. Report to Chairman, Committee on Post Office and Civil Service, House of Representatives.

General Accounting Office (GAO) (1989). Postal Service: Improved labor/management relations at the Oklahoma post office. Report to the Honorable Mickey Edwards, House of Representatives.

General Accounting Office (GAO) (1990). Postal Service: Employee-management relations at the Indianapolis post office are strained. Report to congressional requestors.

General Accounting Office (GAO) (1992). Royal Oaks Tragedy (GAO/GGD-92-29R). Memorandum from L. Nye Stevens, Director, Government Business Operations and Information Issues to the Honorable William S. Broomfield, House of Representatives.

U.S. Congress, House of Representatives (1992). A post office tragedy: The shootings at Royal Oak (Serial 102-7): Hearings before House Post Office and Civil Service Committee. Government Printing House: Washington D.C.

[112] U.S. Congress, House of Representatives (1992). A post office tragedy.

[113] General Accounting Office (GAO) (1986). Postal Service: Employee-management relations.

[114] General Accounting Office (GAO) (1988). Postal Service: Labor-management relations and customer services.

[115] General Accounting Office (GAO) (1989). Postal Service: Improved labor/management relations.

[116] Ibid., 9.

[117] Ibid.,16.

[118] U.S. Congress, House of Representatives (1992). A post office tragedy.

[119] General Accounting Office (GAO) (1990). Postal Service: Employee-management relations.

[120] U.S. Congress, House of Representatives (1992, pp. 63-64). A post office tragedy.

[121] Ibid., 15.

[122] Ibid., 16

[123] Ibid, 17-18.

[124] Ibid., 21.

[125] Ibid., 64.

[126] Ibid., 64.

[127] Ibid., 329.

[128] Ibid., 331.

[129] General Accounting Office (GAO) (1992). Royal Oaks Tragedy (GAO/GGD-92-29R). Memorandum from L. Nye Stevens, Director, Government Business Operations and Information Issues to the Honorable William S. Broomfield, House of Representatives.

[130] Ibid., 2.

[131] Joint hearing to review violence in the U.S. Postal Service: Joint hearings before the Subcommittee on Census, Statistics, and Postal Personnel and the Subcommittee on Postal Operations and Services of the Committee on Post Office and Civil Service, House of Representatives, One Hundred Third Congress, first session, August 5; October 14 and 19, 1993 United States (1994). Congress. House. Committee on Post Office and Civil Service. Subcommittee on Census, Statistics, and Postal Personnel: Washington.

[132] Ibid., 19.

[133] Ibid., 24.

[134] General Accounting Office (GAO) (1994). U.S. Postal Service: Labor management problems persist on the workroom floor. Report to congressional requestors.

[135] General Accounting Office (GAO) (1997). U.S. Postal Service: Little progress made in addressing persistent labor-management problems. Report to Chairman, Subcommittee on Government Reform and Oversight, House of Representatives.

[136] General Accounting Office (GAO) (1994, p. 6). U.S. Postal Service: Labor management problems persist on the workroom floor.

137 General Accounting Office (GAO) (1997, p. 6). U.S. Postal Service: Little progress made in addressing persistent labor-management problems.

138 Postal Reporter Web Site (2008). USPS to eliminate 2,400 supervisor positions? Retrieved 2/19/08 from http://www.postalreporter.com/news/2008/03/19/usps-to-eliminate-2400-supervisor-positions.

139 General Accounting Office (GAO) (1997, p. 1). U.S. Postal Service: Little progress made in addressing persistent labor-management problems.

140 National Center on Addiction and Substance Abuse at Columbia University (2000). Report of the USPS Commission on a Safe and Secure Workplace. New York: Author.

141 Ibid., 34.

142 Ibid., Table C.4.

143 Ibid., 34.

144 Ibid., Table C.4.

145 Ibid., 34.

146 Ibid., 88.

147 Ibid., 50.

148 Fleet, D.D., Griffin, R.W. (2006, p. 704). Dysfunctional organization culture: The role of leadership in motivating dysfunctional work behaviors. Journal of Managerial Psychology, 21(8), 698-708.

Chapter Eight

149 Joint hearing to review violence in the U.S. Postal Service: Joint hearings before the Subcommittee on Census, Statistics, and Postal Personnel and the Subcommittee on Postal Operations and Services of the Committee on Post Office and Civil Service, House of Representatives, One Hundred Third Congress, first session, August 5; October 14 and 19, 1993 United States (1994). Congress. House. Committee on Post Office and Civil Service. Subcommittee on Census, Statistics, and Postal Personnel: Washington.
U.S. Congress, House of Representatives (1992). A post office tragedy: The shootings at Royal Oak (Serial 102-7): Hearings before House Post Office and Civil Service Committee. Government Printing House: Washington D.C.

150 General Accounting Office (GAO) (1994). U.S. Postal Service: Labor management problems persist on the workroom floor. Report to congressional requestors.
General Accounting Office (GAO) (1997). U.S. Postal Service: Little progress made in addressing persistent labor-management problems. Report to Chairman, Subcommittee on Government Reform and Oversight, House of Representatives.

151 Towards postal excellence: The report of the President's Commission on postal organization (1968). Government Printing Office: Washington D.C. Author.
Embracing the future: Making the tough choices to preserve universal mail service: Report of the President's Commission on the United States Postal Service (2003). Retrieved 2/15/08 from http://www.treas.gov/offices/domestic-finance/usps/pdf/freport.pdf.

152 United States Postal Service Strategic Plans from 1998-2013. Retrieved 10/20/08 from http://www.usps.com/strategicplanning/welcome.htm

Chapter Nine

153 Society for Occupational Health Psychology: NIOSH-APA Contributions to Occupational Health Psychology (2008). Retrieved 3/6/08 from http://sohp.psy.uconn.edu/NIOSH-APA.htm.

154 Karasek, R. (1979). Job demands, job decision latitude and mental strain: Implications for job redesign. Administrative Science Quarterly, 24, 285-306.

155 Karasek, R. A., & Theorell, T. (1990). Healthy work: Stress, productivity, and the reconstruction of working life. New York, NY: Basic Books, Inc.

156 Veldhoven, V.M, Jonge, J., Broerson, S., & Kompier. M. (2002, p. 211). Specific relationships between psychosocial job conditions and job-related stress: A three-level analytic approach. Work & Stress, 16 (3), 207-228.

157 Kudielka, B.M., Kanel, V.R., Gander, M., & Fischer, J. (2004). Effort-reward imbalance, over commitment and sleep in a working population. Work & Stress, 18 (2), 167-178.

158 Ibid.,174.

159 Kuper, H. & Marmot, M. (2003). Job strain, job demands, decision latitude, and risk of coronary heart disease within the Whitehall II study. Journal Epidemiology and Community Health, 57 (2), 147-153.

160 Guimont, C., Brisson, C., Dagenais, G.R., Milot, A., Vezina, M., Masse, B., Moisan, J., Laflamme, N., & Blanchette, C. (2006). Effects of job strain on blood pressure: A prospective study of male and female white-collar workers. American Journal of Public Health, 96 (8), 1436-1443.

Chapter Ten

161 Karasek, R. A., & Theorell, T. (1990). Healthy work: Stress, productivity, and the reconstruction of working life. New York, NY: Basic Books, Inc.

162 Joint hearing to review violence in the U.S. Postal Service: Joint hearings before the Subcommittee on Census, Statistics, and Postal Personnel and the Subcommittee on Postal Operations and Services of the Committee on Post Office and Civil Service, House of Representatives, One Hundred Third Congress, first session, August 5; October 14 and 19, 1993 United States (1994, p. 39). Congress. House. Committee on Post Office and Civil Service. Subcommittee on Census, Statistics, and Postal Personnel: Washington.

163 United States Postal Service (2008). Postal Accountability and Enhancement Act & 302 Network Plan. United States Postal Service. June 2008.

164 National Center on Addiction and Substance Abuse at Columbia University (2000, p. 49). Report of the USPS Commission on a Safe and Secure Workplace. New York: Author.

165 Office of Inspector General (1998). OIG PA-MA-98-002: Violence in the Workplace – Identification of Area Hot Spots. Retrieved 2/2/9 from http://www.uspsoig.gov/reading_room.cfm.

Chapter Eleven

166 Report – Assessment of Work Environment Postal District: Non-Bargaining/Field and Plant Operations Employees (2006). Author: Stephen Musacco, Ph.D.

167 United States Postal Service (1997). "Going Postal": Myth or reality. Postal Life. Retrieved 2/10/08 from http://www.usps.com/history/plife/pl011697/cover.htm.
United States Postal Service (2006). USPS commission on a safe and secure workforce. United States Postal Service (2006). Public Affairs and Communications Department, 1/31/06. Retrieved 3/1/08 from http://www.usps.com/communications/news/press/2006/pr06_0131commission.htm.

168 NIOSH (1993). Fatal injuries to workers in the United States, 1980-1989. Retrieved 3/2/08 from http://www.cdc.gov/NIOSH/93-108.html.
Centers for Disease Control and Prevention (CDC) (1994). Occupational injury deaths of postal workers—United States, 1980-1989. MMWR 43(32):587, 593-595. Retrieved 3/2/08 from http://www.cdc.gov/mmwr/preview/mmwrhtml/00032345.htm.

169 National Center on Addiction and Substance Abuse at Columbia University (2000). Report of the USPS Commission on a Safe and Secure Workplace. New York: Author.

170 U.S. Congress, House of Representatives (1992). A post office tragedy: The shootings at Royal Oak (Serial 102-7): Hearings before House Post Office and Civil Service Committee. Government Printing House: Washington D.C.

Joint hearing to review violence in the U.S. Postal Service: Joint hearings before the Subcommittee on Census, Statistics, and Postal Personnel and the Subcommittee on Postal Operations and Services of the Committee on Post Office and Civil Service, House of Representatives, One Hundred Third Congress, first session, August 5; October 14 and 19, 1993 United States (1994). Congress. House. Committee on Post Office and Civil Service. Subcommittee on Census, Statistics, and Postal Personnel: Washington.

171 Postal Reorganization Act of 1970 (39 U.S.C. § 206).

172 Embracing the future: Making the tough choices to preserve universal mail service: Report of the President's Commission on the United States Postal Service (2003). Retrieved 2/15/08 from http://www.treas.gov/offices/domestic-finance/usps/pdf/freport.pdf.

173 H.R. 6407 [109th]: Postal Accountability and Enhancement Act (2006).

174 Ibid.

175 NAPUS (2007). Letter to Postmaster General and Chief Executive Officer. March 7, 2007, from NAPUS, League, and NAPS. Retrieved 2/25/08 from http://www.napus.org/breakingnews_content/lettertopostmaster.gif.

176 Ibid.

177 Testimony of Charles W. Mapa, President, National League of Postmasters: The U.S. Postal Service 101— The Subcommittee on Federal Workforce, Postal Service, and the District of Columbia (2007). Retrieved 2/25/08 from http://federalworkforce.oversight.house.gov/documents/20070504093546.pdf.

Testimony of Charles W. Mapa, President, National League of Postmasters: The U.S. Postal Service, Post-PAEA: What's Next?—The Subcommittee on Federal Workforce, Postal Service, and the District of Columbia (2008). Retrieved 5/10/08 from http://federalworkforce.oversight.house.gov/documents/20080508180054.pdf.

178 National Labor Relations Act (NLRA (1935) 29 U.S.C. §§ 151-169.

179 H.R. 6407 [109th]: Postal Accountability and Enhancement Act (2006).

180 Towards postal excellence: The report of the President's Commission on postal organization (1968). Government Printing Office: Washington D.C. Author.

181 General Accounting Office (GAO) (1994). U.S. Postal Service: Labor management problems persist on the workroom floor. Report to congressional requestors.
General Accounting Office (GAO) (1997). U.S. Postal Service: Little progress made in addressing persistent labor-management problems. Report to Chairman, Subcommittee on Government Reform and Oversight, House of Representatives.

182 U.S. Congress, House of Representatives (1992). A post office tragedy.
Joint hearing to review violence in the U.S. Postal Service: U.S. Congress (1994).

183 National Center on Addiction and Substance Abuse at Columbia University (2000).

184 Inspector General Act of 1978, as amended, (Pub. L. 95-452, Oct. 12, 1978, 92 Stat. 1101, as amended by Pub. L. 96-88).

185 Bullying Institute Website. Retrieved 10/07/07 from http://bullyinginstitute.org/.

186 Yamada, D. (2006). Potential legal protections and liabilities for workplace bullying. Retrieved 10/7/07 from http://bullyinginstitute.org/education/bbstudies/yamada2007.pdf.
Yamada, D. (2000). The phenomenon of workplace bullying and the need for status-blind hostile work environment protection. Georgetown Law Journal, 88 (3), 476-536.

187 Mail Delivery Protection Act (S.1457).

188 Mail Network Protection Act (H.R. 4236).

189 The U.S. Postal Service 101—The Subcommittee on Federal Workforce, Postal Service, and the District of Columbia (2007). Retrieved 2/25/08 from http://federalworkforce.oversight.house.gov/story.asp?ID=1249.

The U.S. Postal Service, Post-PAEA: What's Next?—The Subcommittee on Federal Workforce, Postal Service, and the District of Columbia (2008). Retrieved 5/10/08 from http://federalworkforce. oversight.house.gov/story.asp?ID=1928.

190 APWU (2008). APWU to PRC: Burden of proof. APWU Web News Article #66-08, July 11, 2008. Retrieved 7/13/08 from http://www.apwu.org/news/webart/2008/0866-prc_uso-080711.htm.

191 United States Postal Service (2008). Postal accountability and Enhancement Act & 302 Network Plan. United States Postal Service. June 2008.

192 United States Postal Service (2008). Draft request for proposal concerning a time-definite surface network for U.S. Postal Service. United States Postal Service, July 1, 2008.

193 General Accounting Office (GAO) (2008). U.S. Postal Service: USPS has taken steps to strengthen network.

194 General Accounting Office (GAO-08-787) (2008). United States Postal Service: Data needed to assess the effectiveness of outsourcing. Report to congressional requestors.

Appendix A

195 Northwestern National Life Insurance (1993). Fear and violence in the workplace: A survey documenting the experience of American workers. Minneapolis, MN: Author.

196 Namie, G. (2000). The WBTI report on U.S. hostile workplace survey 2000. Retrieved 9/26/07 from www.bullyinginstitute.org.

197 Namie, G. (2003, p. 1). Workplace bullying: Escalated incivility. Ivey Business Journal, Nov/Dec, 1-6.

198 Lutgen-Sandvik, P., Tracy. S., &, Alberts, J. (2007). Burned by bullying in the American workplace: Prevalence, perception, degree and impact. Journal of Management Studies, 44 (6), 837-862.

199 Namie, G. (2007). The WBTI 2007 U.S. Workplace survey on bullying. Retrieved 9/26/07 from www.bullyinginstitute.org.2007.

200 Northwestern National Life Insurance (1993). Fear and violence in the workplace.

201 Schat, A.C , Frone, M. & Kelloway, K. (2006). In: Kelloway, K., Barling, J., & Hurrel, J.J. (Eds.), 47-61. Handbook of Workplace Violence. Thousand Oaks, CA: Sage.

202 Bureau of Labor Statistics (2006). National census of fatal occupational injuries in 2006. Author. Retrieved 1/20/08 from: http://www.bls.gov/iif/oshcfoi1.htm.

203 DHHS (1993). Fatal injuries to workers in the U.S., 1980-1989: A decade of surveillance national and state profiles. (NIOSH) Publication No. 93-108s. Retrieved 1/20/08 from http://www.cdc. gov/niosh/93-108s.html.

204 Bureau of Labor Statistics (2006). National Census of Fatal Occupational Injuries in 2006.

Appendix B

205 United States Postal Service (2006). Threat assessment team (TAT) orientation—Addendum: National headlines narratives. Developed by USPS EAP/WEI program/September 2006.
National Center on Addiction and Substance Abuse at Columbia University (2000). Report of the USPS Commission on a Safe and Secure Workplace. New York: Author.
Mantell, M. & Albrecht, S. (1994). Ticking Bombs: Defusing violence in the workplace. Irwin Publishing, New York.
Coleman., C. (2004). The Copycat effect: How the media and popular culture trigger the mayhem in tomorrow's headlines. Pocket Books: New York.
Lasseter, D. (1997). Going postal. Kensington Publishing: New York.
Wikipedia (2008). List of postal killings: United States. Retrieved from http://en.wikipedia.org/wiki/List_of_postal_killings
Fearn-Banks, K (2007). Crisis Communications. Lawrence Erlbaum Associates, Publishers: New Jersey.

U.S. Congress, House of Representatives (1992). A post office tragedy: The shootings at Royal Oak (Serial 102-7): Hearings before House Post Office and Civil Service Committee. Government Printing House: Washington D.C.

Ames, M. (2005). Going postal: Rage, murder, and rebellion: from Reagan's workplaces to Clinton's Columbine and beyond. Soft Skull Press: New York, NY.

Denenberg, R., & Braverman, M. (2001). The violence prone workplace: A new approach to dealing with hostile, threatening, and uncivil behavior. Cornell University Press: Ithaca, NY

Baxter, V., & Margavio, A. (1996). Assaultive Violence in the U.S. Post Office. Work & Occupations, 23(3), 277-296.

Appendix C

[206] United States Postal Service Strategic Plans from 1998-2013. Retrieved 3/27/08 from http://www.usps.com/strategicplanning/welcome.htm.

[207] Embracing the future: Making the tough choices to preserve universal mail service: Report of the President's Commission on the United States Postal Service (2003). Retrieved 2/15/08 from http://www.treas.gov/offices/domestic-finance/usps/pdf/freport.pdf.

[208] H.R. 6407 [109th]: Postal Accountability and Enhancement Act (2006)

[209] The U.S. Postal Service 101—The Subcommittee on Federal Workforce, Postal Service, and the District of Columbia (2007). Retrieved 2/25/08 from http://federalworkforce.oversight.house.gov/story.asp?ID=1249.

The U.S. Postal Service, Post-PAEA: What's Next?—The Subcommittee on Federal Workforce.

[210] Government Performance Results Act of 1993.

[211] United States Postal Service Strategic Plan from 1998-2002. Retrieved 3/28/08 from http://www.usps.com/strategicplanning/welcome.htm.

[212] Yoder, Eric (1998). Time for a change. Government. Executive Magazine, May 1. Retrieved 3/15/08 from http://www.govexec.com/story_.cfm?filepath=/features/0598s6.htm.

[213] United States Postal Service Strategic Plan from 1998-2002, p. 21.

[214] United States Postal Service Strategic Plan from 2001-2005. Retrieved 3/27/08 from http://www.usps.com/strategicplanning/welcome.htm.

[215] Ibid., 20.

[216] Ibid., 20.

[217] United States Postal Service Strategic Plan from 2002-2006. Retrieved 3/27/08 from http://www.usps.com/strategicplanning/welcome.htm.

[218] Postal Reorganization Act of 1970 (39 U.S.C. § 206).

[219] United States Postal Service Strategic Plan from 2001-2005, Executive summary, x. Retrieved 3/27/08 from http://www.usps.com/strategicplanning/welcome.htm.

[220] United States Postal Service Strategic Plan from 2004-2008. Retrieved 3/27/08 from http://www.usps.com/strategicplanning/welcome.htm.

[221] Ibid., 54.

[222] Ibid., 56.

[223] United States Postal Service Strategic Plan from 2006-2010. Message from Chairman of the Board James C. Miller III and Postmaster General & CEO John E. Potter. Retrieved 3/27/08 from http://www.usps.com/strategicplanning/welcome.htm .

[224] Ibid., 45.

[225] United States Postal Service Strategic Plan from 2006-2010, 2007 Update. Retrieved 3/27/08 from http://www.usps.com/strategicplanning/welcome.htm.

[226] Ibid., 45.

[227] United States Postal Service Strategic Plan from 2008-2013, Vision 2013. Retrieved 10/20/08 from http://www.usps.com/strategicplanning/welcome.htm

[228] Ibid, 13.

229 Ibid, 13.
230 Embracing the future: Making the tough choices to preserve universal mail service: Report of the President's Commission on the United States Postal Service (2003, p. 161).
231 Magazine Publisher of America (MPA). Postal victory for MPA as USPS forgoes final rate increase under old postal law. Washington E-Newsletter, December 20, 2007. Retrieved 8/1/08 from http://www.magazine.org/news/newsletters/washingtonenews/index.aspx?y=2007.
232 H.R. 6407 [109th]: Postal Accountability and Enhancement Act, Section 505 Noninterference with collective bargaining agreements (2006).
233 The U.S. Postal Service 101—The Subcommittee on Federal Workforce (2007).
      The U.S. Postal Service, Post-PAEA: What's Next?—The Subcommittee on Federal Workforce, Postal Service, and the District of Columbia (2008). Retrieved 5/10/08 from http://federalworkforce.oversight.house.gov/story.asp?ID=1928.
      The U.S. Postal Service, The three R's of the postal network plan: Realignment, right-sizing, and responsiveness. The Subcommittee on Federal Workforce, Postal Service, and the District of Columbia (2008). Retrieved 7/26/08 from http://federalworkforce.oversight.house.gov/story.asp?ID=2100.
234 United States Postal Service (2008). Postal accountability and Enhancement Act & 302 Network Plan. United States Postal Service. June 2008.
235 Testimony of Oscar "Dale" Goff, Jr., President, National Association of Postmasters of the United States: The U.S. Postal Service 101—The Subcommittee on Federal Workforce, Postal Service, and the District of Columbia (2007). Retrieved 2/25/08 from http://federalworkforce.oversight.house.gov/documents/20080508180313.pdf.
236 Ibid., 5.
237 APWU (2008). Federal court dismisses APWU suit: Union vows to challenge USPS secrecy in other forums. APWU Web News Article 28-08, April 2, 2008. Retrieved 4/5/08 from http://www.apwu.org/news/webart/2008/webart-0828-mtac_lawsuit-080402.htm.
238 Ibid.
239 APWU (2008). PRC ruling exposes unhealthy relationship between USPS and influential mailers. Burrus Update #04-08, March 25, 2008. Retrieved 3/28/08 from http://www.apwu.org/news/burrus/2008/update04-2008-032508.htm.
240 APWU (2008). Burrus asks Bush to appoint Postal Service advisory council. APWU Web News Article #31-08, April 14, 2008. Retrieved 4/17/08 from http://www.apwu.org/news/webart/2008/webart-0831-bush_advcouncil-080414.htm.
241 APWU (2008). President Williams Burrus, APWU, letter to President George W. Bush (2008). April 11, 2008. Retrieved 4/15/08 from http://www.apwu.org/news/webart/2008/webart-0831-bush_advcouncil-080414.pdf.
242 APWU (2008). APWU sues bush over failure to appoint USPS advisory council. APWU Web News Article #68-08, July 17, 2008. Retrieved 7/20/08 from http://www.apwu.org/news/webart/2008/0868-bush_lawsuit-080717.htm.
243 APWU to PRC: Burden of proof. APWU Web News Article #66-08, July 11, 2008. Retrieved 7/13/08 from http://www.apwu.org/news/webart/2008/0866-prc_uso-080711.htm.
244 USPS (Oct., 2008). Report on universal service and the postal monopoly. Retrieved 10/20/08 from http://www.usps.com/postallaw/universalserviceobligation.htm.
245 The U.S. Postal Service, The three R's of the postal network plan: Realignment, right-sizing, and responsiveness. The Subcommittee on Federal Workforce, Postal Service, and the District of Columbia (2008).

Appendix D

246 Postal Reorganization Act of 1970 (39 U.S.C. § 206).

247 United States Postal Service Strategic Plans from 1998-2013. Retrieved 3/27/08 from http://www.usps.com/strategicplanning/welcome.htm.

248 Embracing the future: Making the tough choices to preserve universal mail service: Report of the President's Commission on the United States Postal Service (2003). Retrieved 2/15/08 from http://www.treas.gov/offices/domestic-finance/usps/pdf/freport.pdf.

249 NALC (2008). Impasse! Interest arbitration to resolve contract: Postal Service rejects strategic partnership; opt for contractor and contracting out. April 6, 2007 No. 07-05. Retrieved 4/9/08 from http://www.nalc.org/news/bulletin/PDF2007/Bull07-05.pdf.

250 James C. Miller II named honorary title of chairman pro tempore. Retrieved 5/01/08 from http://www.lunewsviews.com/issues.htm.

251 General Accounting Office (GAO) (1994, p. 6). U.S. Postal Service: Labor management problems persist.

252 NALC (2006). NALC presents Postal Service with main contract proposals. NALC Bulletin, October 25, 2006, No. 06-22. Retrieved 4/1/08 from http://www.nalc.org/news/bulletin/PDF2005/bull06-22.pdf.

253 General Accounting Office (GAO) (1994, p. 88). U.S. Postal Service: Labor management problems persist.

254 General Accounting Office (GAO) (1997, appendix IV, pp. 84-85). U.S. Postal Service: Little progress made in addressing persistent labor-management problems.

255 Ibid., 83.

256 NALC (2005, p. 2). Postal Service derails search for better way to adjust routes. Postal Record, January 2005. Retrieved 5/1/08 from http://www.nalc.org/news/precord/ArticlesPDF/0105-RtInspect.pdf.

257 NALC (2006, p. 4). NALC pressing USPS on DOIS flaws, abuses. Postal Record, April 2006. Retrieved 5/1/08 from http://www.nalc.org/news/precord/ArticlesPDF/0406-dois.pdf.

258 NALC (2006, p. 10). What's the deal with DOIS? Postal Record, May 2006. Retrieved 5/1/08 from http://www.nalc.org/news/precord/ArticlesPDF/0506-dois.pdf.

259 Ibid., 11.

260 Dupree, K.E. (2004). Beating up the boss: The prediction and prevention of interpersonal aggression targeting workplace supervisors. Unpublished doctoral dissertation. Queen's University, Kingston, Ontario, Canada.

261 Postal Reporter (2008). USPS to begin GPS tracking project. Retrieved 5/5/08 from http://www.postalreporter.com/news/2008/05/02/usps-to-begin-gps-vehicle-tracking-project/.

262 USPS (2008). Delivery Operations. Joint Area Vice Presidents; Managers, Operations Support; Area Marketing Managers Meeting, September 11, 2008. Retrieved 10/20/08 from http://www.nalcbranch709.com/091108.pdf.

263 Ibid.

264 NALC (2007, pp. 133-134). The 2006-2011 National Agreement between the USPS and the NALC. Retrieved 5/1/08 from http://www.nalc.org/news/bargain/2006-2011%20National%20Agreement%20-%20FINAL.pdf.

265 NALC (2008). NALC-USPS Reach New Agreement on Expedited Route Adjustments. October 27, 2008, NALC Bulletin, No. 08-26. Retrieved 10/20/08 from http://nalc.org/news/bulletin/PDF2008/Bull08-20.pdf.

266 NALC (2007). Young testified to Congress on "contracting out" issue: Appears before House and Senate panels; outlines moratorium on outsourcing work. NALC Bulletin, July 27, 2007, No. 07-13. Retrieved 5/1/08 from http://www.nalc.org/news/bulletin/PDF2007/Bull07-13.pdf.

267 Ibid.

268 Ibid.

269 Quote from Moe Biller in 1982. Retrieved 3/28/08 from http://www.redbanklocal.com/LABOR%20QUOTES.htm#Moe%20Biller.

270 Joint hearing to review violence in the U.S. Postal Service: Joint hearings before the Subcommittee on Census, Statistics, and Postal Personnel and the Subcommittee on Postal Operations and Services of the Committee on Post Office and Civil Service, House of Representatives, One Hundred Third Congress, first session, August 5; October 14 and 19, 1993 United States (1994, p. 58). Congress. House. Committee on Post Office and Civil Service. Subcommittee on Census, Statistics, and Postal Personnel: Washington.

271 Ibid., 58.

272 Ibid., 59.

273 General Accounting Office (GAO) (1997, p. 64). U.S. Postal Service: Little progress made in addressing persistent labor-management problems.

274 Ibid., 65.

275 Ibid., 65.

276 Ibid., 38.

277 Ibid., 36.

278 Ibid., 37.

279 Joint hearing to review violence in the U.S. Postal Service: U.S. Congress (1994, p. 58).

280 General Accounting Office (GAO) (1994, p. 139). U.S. Postal Service: Labor management problems persist on the workroom floor. Report to congressional requestors.

281 Postal Reporter (2008). APWU: USPS rejects pilot program for new retail position. Retrieved 9/13/08 from http://www.postalreporter.com/news/2008/09/13/apwu-usps-rejects-pilot-program-for-new-retail-position/.

282 APWU (2008). Tour 2, Early-outs, Four-Day Workweeks. Burrus Update #13-08, Oct. 15, 2008. Burrus Update #13-08, Oct. 15, 2008. Retrieved 10/20/08 from http://www.apwu.org/news/burrus/2008/update13-2008-101508.htm.

283 APWU (2006). USPS briefs APWU on plans to realign networks. APWU Web News Article, #11-06, February 15, 2006. Retrieved 3/19/08 from http://www.apwu.org/news/nsb/2006/nsb03-021506.pdf.

284 APWU (2006). USPS lists 139 facilities as "potential candidates" for consolidation. APWU Web News Article, #43-06, July 31, 2006. Retrieved 3/19/08 from http://www.apwu.org/news/webart/2006/webart-0643-consolnewlistt-060731.htm.

285 APWU (2006). National executive board acts to fight network consolidation: Dues assessment approved to help pay for ad campaign. APWU News Bulletin, #04-2006, March 10, 2006. Retrieved 3/19/08 from http://www.apwu.org/news/nsb/2006/nsb04-031006.pdf.

286 Mail Delivery Protection Act (S.1457) and Mail Network Protection Act (H.R. 4236).

287 United States Postal Service (2008). Postal Accountability and Enhancement Act & 302 Network Plan. United States Postal Service. June 2008.

288 United States Postal Service (2008). Draft request for proposal concerning a time-definite surface network.

289 General Accounting Office (GAO-08-787) (2008). United States Postal Service: Data needed to assess the effectiveness of outsourcing. Report to congressional requestors.

290 Testimony of Myke Reid, APWU Legislative Director: The U.S. Postal Service, Post-PAEA: What's Next?—The Subcommittee on Federal Workforce, Postal Service, and the District of Columbia (2008, p. 3). Retrieved 5/10/08 from http://federalworkforce.oversight.house.gov/documents/20080508180054.pdf.

291 Testimony of William Quinn, President, National Postal Mail Handlers Union, Joint hearing to review violence in the U.S. Postal Service (1994, p. 72).

292 John F. Hegarty, President, National Postal Mail Handlers Union: The U.S. Postal Service, Post-PAEA: What's Next?—The Subcommittee on Federal Workforce, Postal Service, and the District of Columbia (2008). Retrieved 5/10/08 from http://federalworkforce.oversight.house.gov/documents/20080508180226.pdf.

293 Rural Carrier Postal News (2008). NRLCA Withdraws from QWL-EI. Retrieved 11/14/08 from http://ruralcarriernews.blogspot.com/2008/11/nrlca-withdraws-from-qwl-ei.html.

294 General Accounting Office (GAO) (1997, p. 98). William P. Brennan, President, League, statement to GAO. U.S. Postal Service: Little progress made in addressing persistent labor-management problems.

295 James Miller, President, National Association of Postmasters (NAPUS), Joint hearing to review violence in the U.S. Postal Service (1994, p. 100).

296 NAPUS (2007). Letter to Postmaster General and Chief Executive Officer. March 7, 2007, from NAPUS, League, and NAPS. Retrieved 2/25/08 from http://www.napus.org/breakingnews_content/lettertopostmaster.gif.

297 League (2008). President's Message: Charles W. Mapa, President, National League of Postmasters. Retrieved October 31, 2008 from http://www.postmasters.org/news/message/103008.asp.

298 Testimony of Charles W. Mapa, President, National League of Postmasters: The U.S. Postal Service 101—The Subcommittee on Federal Workforce, Postal Service, and the District of Columbia (2007, p. 4). Retrieved 2/25/08 from http://federalworkforce.oversight.house.gov/documents/20070504093546.pdf.

299 Testimony of Charles W. Mapa, President, National League of Postmasters: The U.S. Postal Service, Post-PAEA: What's Next?—The Subcommittee on Federal Workforce, Postal Service, and the District of Columbia (2008). Retrieved 5/10/08 from http://federalworkforce.oversight.house.gov/documents/20080508180054.pdf.

300 Testimony of Dale Goff, President, National Association of Postmaster of the United States (NAPUS): The U.S. Postal Service, Post-PAEA: What's Next?—The Subcommittee on Federal Workforce, Postal Service, and the District of Columbia (2008). Retrieved 5/10/08 from http://federalworkforce.oversight.house.gov/documents/20080508180313.pdf.

301 Testimony of Ted Keating, President, National Association of Supervisors (NAPS): The U.S. Postal Service, Post-PAEA: What's Next?—The Subcommittee on Federal Workforce, Postal Service, and the District of Columbia (2008). Retrieved 5/10/08 from http://federalworkforce.oversight.house.gov/documents/20080508180342.pdf.

302 NAPS (2008). Letter to the Subcommittee on Federal Workforce, Postal Service, and the District of Columbia from Ted Keating. Retrieved 9/2/08 from http://www.naps.org/Legislative_News/NAPSLtrtoHouseSubComm-NetworkRealignmentHearing_08-05-08.pdf.

Appendix E

303 U.S. Congress, House of Representatives (1992, VIII.). A post office tragedy: The shootings at Royal Oak (Serial 102-7): Hearings before House Post Office and Civil Service Committee. Government Printing House: Washington D.C.

304 Press release (2008). Ponemon Institute announces 2008 privacy trust rankings of U.S. government agencies: U.S. Postal Service once again tops in public perceptions of trust in public institutions, April 7, 2008, Marketwire. Retrieved 4/11/08 from http://www.marketwire.com/press-release/Ponemon-Institute-840922.html.

305 Press release (2008). Postal officials routinely OK requests to monitor mail. March 6, 2008. Indianapolis Star. Retrieved 4/11/08 from http://www.postalnews.com/2008_03_01_archive.html.

306 Press release (2007). Bush warned about mail-opening authority: Recent "signing statement" seen as stretching the law. January 5, 2007, Washington Post. Retrieved 4/11/08 from http://www.washingtonpost.com/wp-dyn/content/article/2007/01/04/AR2007010401702.html.

307 Ibid.

308 ABC News (2008). Exclusive: Top Federal Postal Cop Retires in Wake of ABC News Investigation Official Gambled at a Casino During Conference He Arranged at Nearby Resort, dated October 17, 2008.

Retrieved 10/20/08 from http://abcnews.go.com/Blotter/Nightline/Story?id=5996279&page=1.

309 Ibid.

310 Ibid.

311 Ibid.

312 Inspector General Act of 1978, as amended, (Pub. L. 95-452, Oct. 12, 1978, 92 Stat. 1101, as amended by Pub. L. 96-88).

313 General Accounting Office (GAO) (1994). U.S. Postal Service: Labor management problems persist on the workroom floor. Report to congressional requestors.
General Accounting Office (GAO) (1997). U.S. Postal Service: Little progress made in addressing persistent labor-management problems. Report to Chairman, Subcommittee on Government Reform and Oversight, House of Representatives.

314 Press release (2003). Taxpayers relieved by retirement of postal inspector general; Federal investigation supports CAGW charges of rampant waste, abuse. August 20, 2003, PR Newswire. Retrieved 12/10/07 from http://goliath.ecnext.com/coms2/gi_0199-3093953/Taxpayers-Relieved-by-Retirement-of.html.

315 United States Postal Service Office of Inspector General office (OIG) (1999, p. 11). Semiannual Report to Congress, October 1, 1998-March 31, 1999. Retrieved 4/3/08 from http://www.uspsoig.gov/sarcs/March99.PDF.

316 United States Postal Service Office of Inspector General office (OIG) (1999, p. 73). Semiannual Report to Congress, April 1, 1999-September 30, 1999. Retrieved 4/3/08 from http://www.uspsoig.gov/sarcs/Sept99.PDF.

317 Ibid.

318 United States Postal Service Office of Inspector General office (OIG) (2001). Semiannual Reports to Congress from September 1999 to September 2001. Retrieved 4/3/08 from http://www.uspsoig.gov/sarc.htm.

319 United States Postal Service Office of Inspector General office (OIG) (2003). Semiannual Reports to Congress from March 2001 to September 2003. Retrieved 4/3/08 from http://www.uspsoig.gov/sarc.htm.

320 United States Postal Service Office of Inspector General office (OIG) (2000, p. 86). Semiannual Report to Congress, October 1, 1999-March 31, 2000. Retrieved 4/3/08 from http://www.uspsoig.gov/sarcs/March00.pdf.

321 United States Postal Service Office of Inspector General office (OIG) (2001, p. 42). Semiannual Report to Congress, April 1, 2001-September 1, 2001. Retrieved 4/3/08 from http://www.uspsoig.gov/sarcs/Sept01.pdf.

322 United States Postal Service Office of Inspector General office (OIG) (2001, p. 42). Semiannual Report to Congress, October 1, 2000-March 31, 2001. Retrieved 4/3/08 from http://www.uspsoig.gov/sarcs/March01.pdf.

323 United States Postal Service Office of Inspector General office (OIG) (2003, p. 64). Semiannual Report to Congress, October 1, 2002-March 31, 2003. Retrieved 4/3/08 from http://www.uspsoig.gov/sarcs/March03.pdf.

324 United States Postal Service Office of Inspector General office (OIG) (2001). Contracting practices for the procurement of mail transport equipment services. January 27, 2001, CA-AR-01-001. Retrieved 4/3/08 from http://www.uspsoig.gov/foia_files/CA-AR-01-001.pdf.

325 United States Postal Service Office of Inspector General office (OIG) (2005, p. 9). Semiannual Report to Congress, April 1, 2005-September 30, 2005. Retrieved 4/3/08 from http://www.uspsoig.gov/sarcs/Sept05.pdf.

326 United States Postal Service Office of Inspector General office (OIG) (2006, p. 4). Semiannual Report to Congress, April 1, 2006-September 30, 2006. Retrieved 4/3/08 from http://www.uspsoig.gov/sarcs/Sept06.pdf.

327 United States Postal Service Office of Inspector General office (OIG) (2007, p. 6). Semiannual Report to Congress, April 1, 2007-September 30, 2007. Retrieved 4/3/08 from http://www.uspsoig.gov/sarcs/Sept07.pdf.

328 United States Postal Service Office of Inspector General office (OIG) (2008). Our mission: USPS OIG. Retrieved 4/3/08 from http://www.uspsoig.gov/about.htm.

329 United States Postal Service Office of Inspector General office (OIG) (2008). OIG Audit reports from July 26, 2003 to October, 16, 2006. Retrieved 4/3/08 from http://www.uspsoig.gov/rr_all.cfm.

330 United States Postal Service Office of Inspector General office (OIG) (2008). OIG Audit reports from August 8, 2005 to March 28, 2006: Value Proposition Agreement"—an agreement between the OIG and the Postal Service Vice President of Delivery and Retail. Retrieved 4/3/08 from http://www.uspsoig.gov/rr_all.cfm.

331 United States Postal Service Office of Inspector General office (OIG) (2007). Delivery and retail standard operation procedures – National capping report. February 22, 2007, DR-MA-07-003. Retrieved 4/3/08 from http://www.uspsoig.gov/foia_files/DR-MA-07-003.pdf.

332 APWU (2008). Unions sue USPS, Inspector General over invasion of medical-records privacy. January 30, 2008, APWU News Bulletin, 38 (1). Retrieved 5/4/08 from http://www.apwu.org/news/nsb/2008/nsb01-080130-ms47.pdf.

333 NALC (2008). NALC files suit against OIG to stop invasion of privacy in obtaining medical files. NALC Bulletin, January 18, 2008, No.08-01. Retrieved 5/4/08 from http://www.nalc.org/news/bulletin/PDF2008/Bull08-1.pdf.

334 Ibid.

335 Ibid.

336 APWU (2008). Unions sue USPS, Inspector General over invasion of medical-records privacy. January 30, 2008, APWU News Bulletin, 38 (1). Retrieved 5/4/08 from http://www.apwu.org/news/nsb/2008/nsb01-080130-ms47.pdf.

337 NALC (2007). Taking on the Office of the Inspector General. Postal Record—April 2007. Retrieved 5/4/08 from http://www.nalc.org/news/precord/ArticlesPDF/0407-OIG.pdf.

338 Ibid.

339 NALC (2007). Good cop/bad cop—right here in the USPS. President's Message, Postal Record—December 2007. Retrieved 5/4/08 from http://www.nalc.org/news/precord/PresMesPDF/pres1207.pdf.

340 Regular Arbitration Panel (2007). USPS case Nos: GOIN-4G-D 07034244 and GOIN-4G-D 07072314, Emergency Procedure and Removal, Peter Clarke, Arbitrator, Award Summary, May 2007.

341 NALC (2007). Good cop/bad cop—right here in the USPS. President's Message, Postal Record—December 2007. Retrieved 5/4/08 from http://www.nalc.org/news/precord/PresMesPDF/pres1207.pdf.

342 United States Postal Service Office of Inspector General office (OIG) (2008). Response to National Association of Letter Carriers President's message referencing OIG. Memorandum from David C. Williams, Inspector General. News Release, January 16, 2008. Retrieved 5/4/08 from http://www.uspsoig.gov/press_releases/NALC_response.pdf.

343 APWU (2007). Burrus issues stinging rebuke to USPS Inspector General: Audit lacks relevance, ignores legislative mandate to bargain. APWU Web News Article #108-07, November 27, 2007. Retrieved 5/4/08 from http://www.apwu.org/news/webart/2007/webart07108-usps_oig-071127.htm.

344 United States Postal Service Office of Inspector General office (OIG) (2006). Memorandum from David Williams, Inspector General, to Greg Bell, AWPU Director of Industrial Relations, dated January 11, 2006. Retrieved 5/4/08 from http://www.postalreporter.com/pdfs/oig.pdf.

345 Ibid.

346 APWU (2006). Memorandum from Greg Bell, AWPU Director of Industrial Relations, to David Williams, Inspector General, dated March 27, 2006. Retrieved 5/4/08 from http://www.postalreporter.com/pdfs/gbell.pdf.

347 Inspector General Act of 1978, as amended, (Pub. L. 95-452, Oct. 12, 1978, 92 Stat. 1101, as amended by Pub. L. 96-88).

8912692R0

Made in the USA
Lexington, KY
12 March 2011